Andrew Kennedy Hutchinson Boyd

The Commonplace Philosopher in Town and Country

Andrew Kennedy Hutchinson Boyd

The Commonplace Philosopher in Town and Country

ISBN/EAN: 9783337081287

Printed in Europe, USA, Canada, Australia, Japan

Cover: Foto ©Thomas Meinert / pixelio.de

More available books at **www.hansebooks.com**

THE COMMONPLACE PHILOSOPHER

IN

TOWN AND COUNTRY.

BY THE AUTHOR OF
'THE RECREATIONS OF A COUNTRY PARSON.'

NEW EDITION.

LONDON:
LONGMANS, GREEN, AND CO.
1871.

CONTENTS.

CHAPTER I.
PAGE
TO WORK AGAIN 1

CHAPTER II.
CONCERNING THE WORLD'S OPINION; WITH SOME THOUGHTS ON COWED PEOPLE . . . 13

CHAPTER III.
CONCERNING THE SORROWS OF CHILDHOOD . . 55

CHAPTER IV.
CONCERNING ATMOSPHERES; WITH SOME THOUGHTS ON CURRENTS 90

CHAPTER V.
CONCERNING BEGINNINGS AND ENDS . . . 116

CHAPTER VI.
GOING ON 142

CHAPTER VII.

CONCERNING DISAGREEABLE PEOPLE . . . 188

CHAPTER VIII.

OUTSIDE 229

CHAPTER IX.

GETTING ON 251

CHAPTER X.

CONCERNING MAN AND HIS DWELLING-PLACE . . 281

CHAPTER XI.

CONCERNING A GREAT SCOTCH PREACHER . . 327

CHAPTER XII.

AT THE LAND'S END 371

CONCLUSION 389

CHAPTER I.

TO WORK AGAIN.

IF you had slept last night in any one of the row of houses which forms the north side of a certain street in a certain city, you would almost certainly have been wakened up a little before six o'clock this morning by a most dreadful squall, which was the culmination of a stormy night. It was quite dark. The rain was driven in bitter plashes against the windows. The windows rattled, the doors creaked; the very walls seemed to tremble; and there was a dismal howling in the chimneys. For though the street I have mentioned has the city all round it, yet the ground on which it is built slopes so much, that the houses catch the unbroken force of the wind from the not distant sea. And from the upper windows, if you look to the north, beyond the gleam of a frith six miles in breadth, you may discern a range of hills, not far enough distant to seem blue.

It was a time in which to remember those who

are at sea; and to be thankful that you were safe on shore. But there is a farther association with such a time, which would probably be present to the mind of many who in former days studied at a certain ancient University which the writer will never cease to hold in affectionate remembrance. For this morning was one of the latest mornings of October: and on the selfsame morning in time, and on just such a morning for pleasantness, has many a student risen at six from his bed, that he might be present in the lecture-room, a mile and a half away, at half-past seven. On the previous day, he had gone at a comfortable forenoon hour to the Common Hall of the University, and assisted at the ceremony of opening the session. The ceremony was a simple one. Several hundreds of students, arrayed in gowns of flaming scarlet, assembled in that plain Hall; and heard the Principal give a short address on academic dignity and duty. And if the student were one who had studied at the University in former sessions, he would be cheered up somewhat in the prospect of resuming his studies by the sight of some familiar and kindly faces. But that ceremony in the early forenoon was but the gentle introduction to college work: here is its stern reality. I am well aware that human beings in this world have oftentimes very dark and repulsive prospects to face, on rising from their bed in the morning: and I could think of things so grave as awaiting worthier men, that they make me almost ashamed to chronicle lesser trials.

Yet I can say, from sorrowful experience, that duty and work seldom look more gloomy and disheartening than they do to a student of that ancient University of which the writer is an unworthy son, when he gets up in darkness and cold and hurricane; and hastens through mud and sleet along the gloomy streets to the lecture at half-past seven.

One happy result follows. During all the remainder of his life, the man who for three long winters in succession, each beginning about the twenty-eighth of October, and reaching on till the end of April, has undergone that discipline, can never cease to have a special feeling of thankfulness when on a day of late October or early November he awakes at half-past five in the morning, and hears the rain outside; and then reflects that he need not get up and go out. The remembrance of many mornings past may send a chill through his frame; and various worries and cares which must be faced at rising may painfully suggest themselves: yet at least there is not that dismal rising before he has gathered heart to face the dreary day.

Things which were very far from pleasant when they occurred, are sometimes very pleasant to look back on. I remember well how through months of over-work at College, anything but enjoyable while they passed over, I kept written on a piece of paper, always before my eyes, Virgil's line which says so. I can see it yet, in large letters on my table: I used to look at it, in the silent house, at half-past three in the morning before going to bed, and to repeat it over when getting up wearily at half-past six again. *Forsan et hæc olim meminisse juvabit:* which was the graceful classic way of saying that there is a good time coming, and of advising sensible folk to wait a little longer. That time has come to the writer, and to many of his friends. We like to talk, when we meet, of the old days with their dismal mornings. It rejoiced me, between five and six this morning, to remember these things; and to feel the force of the anniversary. And now, when a new generation is gathering, on this very day, within the gloomy courts so well remembered, the recollection does no worse than call up in the writer many thoughts of the varied ways in which men take to work again. Suffer me to say here, my friendly reader, May the City and the University flourish together; according to the simple and straightforward wish of the pious burghers who first inscribed the motto on the scutcheon of the ancient town. And let me confess that I have already grown so old, that not without a certain mist that dims one's eyes, I can look on the crowd of lads and boys (for most of them are no more) in the Hall on the day of the opening of a session. You look back yourself, my friend: and from a record, not far to seek, you are able to discern a little of the mistakes, the follies, the repentances, the humiliations, the mortifications, the labours, the manifold takings-down, which await those hopeful young fellows, before they are battered, rudely enough, into trim for sober life. The Duke of Wellington said that all war was a series of blunders: it is not too much to say that blunders and repentances make up great part of the career of every mortal, especially in the days when he begins first to think for himself.

The winter session, which is the only one of the year in that University which is not to be named here, begins, as has been said, about the twenty-seventh or twenty-eighth of October. The vacation has lasted since the first of the preceding May. It need not be said, that to the more industrious students, that long vacation is in great part given to diligent study: yet it is always study to which your own sense of duty fixes the times and limits. *Now*, you begin to be under authority, and to have your task allotted to you from day to day. And at this season, it is a curious thing to come from the country to that city. You pass at a step from autumn, still rich with colour, into winter, gloomy and gray. In an inland country region, late October is often a charming time; and the landscape has its own touching and even glowing beauty. Though many leaves have fallen, and make a dry rustle under your feet as you go through woodland ways, yet many of the trees are thickly clad: some wonderfully green; some touched by decay into beauty and glory, in the still sunshine of those beautiful days that come. And the dahlias and hollyhocks are blazing: for as the season advances, the colours of nature deepen; and the pale and delicate hues of the early snowdrops, primroses, and lilies, pass through the gradation of summer blossoms and roses into the glow of the late autumn flowers. It is as gentle maidenhood passes into blooming matronhood, with all its qualities more pronounced. And coming away from the country, at such a season, I daresay you have thought it still looking almost its best. But all these things are not, in the great city of that ancient University. The leaves are gone: all the country round is bare and bleak. The College gardens, large and black-looking, are the most dismal scene that ever bore the pleasant name. You will find no winding walks through thick masses of evergreens, which in winter rain or winter frost look so life-like and warm and cheering. The trees, poor and stunted, are all deciduous: and their leaves are not merely capable of falling, but have fallen in fact. The air is thick, and smoke abounds—the smoke that makes the wealth of that wealthy city. And though you may be willing enough to set to work, and indeed rather weary of idleness or desultory study for some weeks past, you will probably confess that, even apart from the dismal lectures at half-past seven in the morning, it is rather a sad setting to work again.

Let us be thankful, my friend, if our work be such, that, after some escape from it, we can take to it again cheerfully and willingly. When we read in the newspapers about the re-assembling of Parliament, the general effect conveyed to one's mind is a pleasant one. The impression left with us is that the members come back to their work willingly; they have been free from it so long that the appetite for the kind of thing has revived; and each man rises that morning with a positive feeling of exhilaration as he looks on to the event of the day. It is not as it was with Napoleon, even when he was Emperor. You remember how he enjoyed his Saturday and Sunday in the country quiet: and how on Sunday night he was accustomed to say, thinking of his return next morning to Paris and the cares of state, 'To-morrow I must put on the yoke of misery again.' Many people, young and old, feel as Napoleon felt. There is the heartsinking of the nervous little boy, going back to school after the holidays, with vague fears of evil. There is the apprehension of a great mercantile man, entering upon a season in which he foresees many painful difficulties and complications, and does not know how things may turn out. It is as with the little bark, which, from a sheltered nook where it was lying snug and safe, puts out unwillingly into the full fury of winds and waves. And even coming back to work which you like, and to which you thankfully feel yourself in some degree equal, there is a certain shrinking from putting the shoulder to the collar again, and going stoutly at your task. There is a certain inertia, a certain nervous timidity, to be overcome. You would like to quietly sit still where you are, and hide your head in a hole.

You will feel this, I think, in coming back from your autumn holiday-time; especially if you live and work in town. Human beings are never content. When you lived entirely in the country, it is very likely you used to think how pleasant and cheerful it would be to spend the dead months of the year in town; and just as the season is darkening down to winter, and the country beginning to look bleak and desolate, to get in among the warm dwellings and multitudes of your fellow-men. But now, if your home be in the city, you probably think, about this season, how enjoyable a thing it is to stay on in the country still, watching the stages through which it passes into its winter aspect; feeling the weather so much nearer you, and so much a greater part of your life, than it is in the town; looking for the days of the Martinmas summer, beautiful as any in all the year; waiting for the exhilaration of the frost, and the silence of the snow: and finding a value in the dreariest aspect of fields and hills and roads, for the hearty thankfulness with which it teaches you to enjoy the warm fireside, and light and books and music. It is October that gathers many men into town to work again, the yearly holidays over. And if you be a working man, who must earn your family's support by your labour, you may be pleased if you have had six weeks or two months of rest. If you have been away from work during the chief part of August and September, Nemesis might well be angry if you were to complain of coming back now as a hardship. Still you shrink a little. Nobody quite enjoys the idea of setting to work again; unless, indeed, his vacation have been so long that it has ceased to be enjoyed as rest, and come to be felt merely as the misery of idleness.

I suppose it is in human nature, that, after living for a while in a pleasant place, you should shrink from leaving it: many people find it costs them a painful effort to go away from their home; but, once away, they can quite easily stay away a long time. Inertia is unquestionably a property of mind as well as of matter. We don't like to move. Likely enough, my friend, in the autumn of this year, we have each been in half a dozen places, in any one of which we should have been content to have stayed all our days. And though no one can be fonder of his duty than yourself, my friend, or more pleased with the place where God has cast your lot: though it was a great strain and exertion to you to go away from both: yet it was a considerable strain and exertion to rise and come back.

Yes, it is a curious feeling you have, in coming away from any place which has been your home for even a short time; and there are not many things, besides actual physical pain, to which it does not cost a little pang to say Good-bye. The thoughtful reader has probably remarked how different a place looks when you are coming away from it, from what it ever looked before. You observe, almost with a start, a great many little things, and relations of things about it, which you never previously observed. All the familiar objects seem dumbly asking you to stay. And you must know the feeling by your own experience before you can rightly understand it. You cannot evolve it, *à priori*, out of your own consciousness. You may try to imagine what it would be like; but you cannot. Well does this writer remember how, in the days when he was a country clergyman, he used sometimes to pace up and down a certain little walk, every shrub by whose side had the look of an old friend; and to wonder what the feeling would be, and what the place would look like, if he should ever go away from it. But in those days he never thought he would; and his imagination would not serve him. And when the day, vaguely anticipated, came at last, every familiar holly and yew wore a new face; and the aspect of the whole scene was one never beheld before. In a lesser degree, but still a very appreciable degree, you feel all this in quitting a place where you have been staying for even six weeks. And you will be aware of a certain cheerlessness and desolateness, till your roots, thus torn up, get buried anew in the earth of your familiar home and its interests. Once fairly amid your own belongings and duties again, and you are all right. Your home seemed misty and unsubstantial while you were far away from it; but here it is again, real and warm, and with a general look of not unpleased recognition. And if you and I, my reader, in any degree deserve them, some kind looks and words of welcome, in the first busy days of somewhat confused occupation, may probably warm and cheer our spirit, and make us set with all the more hope and heart to work again.

There is no pleasanter incident in the little history of this time of return to very arduous duty, than the sending out of these Essays, which have been written in months past, as some not unsalutary change of occupation from graver thoughts and labours. The writer trusts that they may fall into the right hands. Certain volumes, which the friendly reader may know, have done so; and have gained for the writer the approval of various wise and good men, whose approval is to him among the most prized of earthly possessions. If these pages should fall into the hands of the man they do not suit, I hope he will not take the trouble of reading them: he has but to close the volume, and they will worry him no more. But the people for whom the author writes will understand easily that these chapters contain thoughts which are not unconsidered, and which aim at something beyond the mere amusement of a vacant hour.

In closing a former volume, I said I hoped the chapters it contained might not be the last. And now I am very pleased and thankful that the wish has been indulged. It is but a little part of a life, devoted to the most solemn and the happiest of all work, that has been spared to these Essays. But they have found an audience vastly wider than the writer's voice could reach, or than will ever listen to his sermons. And believing what I like to believe, not in self-conceit, but in thankfulness, I receive and cherish the assurance of very many who have told me that the reading of these pages did some little good to them; as the writing of these pages has done some little good to myself.

CHAPTER II.

CONCERNING THE WORLD'S OPINION:

WITH SOME THOUGHTS ON COWED PEOPLE.

IT seems to me that there are few things in which it is more difficult to hold the just mean, than our feeling as to the opinion of those around us. For the most part, you will find human beings taking a quite extreme position as to what may be called the World's Opinion. They pay either too much regard to it, or too little. Either they are thoroughly cowed by it, or they stand towards it in an attitude of defiance. The cowed people, unquestionably, are in the majority. Most people live in a vague atmosphere of dread of the world, and of what the world is saying of them. You may discern the belief which prevails with the steady-going mass of humankind, in the typical though not historical fact which was taught most of us in childhood,—that Don't Care came to a bad end. The actual idea which is present to very many minds is difficult to define. Even to attempt to define it takes away that vagueness which is of the essence of its nature, and which is a great reason of the fear it excites. And the actual idea varies much in different minds, and in the same mind at different times. Sometimes, if put into shape, it would amount to this:—that some great and uncounted number of human beings is watching the person; is thinking of him; is forming an estimate of him, and an opinion as to what he ought to do. Sometimes the world's opinion becomes a more tangible thing: it means the opinion of the little circle of the person's acquaintance; or the opinion of the family in which he or she lives; or the opinion of even some single individual of a somewhat strong, and probably somewhat coarse and meddlesome nature. In such a case the world becomes personified in the typical Mrs. Grundy; and the fear of the world's opinion is expressed in the question—What will Mrs. Grundy say?

Most people, then, live in a vague fear of that which may be styled Mrs. Grundy; and are cowed into abject submission not merely to her ascertained opinions, but also to what they fancy that possibly her opinions may be. Others, again—a smaller number, and a number lessening as the individuals who constitute it grow older—confront Mrs. Grundy, and defy her. DON'T CARE was a leader of this little band. But even though Don't Care had not come to trouble, it is highly probable that as he advanced in years he would have found that he must care, and that he did care. For a good many years I have enjoyed the acquaintance and the conversation of a man who, even after he became Solicitor-General, held bravely yet temperately by the forlorn hope of which a large part has always consisted of the young and the wrongheaded; and from which, with advancing years and increasing experience, men are so apt to drop away. I know that it was not vapouring in him to say, 'The hissing of collected Europe, provided I knew the hissers could not touch me, would be a grateful sound rather than the reverse—that is, if heard at a reasonable distance.'* But though I believe the words were sincere when he said them, yet I am convinced it was only by a stiffening of the moral nature, implying effort too great to last, that he was able to keep the feeling which these words expressed. I see in these words the expression of a desperate reaction against a strong natural bias; and I believe that time would gradually crumble that resolute purpose down. By a determined effort you may hold out a heavy weight at arm's length for a few minutes; you may defy and vanquish the law of gravitation for that short space; but the law of gravitation, quietly and unvaryingly acting, will beat you at last. And even if Ellesmere could peacefully go about his duty, and tranquilly enjoy his home, with that universal hiss in his ears, I know of those into whose hearts that hiss would sink down—whose hearts that hiss would break. How

* Ellesmere, in *Companions of my Solitude*.

about his wife and children? And how would the strong man himself feel, when day by day he saw by the pale cheek, the lined brow, the anxious eye, the unnatural submissiveness, that *they* were living in a moral atmosphere that was poisoning them? Think of the little children coming in and saying that the other children would not play with them or speak to them. Think of the poor wife going to some meeting of charitable ladies, and left in a corner without one to notice her or take pity on her. Ah, my friend Ellesmere, once you have given hostages to fortune, we know where the world can make you feel!

Let us give a little time to clearing up our minds on this great practical question, as to the influence which of right belongs to the world's opinion; as to the deference which a wise man will accord to it. Let us try to define that great shadowy phantom which holds numbers through all their life in a slavery which extends to all they say and do; to the food they eat, and the raiment they put on, and the home they dwell in; and in many cases even to what they think, and to what they will admit to themselves that they think. The tyranny of the world's opinion is a tyranny infinitely more subtle and farther-reaching than that of the Inquisition in its worse days; one which passes its sentences, though no one knows who are the judges that pronounce them; and one which inflicts its punishments by the hands of numbers who utterly disapprove them. And yet, one has not the comfort of feeling

Concerning the World's Opinion.

able to condemn this strange tribunal out and out; you are obliged to confess that in the main its judgments are just, and its supervision is a wholesome one. Now and then it does things that are flagrantly unjust and absurd; but if I could venture, with my experience of life, to lay down any general principle, it would be the principle, abhorrent to warm young hearts, and to hasty young heads, that in the main the world's opinion is right in those matters to which the world's opinion has a right to extend. I dare say you will think that this is a general principle promulgated with considerable reservation. So it is; and I hardly know to which thing, the principle or the reservation, it seems to me that the greater consideration is due.

It is wrong, doubtless, to be always thinking what people will say. It is a low and wretched state of mind to come to. There is no more contemptible or miserable mortal than one of whom *this* can be said:

> While you, you think
> What others think, or what you think they'll say;
> Shaping your course by something scarce more tangible
> Than dreams, at best the shadows on the stream
> Of aspen trees by flickering breezes swayed—
> Load me with irons, drive me from morn till night,
> I am not the utter slave which that man is
> Whose sole thought, word, and deed are built on what
> The world may say of him!

The condition of mind described in these indignant lines is doubtless wrong and wretched. But still one feels that these lines must be understood with much qualification and restriction. Neither in moral principle, nor in common sense or taste, can one go with those who run to the other extreme. It is as well for most people to be cowed by a rule which in the main will keep them right, as to be suffered to run wild with no rule at all. The road to insanity is even more short and direct to the man who resolves that he shall do nothing like anybody else, than to the poor subdued creature in whom the fear of the world's judgment has run to that morbid excess that she fancies that as she goes along the street everyone is pointing at her. There was nothing fine in Shelley's wearing a round blue jacket after he was a married man, just because men in general do not wear boys' jackets. And his writing *Atheist* after his name in the tourists' book, to shock people, does not strike me for its profanity half so much as for its idiotic silliness and its contemptible littleness. I do not admire the woman who walks about, a limp and conspicuous figure, in the days when crinoline is universally accepted. The extreme of crinoline is silly; the utter absence of it is silly; the wise and safe course is the middle one. I do not think it wise or admirable for a lady to walk a quarter of a mile bareheaded along a crowded street to a friend's house, even though thus she may save the trouble of going upstairs for her bonnet. I do not approve the young fellow who tells you, when you speak to him about some petty flying in the face of the conventional notion of propriety, that he will do exactly what he likes, and that he does not care a straw what anyone may think or say. That young fellow is in a very unsafe and a very unstable position. It is not likely that he will long remain at his present moral stand-point. It is extremely probable that, after a few signal instances of mischief brought upon himself by that defiant spirit, he will be cowed into abject submission to what people may think; and become afraid almost to move or breathe for fear of what may be said by folk whose opinion he secretly despises. He will gain a reputation for want of common sense, which it will be very difficult to get rid of. And even the humblest return to his allegiance to Mrs. Grundy may fail to conciliate that individual's favour, lost by many former insults.

There are some persons who are bound, not merely in prudence, but in principle, to consider the world's opinion a good deal. They are bound, not merely to avoid evil, but to avoid even the appearance of evil. And this because their usefulness in this world may be very prejudicially affected by the unfavourable opinion of those around them. It is especially so with the clergy. A clergyman's usefulness depends very much on the estimation in which he is held by his parishioners. It is desirable that his parishioners should like him : it is quite essential that they should respect him. It is not wise in the parson to shock the prejudices of those around him. It will be his duty sometimes to yield to opinions which he thinks groundless. However fond a clergyman of the Anglican Church may be of a choral service, it will be extremely foolish and wrongheaded in him to endeavour to thrust such a service upon a congregation of people who in their ignorance think it Popish. And it will not be prudent in a clergyman of the Scotch Church, placed in a remote country parish where the population retains a good deal of the old covenanting leaven, to fill his church windows with stained glass, or even to put a cross above the eastern gable. And such a man will also discern that it is his duty to practise a certain economy and reticence in the explaining of his views as to instrumental music in church, and liturgical services. If it be the fact that many rustics in the parish regard these things as marks of the Beast, he need not obtrude the fact that he holds a different opinion. For he would then, in some quarters, bring all his teaching into suspicion. Let Mr. Snarling take notice, that I am counselling no reserve in the grave matters of doctrine: no reserve, that is, in the sense of making your people fancy that you believe what you do not believe, or that you do not believe what you do. The only economy in doctrine which I should approve would be that of bringing out and applying the truth which seems most needful at the time, and best fitted for its exigencies. But as to other things, both in statement and in conduct, I hold by a high authority which states that many things may be lawful for the parson which are not expedient. And I believe that in little things the world's judgment is right in the main. There is a gravitation of society towards common sense: at least to approving it, if not to acting upon it. I am not going to defend hats and the like; or to stand up for our angular Western dress against the flowing garments of the East, though I believe our dress is more convenient if it be less graceful. And I do not believe there is any perverse bent of society to what is ugly and inconvenient, at least in male attire: if any hatter or tailor produced a better covering, which would be as cheap, it would doubtless find acceptance. But I hold that it is not wise for any ordinary man to take issue with his race on any point of dress. He will not be the wisest of judges who shall first lay aside the venerable wig of gray horsehair. It is not expedient that a young clergyman should fly in the face of his parishioners on such a question as the wearing of a shooting-coat or a black neck-tie, or as going out with the hounds. It was not wise in John Foster, the great Baptist preacher, to horrify his simple flock by appearing in his pulpit in a gray coat and a red waistcoat. No doubt, in logic, his position was unassailable. For people who reject all clerical robes as Popish, it is manifestly absurd to make a stand for a black coat and a white neckcloth. By making a stand for these, you cut the ground from under your feet: you admit the principle which justifies satin and lawn. Let me say, a sound and reasonable principle too. It is not fitting that in everyday attire a man should conduct the worship of God's house. But even with folk who thought differently, John Foster acted unwisely. As lawyers would say, it was a bad issue to take. I know how a certain eminent essayist, whom I much revere, stands up for eccentricity. He holds it to be a useful protest against our tendency to a dead conformity. I venture to say that, generally, it is not wise to be eccentric. You find that eccentric people are usually eccentric in little things, not worth fighting about. We all know that there are great and important things in which the world thinks wrongly: take issue *there* with the world, if you like: but it is not worth while to do so in small matters of dress and behaviour. It is not worth while to take a beard into the pulpit where it will interfere with the congregation's attention to the sermon; nor to appear in the same place in lavender gloves in a country where lavender gloves, in such a locality, are unknown. It is wise to give in to the little requirements on which the world's opinion has been plainly expressed. If you are resolved to take a part of opposition to all the world, do so in the behalf of things which are worth the trouble of the strife. Let it not be engraven on your tombstone, Here lies the man who confronted the human race on the question of the wide-awake hat. Stand up for truth and right, if you are fond of fighting: you will have many opportunities in this life. Smite the flunkey, pierce the humbug, violently kick the liar and seducer; and probably you will find abundant occupation. But though you know it is a pleasant and enjoyable thing for yourself and your children to sit on the steps of your country-house in the sunshine after breakfast, you will not gain the approval of wise men by doing the like on the steps of your town-house in a much frequented street: say, for example, in Princes-street in Edinburgh. And though you often roll on the grass with your little boy in the country, do not attempt the like on the pavement of such a public way. For in that case it is conceivable that you may be jeered at by the passers-by, and apprehended by the police. And while you are being conveyed to the station-house, instead of being esteemed as a philosopher and revered as a martyr, it is not impossible that you may be laughed at as a fool. 'We sat on the bridge, and swung our legs over the water:' with these words an eloquent writer lately began an essay. Of course the bridge was in a quiet rural spot. If the writer and his friend had done the like on London-bridge, the small boys would have hallooed at them, and the constable would have moved them on. Yet the merits of the deed are the same in either case. Only in the one case the world says You may; in the other case it says You must not. And the human being who resists the world's judgment in these little matters, shows, not strength, but weakness. Where principle is involved, it is noble to swing your legs, but not otherwise. But doubtless you have remarked that it is a common thing to find great obstinacy in petty concerns in a man who has no real firmness. You will find people who are squeezable and facile in the great affairs of life, and in their larger opinions have not a mind of their own, but adopt the opinion of the last person they heard express one; yet who persistently stick to some little absurd or bad habit which they have often been entreated to leave off, which annoys their friends, and makes them ridiculous. You will find a man whom you might turn round with a straw in his belief on any question political, moral, or literary, but who, having taken up the ground that once one is three, would go to the stake rather than give into the world's way of thinking on that point.

I beg the reader to observe, that I do not counsel a general conformity to the appointments of his particular world, merely on the ground that non-conformity may cause him to be derided, or disliked, or suspected. I wish him to think of the injury which his non-conformity may occasion to others. If your shooting-coat, my clerical brother, however light and easy to walk in on a hot summer day, is to stand between a poor dying girl and the comfort and profit she might get from your counsels and prayers, why, I think, if your are the man I mean, that you will determine never to go beyond your own gate but in the discomfort (often very great in country parishes) of severely clerical attire. Possibly few of my readers know that in various rural districts of Scotland a sermon, however admirable, will do no good if the preacher reads it: he must either give it extempore, or appear to do so by having previously written it and committed it to memory. 'I canna thole the paper,' I have heard an intelligent farmer say. He meant, he could not bear the sight of the manuscript discourse. It is fair to add that this prejudice is fast dying out, even in rural parishes; while in large towns in Scotland it has entirely disappeared. But however unreasonable and stupid may have been the prejudice which condemned overwrought ministers to several hours weekly of the irksome schoolboy labour of getting their sermons by heart; and however painful the anxiety which a man with an uncertain memory must often have felt on a Sunday morning, in the fear that he might forget what he had painfully prepared, and be reduced to a state of utter blankness, and ignominiously stick in his sermon; still, you will think that a conscientious man, earnest to do good, would make this painful sacrifice, not to his popularity, but to his usefulness. Let me confess, for myself, that I cannot imagine how the elder clergy of the Scotch Church were able to accomplish this awful toil. The father of the present writer, for thirty years, wrote and committed to memory two sermons of forty minutes each, every week; and hundreds of his brethren did the same. I could not do it, to save my life. Surely the intellectual fibre of the new generation is less muscular than that of their fathers. I have made mention of a judicious economy in giving instruction. You may discern the result of the want of it in what we are told about a poor dying labourer in one of the midland counties of England. It is quite unquestionable that the world goes round the sun; but it is not in the weakness of the parting hours of life that a poor uneducated man should be called to reconstruct the theory of the universe under which he had lived all his days. And though it was certainly needful to explain to the dying man the meaning of Christian faith, it might have been done without going into anything like metaphysics; and in a way in which a child of six years old might understand it, possibly as well as the parson himself. But a young parson could not see this. He would correct all the intellectual errors of his humble parishioner. He would pour upon him a flood of knowledge. Possibly you may smile at the odd expressions; but I remember few sentences which have so touched me with their hopeless pathos, as that with which the dying man feebly turned to the wall, and spoke no more. 'Wut wi' faeth,' he said, 'and wut wi' the earth goin' round the sun, and wut wi' the railways all a-whuzzin' and a-buzzin', I'm clean muddled, confoozled, and bet!' Well, let us hope that light came at the evening-time upon that blind, benighted way.

It should be borne in mind, that, as to any particular subject, there is sometimes great difficulty in ascertaining what the world (by which I mean our own particular world) is actually saying. It seems to me especially difficult to know, in a small community, what is the general opinion upon almost any matter. For you may fall in with people holding quite exceptional opinions. And exceptional opinions are often very strongly held; and held by very clever men. I remember hearing a really able man (one whom the great world has recognized as such) declare that in his judgment a certain clergyman, not remarkable for talent, earnestness, oddity, or anything but self-conceit, was the greatest preacher he had ever listened to; incomparably greater than A, B, C, or D, each of whom is well known to fame. The man who expressed this opinion was one you would have been obliged to admit as most competent to form an opinion; yet somehow, for some inexplicable reason, some sympathy or antipathy beyond the reach of reasoning, he had come firmly to hold an opinion which was entirely exceptional, which was shared by no other human being. And thus the world may be saying one thing at one tea-table, and just the opposite at another tea-table, in some little country town. At one tea-table, the sermon of last Sunday may be very good; at the other, it may be very bad. The like difference of opinion may exist as to the efficiency of the member of parliament. At one table, he may be a worthy, hard-working man; at the other, a poor silly creature. So with the singing of Miss X. If you are enjoying the cup that does not particularly cheer with Mrs. Smith and her set of friends, you may be informed, as a stranger to the town, that a great treat awaits you in listening to Miss X's songs. Her voice is splendid, and admirably cultivated; her taste exquisite. She is generally regarded as singing better than Jenny Lind. You naturally go away with the belief that, in the opinion of the world at Drumsleekie, Miss X is a very great singer. But all this is due to the accident of your taking tea with Mrs. Smith. Had it been Mrs. Jones, you would have been told that Miss X overstrained her voice; that she sang untruly; that she sang flat; that she sang harshly; that her affectation in singing was such that it was hard to refrain from throwing something at her head; and finally, that she could not sing at all. All this is perplexing. It would be a comfort to get over the preliminary difficulty, and to find out what it is that the world actually does say. Its voice, however, conveys an uncertain sound. And it would cost more time and trouble than the result would be worth, to add up the tea-tables on one side, and the tea-tables on the other side, and then discover on which side is the preponderant weight. And in case it should be found that the tea-tables on either side exactly balanced each other, the difficulty would arise, that it would appear that in Drumsleekie, on the subject of Miss X's singing, the world had no opinion at all. The favourable and unfavourable would just neutralize one another. And as with the singing of Miss X, so will you find it with the beauty of Miss Y, and the manners of Miss Z. Likewise with the horses of Mr. Q, and the poems of Mr. R. In short, to sum the matter up, it depends entirely on the set into which you get in a small community, what impression you are to carry away as to the general opinion upon any question. For though one slice taken from a leg of mutton will give you a fair idea of the general flavour of all the joint; yet you may (so to speak) cut a slice out of the talk of the town which shall be entirely different from all the rest. You may have chanced on the faction which cries up the new town-hall, or on the faction which cries it down. You may have chanced on the party which thinks the parson the greatest of men, or on the party which esteems him as one of the least.

Then it is certain that Mrs. Grundy may be made to appear to say almost anything, by the skilful management and the energy of two or three pushing individuals. It is possible for a very small number of persons to *get up a sough* (to use the Scotch phrase) either for or against a man. A few clacking busybodies, running about from house to house, may disseminate a vague unfavourable impression. A few hearty, active, energetic friends may cause the world's opinion, in a little place, to seem to be setting very strongly in a man's favour. You have probably heard the legend, which very likely is fabulous, of the fashion in which the blacking of a certain eminent man rose into universal fame. The eminent man hired four footmen, of loud and fluent power of expression, and of brazen countenance. He arrayed them in gorgeous liveries; the livery of each being quite different from that of the other three. Then, each alone, from morning to evening, they pervaded London; and this was what they did. When each footman saw a shop in which blacking appeared likely to be sold, he rushed into it with great appearance of excitement, and exclaimed in a hurried manner, 'Give me some of Snooks's blacking instantly.' Snooks, it should be mentioned, was the name of his eminent employer. 'Snooks's blacking,' said the man in the shop; 'we never heard of it!' 'Not heard of Snooks's blacking!' exclaimed the footman; 'why, my master won't let me brush his boots with any other; and just now he is roaring at me for brushing his boots this morning with that of Stiggins; I must be off elsewhere and get Snooks's blacking forthwith.' This interview naturally startled the man in the shop; he began to think, 'I must get some of Snooks's blacking; everybody must be using Snooks's blacking!' And when, in the course of the day, the other three footmen severally visited his shop as the first had done; one exclaiming, 'The Chancellor won't use anything but Snooks's blacking;' another, 'His Grace won't use anything but Snooks's blacking;' the last (in crimson livery), 'His Majesty won't use anything but Snooks's blacking;' the man in the shop took his resolution. He found out the factory of Snooks, and ordered a large quantity of his blacking.

That which has pushed blacking into fame, has done the like for other things. Two or three individuals, vigorously puffing a book, may cause it to seem that the world's judgment in the locality where they live is in that book's favour. And most people will bow to that judgment. Not very many people have so much firmness, or confidence in themselves, as to hold their own opinion in the presence of the strongly expressed opinion of the world on the other side. And a loud and confident declaration that something is very bad, will silence and put down many people who in their secret soul think it very good.

The *sough*, or general opinion and belief in a country district, may occasionally be got up by persons who are little better than idiots. Let me relate certain important facts. A very distinguished preacher once went to preach in the parish church of a certain big and ugly village in Scotland. The village lies among the hills, in a pastoral district. It had no railway communication; no near neighbours; no large town within many miles. The people, many of them, were very ignorant, very pragmatical and self-conceited. The big and ugly village thought it was the centre of the world; possibly, that it was the whole world. Its population formed an unfavourable estimate of the preaching of the great orator. It was generally said in the village that 'his sermons were no' very weel conneckit.' It happens that the discourses of that clergyman are remarkable for their logical linkedness of thought; for the symmetry and beauty of their skeleton, no less than for the brilliance and range of their illustrations. But some blockhead said (not having anything particular to say) that they were 'no' very weel conneckit.' Other blockheads grasped at this. It was something to say; and to say it seemed to imply the possession of some critical acumen. So the voice of Mrs. Grundy in that village re-echoed that statement on every side. The statement was, indeed, absurd. You might as well have said that the sermons were distinguished by their ignorant impatience of the relaxation of taxation, or by their want of mezzo-tinto. But people seized it, and repeated it. I remember going as a boy to that locality; and hearing several persons, all densely stupid, and most of them very conceited, speak of the great preacher. They all criticised him in the selfsame terms: 'His sermons were no' very weel conneckit!' But there is no opinion expressed with so great confidence as the opinion of the man who is incapable of forming any opinion. I remember an old gentleman telling me how he went to hear Dr. Chalmers. 'I could not understand the man,' said he; 'I could not see what he was driving at.' I am entirely satisfied that the old gentleman told the truth. Like the Squire in the *Vicar of Wakefield*, Dr. Chalmers could supply argument, but he could not supply argument, but he could not supply intellect to comprehend it.

An unfavourable *sough* may be got up in a rural district, by a man who combines caution with malignity; and all in such a way that you cannot lay hold of the malicious but cautious man. Let us suppose a new doctor is coming to the village. You, the old doctor, may go about the village and beg the people to try and receive him civilly; he may not be such a bad man after all. The truth probably is, that nobody supposes him a bad man, or intends to receive him otherwise than civilly; but a few days judiciously spent may excite a prejudice which it will take some time to allay. Some one speaks to you in praise of an acquaintance. You may reply, in a hesitating way, ' Yes; he is rather a nice fellow; but——well, I don't want to say anything bad of anyone.' In this way you have not committed yourself; but you have conveyed a worse impression than you could probably have conveyed by any definite charge you could have made against the man. Honest and manly folk, indeed, may possibly call you a sneak. What do you care? Some muscular Christian may kick you. In that case you will have the comfort of knowing that it unquestionably serves you right.

There is something worrying and vexatious in thinking that the *sough of the country side*, which in Scotland signifies the general opinion of the neighbourhood, is running against yourself and your possessions; even though you heartily despise the individuals whose separate judgments go to make up that *sough*. For you gradually come to attach considerable importance to the opinion of the people among whom you live, even though that opinion be in itself worth nothing. There is compensation, however, in the fact, that, if the unfavourable opinions of stupid and incompetent people are able to depress a man, the favourable opinions of stupid and incompetent people are able to elate and encourage even a very clever and wise man. Many such men are kept up to the mark at which they do good and even great things, by rumours of the high estimation in which they are held by Mrs. Grundy. There is probably as much happiness communicated to a human being by the favourable estimate of those around him—though they are people of no great standing, and not very wise—as if they were the wisest and noblest of the land. For, by degrees, even the wise man begins to fancy that these people who think so highly of him are not quite ordinary folk; they are more capable judges of human excellence than people in their station in life usually are. I can quite understand that the author who finds his book praised in the *Little Peddlington Gazette*, or the *Whistlebinkie Banner of Freedom*, will conclude that these are important newspapers, conducted with intelligence much surpassing that of country papers in general. He will be quite cheerful for a whole forenoon after reading in either of those journals that he is one of the most original thinkers of the age. So a clergyman, who is popular in his own parish, will quite honestly come to think that its population is remarkable for its intelligence and its power of appreciating a good sermon. Of course, as has been said, the converse case holds good. The ill opinion of those around you, if quite universal, is depressing, however much you may despise that opinion. Not only is that unfavourable estimate always around you, like an unhealthy atmosphere; but you gradually come to think that the people who hold it are rather wise and important people. A parson, going from a large and intelligent parish to one where the people are few and uncultivated, knows at first very nearly what is the mark of his present position and his present congregation. He knows that, seriously, the opinion which his parishioners form of him is neither here nor there. But he learns very soon that comfort and discomfort may be caused by judgments which are absolutely valueless. You may remember what Philip Van Artevelde says of that which may be regarded as the most favourable of all individual estimates of man :—

>How little flattering is a woman's love !—
>Worth to the heart, come how it may, a world;
>Worth to men's measures of their own deserts,
>If weighed in wisdom's balance, merely nothing!

And gradually you go farther than Van Artevelde.

Probably even that philosophic man, as he found day by day new indications of the warm affection and the hearty admiration of the woman he had in his mind when he said such words, began to think that, after all, there must be something unusual about him to elicit all that devotion; began to think that her opinion was sound and just; and that she must be a person of no ordinary sagacity who arrived at a judgment so true. You will do all that. You will not only be pleased by the favourable estimate of incompetent judges: you will come to think that they are very competent judges. A clergyman who at one time used to preach to a great crowd of cultivated folk in London, told me that, after he had been a few months in a little country parish, he felt quite pleased when he found the mill-girls of a manufacturing town four miles off walking over on Sundays to hear him preach; and also that he began to think those mill-girls very intelligent people, whose appreciation was worth having. Your 'nature is subdued to what it works in.' You stand in considerable awe of things amid which you always live. And the truth is, that almost everything, when you come to know it well, is bigger than the stranger fancies it. It is because things, when you come to know them, are really so good, that the *lues Boswelliana* prevails to such a degree in biographers; that each parson thinks his own church in some one respect superior to the general run; and that the rustics of each parish think their own the finest in the country. The things are really very good ; and it is difficult to estimate how good, relatively to others. When a wise man finds himself second, or ninth, or nineteenth in competition with others, whether the competition be in the size of his turnips, the speed of his horses, the beauty of his pictures, the bitterness of his reviews, the amiability of his children, or the badness of his headaches (all matters of which people are given to boast), the wise man will not necessarily conclude that he himself or his belongings are less good or great than he had previously supposed. The right conclusion is this : that other men and their belongings are better or bigger than he had fancied them. And though the favourable appreciation of judges, barristers, cabinet ministers, and the like, is undoubtedly worth more than that of factory girls, still the favourable appreciation of the factory girls may be regarded as worth a good deal by one who lives exclusively among factory girls.

Besides this, there is a farther consideration that comes in to give weight to the unfavourable judgment of Mrs. Grundy. A wise man, knowing how human vanity leads people to over-estimate their own merits, would, if he found that everybody thought he was a fool, begin to fear that he was one ; and also to fear that the fact that he could not see he was a fool showed the hopelessness of his condition ; as we know that a maniac occasionally believes that he is the only sane person in the world. I believe that there is nothing that can hold a man up against the depressing effect of being held in little esteem by those around him, as his family, or his neighbours; but the fact of his being held in good estimation by some person or persons elsewhere, whom he can regard as wiser and worthier judges of him than those around him are. I have known a great preacher, whose church was nearly empty on Sundays. It was in a remote rural district. But whenever he went to preach in any large town, the church in which he preached was crowded to excess. So he could set the opinion of the remote Mrs. Grundy against that of the near Mrs. Grundy: and, though surrounded by the unfavourable estimation of the near Mrs. Grundy, he could retain composure and confidence in himself, by backing up his estimate of himself with that of the distant world. And there are people with no distant friends to lean on, who yet, in a remote situation, find the support and sympathy they want, in the better part of our periodical literature. The *Times*, coming daily to an educated man in a very rustic place, is a great blessing. So is the *Saturday Review* to the country parson. So are the Quarterly Reviews generally. He will find much in them with which he cannot agree; a good deal which is extremely distasteful to him. But in reading them, he breathes a different atmosphere from that in which he is placed by many of his daily concerns and acquaintances. He finds in them something to prevent him from being cowed into conformity. He finds the thoughts of cultivated men, holding the same canons of taste with himself; and in the main, holding nearly the same great points of belief on more important things. I felt it as a comfort, after lately hearing a man say that a certain noble cathedral was 'a great ugly jail of a place,' to read a brilliant article in praise of Gothic architecture. And when you are building a pretty Elizabethan house, with all its graceful characteristics, you do not mind a bit that Mrs. Grundy, Mr. Snarling, and Miss Lime-juice go about saying that it is gimcrack, barbarous, Popish, inconvenient, dark, and fit only for monks and nuns, when you are able to turn to many pages on which competent men have set out the beauties and comforts of that delightful style, and shown up the nonsense of the stupid and tasteless folk who abuse it. But if you stood alone in the world in your love for the well-shown gable and the pointed arch, it may be feared that, unless you had the determination of the martyr, you would be badgered into keeping your opinions to yourself, and into conforming your practice to that of other people. There are few more delightful things to any one who has long lived among those with whom he feels no sympathy, than to find himself among people who think and feel as he does. And there is more than pleasure in the case; there is something in this that will strengthen and vivify his tastes and beliefs into redoubled energy.

You will not unfrequently find people who loudly

profess their contempt for the world's opinion, who are really living in abject terror of it. A coward, you know, often assumes a bullying manner. And there is no weaker or sillier way of considering Mrs. Grundy, than to be ever on the watch for opportunities of shocking her. It is for the most part nervous people, very much afraid of her, who do this. We all know persons who take great delight in trying to astonish mankind by the awful opinions they express, and by conduct flatly opposed to the rules of civilized society. You will find parsons who in their sermons like to frighten people, by sailing as near unsound doctrine as possible; or by a manner very devoid of that gravity which becomes the time and place. So with young ladies who smoke cigars, or talk in a fast manner to gentlemen on subjects and about people of which they ought to know nothing. So with the greater part of all eccentricity. One can bear eccentricity, however great, when it is genuine. One can bear the man, however oddly he may act, who acts in Mrs. Grundy's presence as though he saw her not; and who *bonâ fide* does not see her. But it is a very wretched and contemptible thing to witness a man doing very bold things, going through all kinds of eccentric gyrations, with a side glance all the while at Mrs. Grundy, and with an ear upon the stretch to remark what she is going to say.

There are men who are right in carefully observing the world's opinion of them and their doings : whose duty it is to observe these things carefully. There are men who know for certain that the world has an opinion of them : an opinion varying from day to day; and an opinion upon whose variations very tangible results depend. Such a man is the Prime Minister in this country. His possession of actual power and of profitable place depends just upon the world's opinion of him : an opinion which ebbs and flows from week to week ; which is indicated unmistakeably by his parliamentary majority as it rises and sinks; and which is affected by a host of circumstances quite away from the Premier's merits. If the Premier is desirous to retain his place, I should fancy that, till he gets indurated to it, it must be a most disagreeable one. From what a variety of quarters the voice of Mrs. Grundy must be borne to his ears; and how difficult it must be to know precisely what importance to attach to this or that specific bellow! Judging from the easy way in which the present head of the Government bears his functions, one would suppose that to be Prime Minister must be like being stoker of an American high-pressure steamer. At first, you will be in momently expectation of being blown up; but by-and-by you will come to take it quite coolly ; indeed with a hardihood rather appalling to most people to see. There is no one who has it in his power to know so certainly and immediately what his own world thinks of him, as a great actor. It is an index of his popularity, as certain as the mercury in the thermometer is of the temperature, how the theatre fills at which he performs. And to him, popularity is more than empty praise. It is substantial pudding. The bread and butter of his wife and children depend upon it. There are cases in which it is a miserable spectacle to see a man eagerly anxious about the world's opinion. There is no more contemptible and degrading sight than a clergyman who sets his heart upon popularity as a preacher; who is always fishing for compliments, and using claptrap arts to draw a crowd and amaze people. You come to hear of preachers who, it is plain, are prepared to go any length: men who would preach standing on their head rather than fail of creating a sensation. I thank God I never listened to such; but I have read in print addresses described as having been given in buildings professedly used for the worship of the Almighty, which addresses, in their title, subject, and entire tone, were perfectly analogous to the advertisements and exhibitions of Barnum. Their vulgar buffoonery and disgusting profanity were intended as a bait to the lowest and worst classes in the community. You may have known persons, in various walks of life, who were in the possession of the world's good opinion, but who could not be said to be in the enjoyment of it. It did not make them happy to have it, but it would have made them miserable to lose it. To go down a peg or two in the scale of fame would have been unendurable. And you would find them occasionally putting out feelers, to try whether the popular gale was slackening. Should it show signs of slackening, you have various acquaintances who will be careful to inform you. I knew a young divine who preached for almost the first time at a certain country church. A few days after, a man from the parish, a vulgar person, and almost a stranger, came and assured him that his sermon did not by any means guv sahtisfawkshun. I have known a person, a stupid and ignorant blockhead, who devoted himself to going about and retailing to every one he knew, any wretched little piece of tattle which might be disagreeable to hear. I don't believe the man was malignant. I suppose he yielded to an impulse analogous to that which makes a hen cackle when it has laid an egg. Unhappily, some men are so weak that, though they find it unpleasant to be informed that the world is pronouncing opinion against them, they yet find a certain fascination impelling them to learn all particulars as to this unfriendly opinion. And so the ignorant blockhead found many attentive auditors. Doubtless this gratified him. My readers, cut such a man short at once. Snub him. Shut him up. As you would close the window through which a bitter north-east wind is blowing into your chamber on a winter day, so shut up this wretched gutter that conveys to you the dregs of Mrs. Grundy!

As you go on through life, my friend, you will discover a good many *Cowed People*. These people have been fairly beaten by the fear of what the world will say. They are always in a vague alarm. They are afraid of doing or saying the most innocent thing, lest in some way, they cannot say how, it may turn to their prejudice. They are in mortal dread of committing themselves. They live in some general confused apprehension of what may come next. They are always thinking that Mr. A bowed rather stiffly to them, and wondering what it can mean; that Mrs. B looked the other way as they passed, and no doubt intends to finally cut their acquaintance; and the like. All this shades off into developments which pass the limit of sanity; as believing that the entire population of the place have combined against them, and that the human race at large is resolved to thwart their plans and crush their hopes. I do not mention these things to be laughed at. The sincerest sympathy is due to such as suffer in this way. No doubt all this founds upon a nervous, anxious nature; but it has been greatly fostered by lending a ready ear to such stupid, if not malicious, tattlers as have just been mentioned. There is, indeed, much of natural temperament here; much of physical constitution. There are boys who go to school each morning, trembling with vague apprehension, they cannot say of what. Possibly there is some idea that all their companions may league against them. There is not much of the magnanimous about boys; and such a poor little fellow probably leads a sad enough school life. And years afterwards, when he is a man in business, you may find him going away

Concerning the World's Opinion. 45

from his cottage on the outskirts into town each morning, to get his letters and attend to the day's transactions, as Daniel might have gone into the den. To many human beings the world is as a great, fierce machine, whirring and grinding inexorably on; and their great desire is to keep away from it. And possibly the man who is most thoroughly cowed by the world is not the man who lives in an even and equable awe of it; but rather he who now and then rebels, makes a frantic, foolish fight for freedom, gets terribly mauled in a quarrel with the world on some stupid issue, and then gives up, and sinks down beaten into a state of utter prostration. Probably such a man, for a while after each desperate rally, is the most cowed of cowed men.

There are human beings of this temperament who seem to feel as though any street in which an acquaintance lives were barricaded against their passage. They will tell you they don't like to pass Mr. Smith's house, lest he should see them. You listen with wonder; and possibly you reply, 'Suppose he does, what then?' Of course they cannot answer your question; they cannot fix on any specific evil result which would follow if Mr. Smith did happen to see them; they have simply a vague fear of the consequences of that event. You will find such people, if they are walking along the street, and see any one they know coming in their direction, instantly get out of the way by turning down some side lane. I believe that in the hunting-field the cry of *Ware wheat* warns the horseman to keep off the ground sown with that precious grain, lest the crop suffer damage. I think I have seen human beings, the voice of whose whole nature, as they advanced through creation, appeared to be *Ware friends*! Their wish was just to keep out of anybody's way. It was vain to ask what harm would follow even if they met Mr. Green or the Miss Browns. They did not know exactly why they were afraid: they were vaguely cowed. Is it because the present writer feels within himself something which might ultimately land him in that wretched condition of moral prostration, that he is anxious to describe it accurately and protest against it bitterly? You find people so thoroughly cowed, that they appear to be always apologising for venturing to be in this world. They seem virtually to say to every one they meet, but especially to all baronets, lords, and the like, ' I beg your pardon for being here.' You will find them saying this even to wealthy mercantile men. Not only is this a painful and degrading point to arrive at; I do not hesitate to say that it is a morally wrong one. It implies a forgetfulness of Who put you in this world, my friend, that you should wish to skulk through it in that fashion. Is not *this* the right thing for a human being to feel—The Creator put me here, in my lowly place indeed; but I have as good a right in this world, in my own place in it, as the Queen or the Emperor. My title to be here is exactly the same as that of the greatest and noblest; it is the will of my Maker. And I shall follow the advice of a good and resolute man in an early century, who was always ready to give honour to whom it was due, but who would not abnegate his rights as man, for mortal. I intend to do what he said should be done by 'every man'—I intend, 'wherein I am called, therein to abide with God.'

There are few more contemptible exhibitions of human slavery than you may find in cowed people who, in every little thing they do, are guided not by their notion of what is right, but by their belief as to what Mrs. Grundy may say; more especially the Grundy whose income and social standing somewhat surpass their own. I once heard a parson, who had a large income, say that he could not venture to put his man-servant into livery, because the gentry in his parish would not like it! I suggested that it was no concern of the gentry how he might attire his servant; that the questions to be considered concerned only himself, and appeared to me to be these:—

1. Whether he could afford it;
2. Whether he would like it.

And that for myself, if I could answer these questions in the affirmative, I should like to see the man in my parish who would venture to interfere with what I thought fit to do in the matter. Not but what I believe that vulgar and impertinent individuals might be found who would not like to see my friend approximating too closely to their own magnificence; but if there be a thing in this world to be decisively and instantly snubbed, it assuredly would be the insolence of venturing to express, in my friend's presence, either liking or dislike in the case. I have known a talking busybody, a relation of Miss Limejuice, who called at the house of a family lately come to settle in a remote country region, to inform them that their dining so late as they did was regarded as presumptuous; and that various neighbouring families felt aggrieved that their own dinner-hour, hitherto esteemed the most advanced in fashion, had been transcended by the new comers. It may suffice to say, that, though the relation of Miss Limejuice was treated with entire civility, she never ventured in that house to recur to that topic again. It is curious how rapidly it comes to be understood, whether any individual possesses that cowed and abject nature which permits impertinent interference in his private concerns, or not. The most meddlesome of tattling old women knows when she may venture to repeat Mrs. Grundy's opinion, and when she had better not. And all this without the least noisy demonstration; all this with very little reference to the absolute social position of the person to be interfered with. It is a question of the nature of the animal. An eagle, you know, is a smaller animal than a goose; but it is inexpedient to interfere with the former bird. If you have any unpleasant advice to offer, stick to the goose, my friend!

In this country, when a man gets on in life, and begins to evince signs of wealth, the only hostile feeling he is likely to encounter is that of the superior class into which he is now seeking admission. It is natural enough that those who have long been in an elevated place, should feel disquieted when they find some one on whom they have been accustomed to look downwards, rising up to their own level, or even transcending it. The feeling, of course, is an unworthy one; and worthy people struggle with it, and soon get over it. A still more disagreeable manifestation is one which I am told is not uncommon in democratic countries. It is that the man who rises is pursued by the envy and hatred of the class from which he rises; and that the people of that class desire to keep him down to his original level. I have been told that in the United States men who have reached great fortune are afraid to take the use of it, lest by doing so they should draw upon themselves the popular enmity. It is quite certain that a rich man in a certain Atlantic city put up a gilded lamp over his front door; and that in a few days a deputation of his neighbours waited upon the rich man, and informed him that the gilded lamp would not do; that it was esteemed as 'too aristocratic;' and that, if he did not wish his windows smashed, he had better have it taken away. In this country, the rich man would have shown the deputation the door; if, indeed, one can imagine the deputation even coming to him. But in that country of unlimited freedom, where the people are free to force other people to do what *they* like, and what the other people don't like, a different course was advisable. The rich man humbly bowed to the expressed judgment of Mrs. Grundy; and he removed the gilded lamp. As the old Scotch poet said, 'Ah, Freedom is a nobill thing!' The misfortune is, that in a perfectly free country, it seems essential that the cultivated minority should be the most cowed people —i.e. the most abject slaves—on the face of the earth.

It is worthy of notice, that, in the respect of the attitude which men assume towards the world's opinion, the most remarkable change sometimes passes over them. We all know that human beings in the course of their lives go through many phases of opinion and feeling as to most matters: but I think there is no single matter in which they may exhibit extremes so far apart as in the matter of confidence and cowedness. You will find men who as schoolboys were remarkable for their forwardness; who were always ready to start up and roar out an answer in their class; and who even at college were pushing and confident, and quite willing to take a lead among their fellow-students; but who, ten years after leaving the university, have shrunk into very modest and retiring and timid men. I have known several cases in which this was so; always in the case of men who had carried off very high honours. Doubtless this loss of confidence is in some measure the result of growing experience, and of the lowlier estimate of one's own powers which *that* seldom fails to bring to men of sense; but I believe that it is in no small measure the result of a nervous system early over-driven, and of a mental constitution from which the elasticity has been taken by too hard work, gone through too soon. You know that, if you put a horse in harness at three years old, he will, if he be a good horse, do his work splendidly; but he will not do it long. At six years old, he will be a spiritless, broken-down creature. You took it out of him too soon. He is used up. And the cleverest young men at the universities are often like the horse set to hard work at three. By the time they are two-and-twenty, you have sometimes taken out of them the best that will ever come. They will probably die about middle age; and till that time they will go heavily through life, with little of the cheerful spring. They will not rise to the occasion. They cannot answer the spur. They are prematurely old: weary, jaded, cowed. Oh that the vile system of midnight toil at the universities, both of England and Scotland, were finally abolished! It directly encourages many of the most promising of the race to mortgage their best energies and their future years, to sustain the reckless expenditure of the present. It would be an invaluable blessing if it were made a law, inexorable as those of the Medes, that no honours should ever be given to any student who was not in bed by eleven o'clock at latest.

It is a sad thing when any person, old or young, goes through his work in a cowed spirit. I do not mean, goes through his work in a jaded, heartless way merely, but goes through his work in the bare hope of escaping blame. A great part of all that is done in this world is done in this way. Many children, many servants, many clerks, and even several parsons, go through their daily round thus. I need not say how poorly that work will usually be done which the man wishes just to get through without any great reprobation; but think how unhappily it will be done, and what a miserable training of mind and heart it is! It seems to me that few people do their work heartily, and really as well as they can. And people whose desire is merely to get through somehow, seem to stand to their work as at a level below it. The man who honestly does his best, works from above; his task is below him; he is master of it, however hard it may be. The man who hopes no more than to escape censure, and who accordingly aims at nothing more, seems to work from below; his task is above him; he is cowed by it. Let us resolve that we shall always give praise when we can. You will find many people who are always willing to find fault with their servants, if their servants do anything wrong, but who never say an approving word when their servants do right. You will find many people who do the like as to their children. And only too often that wretched management breaks the spring of the youthful spirit. Yes, many little children are cowed; and the result is either a permanent dull quiescence, never to be got over, or a fierce reaction against the accursed tyranny that embittered early years—a reaction which may sometimes cast off entirely the bonds of natural affection, and even of moral restraint. How it encourages and cheers the cowed little fellow, growing up in the firm belief that he is hopelessly wicked, and never can do anything to please any one, to try reward as a change from constant punishment and bullying! I have seen the good effect upon such a one of the kind approving word. How much more cheerfully the work will be done; how much better it will be done; and how much happier a man he will be that does it! A poor fellow who never expects that he can please, and who barely hopes that he may pass without censure and abuse, will do his task very heartlessly. Let us praise warmly and heartily wherever praise is deserved. And if we weigh the matter, we shall find that a great deal of hearty praise is deserved in this world on every day that shines upon it.

May I conclude by saying, that many worthy people go through their religious duties in a thoroughly cowed spirit? They want just to escape God's wrath—not to gain His kind favour. The great spring of conduct within them is not love, but abject terror. Truly a mistaken service! You have heard of the devil-worshippers in India; do you know why they worship the devil? Because they think him a very powerful being, who can do them a mischief if they don't. Does not the worship of the Almighty, rendered in that cowed spirit, partake of the essential nature of devil-worship? Let us not love and serve our Maker, my reader, because we are in fear that He will torment us if we do not. Let us humbly love and serve him because He is so good, so kind to you and me, because He loved us first, and because we can see Him and His glory in the kindest face this world ever saw! I do not think we should have been afraid of Jesus of Nazareth. I do not think we need have gone in a cowed spirit to Him. And in Him we have the only manifestation that is level to our understanding, of the Invisible God. I think we could have gone to Him confidingly as a little child to a kind mother. I think we should have feared no repulse, no impatience, as we told to Him the story of all our sins and wants and cares. We can picture to ourselves, even yet, the kindly, sorrowful features which little children loved, and which drew those unsophisticated beings to gather round him without a fear. Let there be deep humility, but nothing of that unworthy terror. You remember what we know on the best of all authority is the first and great thing we are to do. It is not to cultivate a cowed spirit. It is to LOVE our Maker with heart and soul and mind.

CHAPTER III.

CONCERNING THE SORROWS OF CHILDHOOD.

ONCE upon a time, Mr. Smith, who is seven feet in height, went out for a walk with Mr. Brown, whose stature is three feet and a half. It was in a distant age, in which people were different from what they are now; and in which events occurred such as do not usually occur in these days. Smith and Brown, having traversed various paths, and having passed several griffins, serpents, and mail-clad knights, came at length to a certain river. It was needful that they should cross it; and the idea was suggested that they should cross it by wading. They proceeded, accordingly, to wade across; and both arrived safely at the farther side. The water was exactly four feet deep; not an inch more or less. On reaching the other bank of the river, Mr. Brown said, 'This is awful work; it is no joke crossing a river like *that*. I was nearly drowned.' 'Nonsense!' replied Mr. Smith; 'why make a fuss about crossing a shallow stream like this? why, the water is only four feet deep; *that* is nothing at all !' 'Nothing to you, perhaps,' was the response of Mr. Brown, 'but a serious matter for me. You observe,' he went on, 'that water four feet deep is just six inches over my head. The river may be shallow to you, but it is deep to me.' Mr. Smith, like many other individuals of great physical bulk and strength, had an intellect not much adapted for comprehending subtle and difficult thoughts. He took up the ground that things are what they are in themselves; and was incapable of grasping the idea that greatness and littleness, depth and shallowness, are relative things. An altercation ensued, which resulted in threats on the part of Smith that he would throw Brown into the river; and a coolness was occasioned between the friends which subsisted for several days.

The acute mind of the reader of this page will perceive that Mr. Smith was in error; and that the principle asserted by Mr. Brown was a sound and true one. It is unquestionable that a thing which is little to one man may be great to another man. And it is just as really and certainly great in this latter case as anything ever can be. And yet, many people do a thing exactly analogous to what was done by Smith. They insist that the water which is shallow to them shall be held to be absolutely shallow; and that, if smaller men declare that it is deep to themselves, these smaller men shall be regarded as weak, fanciful, and mistaken. Many people, as they look back upon the sorrows of their own childhood, or as they look round upon the sorrows of existing childhood, think that these

Sorrows of Childhood. 57

sorrows are or were very light and insignificant, and their causes very small. These people do this, because to them, as they are now, *big people* (to use the expressive phrase of childhood), these sorrows would be light if they should befal. But though these sorrows may seem light to us now, and their causes small, it is only as water four feet in depth was shallow to the tall Mr. Smith. The same water was very deep to the man whose stature was three feet and a half; and the peril was as great to him as could have been caused by eight feet depth of water to the man seven feet high. The little cause of trouble was great to the little child. The little heart was as full of grief, and fear, and bewilderment as it could hold. Yes, I stand up against the common belief that childhood is our happiest time. And whenever I hear grown-up people say that it is so, I think of Mr. Smith, and the water four feet deep. I have always, in my heart, rebelled against that common delusion. I recal it, as if it were yesterday, a day which I have left behind me more than twenty years. I see a large hall, the hall of a certain educational institution, which helped to make the present writer what he is. It is the day of the distribution of the prizes. The hall is crowded with little boys, and with the relations and friends of the little boys. And the chief magistrate of that ancient town, in all the pomp of civic majesty, has distributed the prizes. It is neither here nor there what honours were borne off by me; though I remember well that *that* day was the proudest that

ever had come in my short life. But I see the face
and hear the voice of the kind-hearted old dignitary,
who has now been for many years in his grave. And
I recal especially one sentence he said, as he made a
few eloquent remarks at the close of the day's pro-
ceedings. 'Ah, boys,' said he, ' I can tell you this is
the happiest time of all your life !' ' Little you know
about the matter,' was my inward reply. I knew that
our worries, fears, and sorrows were just as great as
those of any one else. The sorrows of childhood and
boyhood are not sorrows of that complicated and perplexing nature which sit heavy on the heart in after
years ; but in relation to the little hearts that have to
bear them, they are very overwhelming for the time.
As has been said, great and little are quite relative
terms. A weight which is not absolutely heavy, is
heavy to a weak person. We think an industrious flea
draws a vast weight if it draw the eighth part of an
ounce. And I believe that the sorrows of childhood
task the endurance of childhood as severely as those of
manhood do the endurance of the man. Yes, we look
back now, and we smile at them, and at the anguish
they occasioned, because they would be no great matter to us now. Yet in all this we err just as Mr. Smith
the tall man erred, in that discussion with the little
man Mr. Brown. Those early sorrows were great
things then. Very bitter grief may be in a very little
heart. 'The sports of childhood,' we know from
Goldsmith, ' satisfy the child.' The sorrows of child-

Sorrows of Childhood.

hood overwhelm the poor little thing. I think a sympathetic reader would hardly read, without a tear as well as a smile, an incident in the early life of Patrick Fraser Tytler, recorded in his biography. When five years old, he got hold of the gun of an elder brother, and broke the spring of its lock. What anguish the little boy must have endured; what a crushing sense of having caused an irremediable evil; before he sat down and printed in great letters the following epistle to his brother, the owner of the gun:— 'Oh, Jamie, think no more of guns, for the mainspring of that is broken, and *my heart is broken*!' Doubtless the poor little fellow fancied that for all the remainder of his life he never could feel as he had felt before he touched the unlucky weapon. And looking back over many years, most of us can remember a child crushed and overwhelmed by some trouble which it thought could never be got over; and we can feel for our early self as though sympathizing with another being.

What I wish in this essay is, that we should look away along the path we have come in life; and that we should see that, though many cares and troubles may now press upon us, still we may well be content. I speak to ordinary people, whose lot has been an ordinary lot. I know there are exceptional cases; but I firmly believe that, as for most of us, we never have seen better days than these. No doubt, in the retrospect of early youth, we seem to see a time when the summer was brighter, the flowers sweeter, the snowy days of winter more cheerful, than we ever find them now. But, in sober sense, we know that it is all an illusion. It is only as the man travelling over the burning desert sees sparkling water and shady trees where he knows there is nothing but arid sand.

I dare say you know that one of the acutest of living men has maintained that it is foolish to grieve over past suffering. He says, truly enough in one sense, that the suffering which is past is as truly non-existent as the suffering which has never been at all; that, in fact, past suffering is now nothing; and is entitled to no more consideration than that to which nothing is entitled. No doubt, when bodily pain has ceased, it is all over: we do not feel it any more. And you have probably observed that the impression left by bodily pain passes very quickly away. The sleepless night, or the night of torment from toothache, which seemed such a distressing reality while it was dragging over, looks a very shadowy thing the next forenoon. But it may be doubted whether you will ever so far succeed in overcoming the fancies and weaknesses of humanity, as to get people to cease to feel that past sufferings and sorrows are a great part of their present life. The remembrance of our past life is a great part of our present life. And, indeed, the greater part of human suffering consists in its anticipation and in its recollection. It is so by the inevitable law of our being. It is because we are rational creatures that it is so. We cannot help looking forward to that which

Sorrows of Childhood.

is coming, and looking back on that which is past; nor can we suppress, as we do so, an emotion corresponding to the perception. There is not the least use in telling a little boy who knows he is to have a tooth pulled out to-morrow, that it is absurd in him to make himself unhappy to-night through the anticipation of it. You may show, with irrefragable force of reason, that the pain will last only for the two or three seconds during which the tooth is being wrenched from its place; and that it will be time enough to vex himself about the pain when he has actually to feel it. But the little fellow will pass but an unhappy night in the dismal prospect; and by the time the cold iron lays hold of the tooth, he will have endured by anticipation a vast deal more suffering than the suffering of the actual operation. It is so with bigger people, looking forward to greater trials. And it serves no end whatever to prove that all this ought not to be. The question as to the emotions turned off in the workings of the human mind is one of fact. It is not how the machine ought to work, but how the machine does work. And as with the anticipation of suffering, so with its retrospect. The great grief which is past, even though its consequences no longer directly press upon us, cast its shadow over after years. There are, indeed, some hardships and trials upon which it is possible that we may look back with satisfaction. The contrast with them enhances the enjoyment of better days. But these trials, it seems to me, must be such as come through the direct intervention of Providence; and they must be clear of the elements of human cruelty or injustice. I do not believe that a man who was a weakly and timid boy can ever look back with pleasure upon the ill-usage of the brutal bully of his school-days; or upon the injustice of his teacher in cheating him out of some well-earned prize. There are kinds of great suffering which can never be thought of without present suffering, so long as human nature continues what it is. And I believe that past sorrows are a great reality in our present life, and exert a great influence over our present life, whether for good or ill. As you may see in the trembling knees of some poor horse, in its drooping head, and spiritless paces, that it was over-wrought when young; so, if the human soul were a thing that could be seen, you might discern the scars where the iron entered into it long ago; you might trace not merely the enduring remembrance, but the enduring results, of the incapacity and dishonesty of teachers, the heartlessness of companions, and the idiotic folly and cruelty of parents. No, it will not do to tell us that past sufferings have ceased to exist, while their remembrance continue so vivid, and their results so great. You are not done with the bitter frosts of last winter, though it be summer now, if your blighted evergreens remain as their result and memorial. And the man who was brought up in an unhappy home in childhood, will never feel that *that* unhappy home has ceased to be a present reality, if he knows that its

Sorrows of Childhood.

whole discipline fostered in him a spirit of distrust in his kind, which is not yet entirely got over ; and made him set himself to the work of life with a heart somewhat soured, and prematurely old. The past is a great reality. We are here the living embodiment of all we have seen and felt through all our life ; fashioned into our present form by millions of little touches ; and by none with a more real result than the hours of sorrow we have known.

One great cause of the suffering of boyhood is the bullying of bigger boys at school. I know nothing practically of the English system of *fagging* at public schools, but I am not prepared to join out and out in the cry against it. I see many evils inherent in the system ; but I see that various advantages may result from it too. To organise a recognised subordination of lesser boys to bigger ones must unquestionably tend to cut the ground from under the feet of the unrecognised, unauthorised, private bully. But I know that, at large schools where there is no fagging, bullying on the part of youthful tyrants prevails to a great degree. Human nature is beyond doubt fallen. The systematic cruelty of a school bully to a little boy is proof enough of *that*, and presents one of the very hatefullest phases of human character. It is worthy of notice that, as a general rule, the higher you ascend in the social scale among boys, the less of bullying there is to be found. Something of the chivalrous and the magnanimous comes out in the case of the sons of gentlemen : it is only among such that you will ever find a boy, not personally interested in the matter, standing up against the bully in the interest of right and justice. I have watched a big boy thrashing a little one, in the presence of half-a-dozen other big boys, not one of whom interfered on behalf of the oppressed little fellow. You may be sure I did not watch the transaction longer than was necessary to ascertain whether there was a grain of generosity in the hulking boors; and you may be sure, too, that *that* thrashing of the little boy was to the big bully one of the most unfortunate transactions in which he had engaged in his bestial and blackguard, though brief, life. *I* took care of *that*, you may rely on it. And I favoured the bully's companions with my sentiments as to their conduct with an energy of statement that made them sneak off, looking very liked whipped spaniels. My friendly reader, let us never fail to stop a bully when we can; and we very often can. Among the writer's possessions might be found by the curious inspector several black kid gloves, no longer fit for use, though apparently not very much worn. Surveying these integuments minutely, you would find the thumb of the right hand rent away, beyond the possibility of mending. Whence the phenomenon ? It comes of the writer's determined habit of stopping the bully. Walking along the street or the country road, I occasionally see a big blackguard fellow thrashing a boy much less than himself. I am well aware that some prudent individuals would pass by on the other side, possibly addressing an admonition to the big blackguard. But I approve Thomson's statement, that 'prudence to baseness verges still;' and I follow a different course. Suddenly approaching the blackguard, by a rapid movement, generally quite unforeseen by him, I take him by the arm, and occasionally (let me confess) by the neck; and shake him till his teeth rattle. This being done with a new glove on the right hand will generally unfit that glove for further use; for the bully must be taken with a gripe so firm and sudden as shall serve to paralyse his nervous system for the time. And never once have I found the bully fail to prove a whimpering coward. The punishment is well deserved, of course; and it is a terribly severe one in ordinary cases. It is a serious thing, in the estimation both of the bully and his companions, that he should have so behaved as to have drawn on himself the notice of a passer-by, and especially of a parson. The bully is instantly cowed; and by a few words to any of his school associates who may be near, you can render him unenviably conspicuous among them for a week or two. I never permit bullying to pass unchecked; and so long as my strength and life remain, I never will. I trust you never will. If you could stand coolly by and see the cruelty you could check, or the wrong you could right, and move no finger to do it, you are not the reader I want, nor the human being I choose to know. I hold the cautious and sagacious man, who can look on at an act of bullying without stopping it and punishing it, as a worse and more despicable animal than the bully himself.

Of course, you must interfere with judgment; and you must follow up your interference with firmness. Don't intermeddle, like Don Quixote, in such a manner as to make things worse. It is only in the case of continued and systematic cruelty that it is worth while to work temporary aggravation, to the end of ultimate and entire relief. And sometimes that is unavoidable. You remember how, when Moses made his application to Pharaoh for release to the Hebrews, the first result was the aggravation of their burdens. The supply of straw was cut off, and the tale of bricks was to remain the same as before. It could not be helped. And though things came right at last, the immediate consequence was that the Hebrews turned in bitterness on their intending deliverer, and charged their aggravated sufferings upon him. Now, my friend, if you set yourself to the discomfiture of a bully, see you do it effectually. If needful, follow up your first shaking. Find out his master, find out his parents; let the fellow see distinctly that your interference is no passing fancy. Make him understand that you are thoroughly determined that his bullying shall cease. And carry out your determination unflinchingly.

I frequently see the boys of a certain large public

Sorrows of Childhood.

school which is attended by boys of the better class; and judging from their cheerful and happy aspect, I judge that bullying among boys of that condition is becoming rare. Still, I doubt not, there yet are poor little nervous fellows whose school-life is embittered by it. I don't think any one could read the poet Cowper's account of how he was bullied at school, without feeling his blood a good deal stirred, if not entirely boiling. If I knew of such a case within a good many miles I should stop it; though I never wore a glove again that was not split across the right palm.

But, doubtless, the greatest cause of the sorrows of childhood is the mismanagement and cruelty of parents. You will find many parents who make favourites of some of their children to the neglect of others: an error and a sin which is bitterly felt by the children who are held down, and which can never by possibility result in good to any party concerned. And there are parents who deliberately lay themselves out to torment their children. There are two classes of parents who are the most inexorably cruel and malignant; it is hard to say which class excels, but it is certain that both classes exceed all ordinary mortals. One is the utterly blackguard: the parents about whom there is no good nor pretence of good. The other is the wrongheadedly conscientious and religious; probably, after all, there is greater rancour and malice about these last than about any other. **These act** upon a system of unnatural repression, and systematized weeding **out** of all enjoyment from life. These are the people whose very crowning act of hatred and **malice towards** any one, is to pray **for** him, or to threaten to pray for him. These are the people who, **if their** children complain of their bare and joyless life, **say** that such complaints indicate a wicked heart, or Satanic possession; and have recourse to farther persecution to bring about a happier frame of mind. Yes; the wrongheaded and wronghearted religionist is probably the very worse type of man or woman on whom the sun **looks down.** And oh! **how sad to** think of the fashion in which stupid, conceited, malicious blockheads set up their **own** worst passions as the fruits of the working of the Blessed Spirit; and caricature, to the lasting injury of many a young heart, the pure and kindly religion of the Blessed Redeemer! These are the folk who inflict systematic and ingenious torment on their children; and unhappily a very contemptible parent can inflict much suffering on a sensitive child. But of this there is more to be said **hereafter;** and before going on to it, **let us** think of another evil influence which darkens **and** embitters **the** early years of many.

It is the cruelty, injustice, and incompetence of many schoolmasters. I know a young man of twenty-eight, who **told me** that when at school in a certain large city in Peru (let us say), he never went into his

Sorrows of Childhood.

class any day without feeling quite sick with nervous terror. The entire class of boys lived in that state of cowed submission to a vulgar, stupid, bullying, flogging barbarian. If it prevents the manners from becoming brutal, diligently to study the ingenuous arts, it appears certain that diligently to teach them sometimes leads to a directly contrary result. The bullying schoolmaster has now become an almost extinct animal; but it is not very long since the spirit of Mr. Squeers was to be found, in its worst manifestations, far beyond the precincts of Dotheboys Hall. You would find fellows who showed a grim delight in walking down a class with a cane in their hand, enjoying the evident fear they occasioned as they swung it about; occasionally coming down with a savage whack on some poor fellow who was doing nothing whatsoever. These brutal teachers would flog, and that till compelled to cease by pure exhaustion, not merely for moral offences, which possibly deserve it (though I do not believe any one was ever made better by flogging); but for making a mistake in saying a lesson, which the poor boy had done his best to prepare, and which was driven out of his head by the fearful aspect of the truculent blackguard with his cane and his hoarse voice. And how indignant, in after years, many a boy of the last generation must have been, to find that this tyrant of his childhood was in truth a humbug, a liar, a fool, and a sneak! Yet how that miserable piece of humanity was feared!

How they watched his eye, and laughed at the old idiot's wretched jokes! I have several friends, who have told me such stories of their schooldays, that I used to wonder that they did not, after they became men, return to the schoolboy spot that they might heartily shake their preceptor of other years, or even kick him!

If there be a thing to be wondered at, it is that the human race is not much worse than it is. It has not a fair chance. I am not thinking now of an original defect in the material provided: I am thinking only of the kind of handling it gets. I am thinking of the amount of judgment which may be found in most parents and in most teachers; and of the degree of honesty which may be found in many. I suppose there is no doubt that the accursed system of the cheap Yorkshire schools was by no means caricatured by Mr. Dickens in *Nicholas Nickleby*. I believe that starvation and brutality were the rule at these institutions. And I do not think it says much for the manliness of Yorkshire men and of Yorkshire clergymen, that these foul dens of misery and wickedness were suffered to exist so long, without a voice raised to let the world know of them. I venture to think that, if any one of five or six men I know had lived anywhere near Greta Bridge, Mr. Squeers and his compeers would have attained a notoriety that would have stopped their trade. I cannot imagine how any one, with the spirit of a man in him, could

Sorrows of Childhood.

sleep and wake within sight of one of these schools, without lifting a hand or a voice to stop what was going on there. But without supposing these extreme cases, I can remember what I have myself seen of the incompetence and injustice of teachers. I burn with indignation yet, as I think of a malignant blockhead who once taught me for a few months. I have been at various schools, and I spent six years at one venerable university (where my instructors were wise and worthy); and I am now so old that I may say, without any great exhibition of vanity, that I have always kept well up among my school and college companions; but that blockhead kept me steadily at the bottom of my class, and kept a frightful dunce at the top of it, by his peculiar system. I have observed (let me say) that masters and professors who are stupid themselves, have a great preference for stupid fellows, and like to keep down clever ones. A professor who was himself a dunce at college, and who has been jobbed into his chair, being quite unfit for it, has a fellow-feeling for other dunces. He is at home with them, you see; and is not afraid that they see through him and despise him. The injustice of the malignant blockhead who was my early instructor, and who succeeded in making several months of my boyhood unhappy enough, was taken up and imitated by several lesser blockheads among the boys. I remember particularly one sneaking wretch, who was occasionally set to mark down on a slate the names of such boys as talked in school; such boys being punished by being turned to the bottom of their class. I remember how that sneaking wretch used always to mark my name down, though I kept perfectly silent; and how he put my name last on the list, that I might have to begin the lesson the very lowest in my form. The sneaking wretch was bigger than me, so I could not thrash him; and any representation I made to the malignant blockhead of a schoolmaster was entirely disregarded. I cannot think, but with considerable ferocity, that probably there are many schools to-day in Britain, containing a master who has taken an unreasonable dislike to some poor boy, and who lays himself out to make that poor boy unhappy. And I know that such may be the case where the boy is neither bad nor stupid. And if the school be one attended by a good many boys of the lower grade, there are sure to be several sneaky boys among them who will devote themselves to tormenting the one whom the master hates and torments.

It cannot be denied that there is a generous and magnanimous tone about the boys of a school attended exclusively by the children of the better classes, which is unknown among the children of uncultivated boors. I have observed that, if you offer a prize to the cleverest and most industrious boy of a certain form in a school of the upper class, and propose to let the prize be decided by the votes of the boys themselves, you will

Sorrows of Childhood. 73

almost invariably find it fairly given; that is, given to the boy who deserves it best. If you explain, in a frank, manly way, to the little fellows, that, in asking each for whom he votes, you are asking each to say, upon his honour, whom he thinks the cleverest and most diligent boy in the form, nineteen boys out of twenty will answer honestly. But I have witnessed the signal failure of such an appeal to the honour of the bumpkins of a countryschool. I was once present at the examination of such a school, and remarked carefully how the boys acquitted themselves. After the examination was over the master proposed, very absurdly, to let the boys of each class vote the prize for that particular class. The voting began. A class of about twenty was called up: I explained to the boys what they were to do. I told them they were not to vote for the boy they liked best; but were to tell me faithfully who had done best in the class-lessons. I then asked the first boy in the line for whom he gave his vote. To my mortification, instead of voting for a little fellow who had done incomparably best at the examination, he gave his vote for a big sullen-looking blockhead who had done conspicuously ill. I asked the next boy, and received the same answer. So all round the class: all voted for the big sullen-looking blockhead. One or two did not give their votes quite promptly; and I could discern a threatening glance cast at them by the big sullen-looking blockhead, and an ominous clenching of the blockhead's right fist. I went round the class without remark; and the blockhead made sure of the prize. Of course this would not do. The blockhead could not be suffered to get the prize; and it was expedient that he should be made to remember the occasion on which he had sought to tamper with justice and right. Addressing the blockhead, amid the dead silence of the school, I said: You shall not get the prize, because I can judge for myself that you don't deserve it. I can see that you are the stupidest boy in the class; and I have seen reason, during this voting, to believe that you are the worst. You have tried to bully these boys into voting for you. Their votes go for nothing; for their voting for you proves either that they are so stupid as to think you deserve the prize, or so dishonest as to say they think so when they don't think so. Then I inducted the blockhead into a seat where I could see him well, and proceeded to take the votes over again. I explained to the boys once more what they had to do; and explained that any boy would be telling a lie who voted the prize unfairly. I also told them that I knew who deserved the prize, and that they knew it too; and that they had better vote fairly. Then, instead of saying to each boy, For whom do you vote? I said to each, Tell me who did best in the class during these months past. Each boy in reply named the boy who really deserved the prize; and the little fellow got it. I need not record the means I adopted to prevent the sullen-looking blockhead from carrying out his purpose of thrashing the little fellow. It may suffice to say that the means were thoroughly effectual ; and that the blockhead was very meek and tractable for about six weeks after that memorable day.

But, after all, the great cause of the sorrows of childhood is unquestionably the mismanagement of parents. You hear a great deal about parents who spoil their children by excessive kindness ; but I venture to think that a greater number of children are spoiled by stupidity and cruelty on the part of their parents. You may find parents who, having started from a humble origin, have attained to wealth ; and who, instead of being glad to think that their children are better off than they themselves were, exhibit a diabolical jealousy of their children. You will find such wretched beings insisting that their children shall go through needless trials and mortifications, because they themselves went through the like. Why, I do not hesitate to say that one of the thoughts which would most powerfully lead a worthy man to value material prosperity, would be the thought that his boys would have a fairer and happier start in life than he had; and would be saved the many difficulties on which he still looks back with pain. You will find parents, especially parents of the pharisaical and wrongheadedly religious class, who seem to hold it a sacred duty to make the little things unhappy ; who systematically endeavour to render life as bare, ugly, and wretched a thing as possible; who never praise their children when they do right, but punish them with great severity when they do wrong; who seem to hate to see their children lively or cheerful in their presence; who thoroughly repel all sympathy or confidence on the part of their children, and then mention as a proof that their children are possessed by the devil, that their children always like to get away from them; who rejoice to cut off any little enjoyment; rigidly carrying out into practice the fundamental principle of their creed, which undoubtedly is that 'nobody should ever please himself, neither should anybody ever please anybody else, because in either case he is sure to displease God.' No doubt Mr. Buckle, in his second volume, caricatured and misrepresented the religion of Scotland as a country; but he did not in the least degree caricature or misrepresent the religion of some people in Scotland. The great doctrine, underlying all other doctrines, in the creed of a few unfortunate beings, is that God is spitefully angry to see his creatures happy; and of course the practical lesson follows, that they are following the best example when they are spitefully angry to see their children happy.

Then a great trouble, always pressing heavily on many a little mind, is that it is over-tasked with lessons. You still see, here and there, idiotic parents striving to make infant phenomena of their children; and recording with much pride how their children

Sorrows of Childhood. 77

could read and write at an unnaturally early age. Such parents are fools; not necessarily malicious fools, but fools beyond question. The great use to which the first six or seven years of life should be given, is the laying the foundation of a healthful constitution in body and mind; and the instilling of those first principles of duty and religion which do not need to be taught out of any books. Even if you do not permanently injure the young brain and mind by prematurely overtasking them; even if you do not permanently blight the bodily health, and break the mind's cheerful spring; you gain nothing. Your child, at fourteen years old, is not a bit further advanced in his education than a child who began his, years after him; and the entire result of your stupid driving has been to overcloud some days which should have been among the happiest of his life. It is a woful sight to me to see the little forehead corrugated with mental effort, though the effort be to do no more than master the multiplication table; it was a sad story I lately heard of a little boy repeating his Latin lesson over and over again in the delirium of the fever of which he died, and saying piteously that indeed he could not do it better. I don't like to see a little face looking unnaturally anxious and earnest about a horrible task of spelling: and even when children pass that stage, and grow up into schoolboys who can read Thucydides and write Greek iambics, it is not wise in parents to stimulate a clever boy's anxiety to hold the first place in his class. That anxiety is strong enough already; it needs rather to be repressed. It is bad enough even at college to work on late into the night; but at school it ought not to be suffered for one moment. If a lad takes his place in his class every day in a state of nervous tremor, he may be in the way to get his gold medal, indeed; but he is in the way to shatter his constitution for life.

We all know, of course, that children are subjected to worse things than these. I think of little things, early set to hard work, to add a little to their parents' scanty store. Yet if it be only work, they bear it cheerfully. This afternoon I was walking through a certain quiet street, when I saw a little child standing with a basket at a door. The little man looked at various passers-by; and I am happy to say that when he saw me, he asked me to ring the door-bell for him. For though he had been sent with that basket, which was not a light one, he could not reach up to the bell. I asked him how old he was. 'Five years past,' said the child, quite cheerfully and independently. God help you, poor little man, I thought; the doom of toil has fallen early upon you! If you visit much among the poor, few things will touch you more than the unnatural sagacity and trustworthiness of children who are little more than babies. You will find these little things left in a bare room by themselves; the eldest six years old; while the poor mother is out at her work. And the eldest will reply to your questions in

Sorrows of Childhood.

a way that will astonish you, till you get accustomed to such things. I think that almost as heartrending a sight as you will readily see, is the misery of a little thing who has spilt in the street the milk she was sent to fetch, or broken a jug; and who is sitting in despair beside the spilt milk or the broken fragments. Good Samaritan, never pass by such a sight; bring out your twopence; set things completely right; a small matter and a kind word will cheer and comfort an overwhelmed heart. That child has a truculent stepmother or (alas!) mother at home, who would punish that mishap as nothing should be punished but the gravest moral delinquency. And lower down the scale than this, it is awful to see want, cold, hunger, rags, in a little child. I have seen the wee thing, shuffling along the pavement in great men's shoes, holding up its sorry tatters with its hands; and casting on the passers-by a look so eager, yet so hopeless, as went to one's heart. Let us thank God that there is one large city in the empire where you need never see such a sight; and where, if you do, you know how to relieve it effectually; and let us bless the name and the labours and the genius of Thomas Guthrie! It is a sad thing to see the toys of such little children as I can think of. What curious things they are able to seek amusement in! I have known a brass button at the end of a string a much prized possession. I have seen a grave little boy standing by a broken chair in a bare garret, solemnly arranging and rearranging two pins upon the broken chair. A machine much employed by poor children in country places is a slate tied to a bit of string. This, being drawn along the road, constitutes a cart; and you may find it attended by the admiration of the entire young population of three or four cottages, standing in the moorland, miles from any neighbour.

You will not unfrequently find parents who, if they cannot keep back their children from some little treat, will try to infuse a sting into it, so as to prevent the children from enjoying it. They will impress on their children that they must be very wicked to care so much about going out to some children's party; or they will insist that their children should return home at some preposterously early hour, so as to lose the best part of the fun, and so as to appear ridiculous in the eyes of their young companions. You will find this amiable tendency in people intrusted with the care of older children. I have heard of a man whose nephew lived with him, and lived a very cheerless life. When the season came round at which the lad hoped to be allowed to go and visit his parents, he ventured, after much hesitation, to hint this to his uncle. Of course the uncle felt that it was quite right the lad should go, but he grudged him the chance of the little enjoyment; and the happy thought struck him that he might let the lad go, and at the same time make the poor fellow uncomfortable in going. Accordingly he conveyed his permission to the lad to go by roaring out in a savage manner, '*Begone!*' This made the poor lad feel as if it were his duty to stay, and as if it were very wicked in him to wish to go; and though he ultimately went, he enjoyed his visit with only half a heart. There are parents and guardians who take great pains to make their children think themselves very bad; to make the little things grow up in the endurance of the pangs of a bad conscience. For conscience, in children, is a quite artificial thing; you may dictate to it what it is to say. And parents, often injudicious, sometimes malignant, not seldom apply hard names to their children, which sink down into the little heart and memory far more deeply than they think. If a child cannot eat fat, you may instil into him that it is because he is so wicked; and he will believe you for a while. A favourite weapon in the hands of some parents, who have devoted themselves diligently to making their children miserable, is to frequently predict to the children the remorse which they (the children) will feel, after they (the parents) are dead. In such cases, it would be difficult to specify the precise things which the children are to feel remorseful about. It must just be, generally, because they were so wicked, and because they did not sufficiently believe the infallibility and impeccability of their ancestors. I am reminded of the woman metioned by Sam Weller, whose husband disappeared. The woman had been a fearful termagant; the husband, a very inoffensive man. After his disappearance, the woman issued an advertisement, assuring him that if he returned he would be fully forgiven; which, as Mr. Weller justly remarked, was very generous, seeing he had never done anything at all.

Yes, the conscience of children is an artificial and a sensitive thing. The other day a friend of mine, who is one of the kindest of parents and the most amiable of men, told me what happened in his house on a certain *Fast day*. A Scotch Fast day, you may remember, is the institution which so completely puzzled Mr. Buckle. That historian fancied that *to fast* means in Scotland to abstain from food. Had Mr. Buckle known anything whatever about Scotland, he would have known that a Scotch Fast day means a week day on which people go to church; but on which (especially in the dwellings of the clergy) there is a better dinner than usual. I never knew man or woman in all my life who on a Fast day refrained from eating. And quite right too. The growth of common sense has gradually abolished literal fasting. In a warm Oriental climate, abstinence from food may give the mind the pre-eminence over the body, and so leave the mind better fitted for religious duties. In our country, literal fasting would have just the contrary effect; it would give the body the mastery over the soul; it would make a man so physically uncomfortable, that he could not attend with profit to his religious duties at all. I am aware, Anglican reader, of the defects of my countrymen; but commend me to the average Scotchman for sound practical sense. But to return. These Fast days are by many people observed as rigorously as the Scotch Sunday. On the forenoon of such a day, my friend's little child, three years old, came to him in much distress. She said, as one who had a fearful sin to confess, 'I have been playing with my toys this morning;' and then began to cry as if her little heart would break. I know some stupid parents who would have strongly encouraged this needless sensitiveness; and who would thus have made their child unhappy at the time, and prepared the way for an indignant bursting of these artificial trammels when the child had grown up to maturity. But my friend was not of that stamp. He comforted the little thing; and told her that though it might be as well not to play with her toys on a Fast day, what she had done was nothing to cry about. I think, my reader, that even if you were a Scotch minister, you would appear with considerable confidence before your Judge, if you had never done worse than failed to observe a Scotch Fast day with the covenanting austerity.

But when one looks back and looks round, and tries to reckon up the sorrows of childhood arising from parental folly, one feels that the task is endless. There are parents who will not suffer their children to go to the little feasts which children occasionally have, either on that wicked principle that all enjoyment is sinful, or because the children have recently committed some small offence, which is to be thus punished. There are parents who take pleasure in informing strangers, in their children's presence, about their children's faults, to the extreme bitterness of the children's hearts. There are parents who will not allow their children to be taught dancing, regarding dancing as sinful. The result is, that the children are awkward, and unlike other children ; and when they are suffered to spend an evening among a number of companions who have all learned dancing, they suffer a keen mortification which older people ought to be able to understand. Then you will find parents, possessing ample means, who will not dress their children like others, but send them out in very shabby garments. Few things cause a more painful sense of humiliation to a child. It is a sad sight to see a little fellow hiding round the corner when some one passes who is likely to recognise him; afraid to go through the decent streets, and creeping out of sight by back ways. We have all seen *that*. We have all sympathized heartily with the reduced widow, who has it not in her power to dress her boy better ; and we have all felt lively indignation at the parents who had the power to attire their children becomingly, but whose heartless parsimony made the little things go about under a constant sense of painful degradation.

An extremely wicked way of punishing children, is by shutting them up in a dark place. Darkness is naturally fearful to human beings, and the stupid ghost stories of many nurses make it especially fearful to a

Sorrows of Childhood. 85

child. It is a stupid and wicked thing to send a child with a message out into a dark night. I do not remember passing through a greater trial in my youth, than once walking three miles alone (it was not going a message) in the dark, along a road thickly shaded with trees. I was a little fellow; but I got over the distance in half-an-hour. Part of the way was along the wall of a churchyard; one of those ghastly, weedy, neglected, accursed-looking spots, where stupidity has done what it can, to add circumstances of disgust and horror to the Christian's long sleep. Nobody ever supposed that this walk was a trial to a boy of twelve years old; so little are the thoughts of children understood. And children are reticent; I am telling now about that dismal walk for the very first time. And in the illnesses of childhood, children sometimes get very close and real views of death. I remember, when I was nine years old, how every evening when I lay down to sleep, I used for about a year to picture myself lying dead, till I felt as though the coffin were closing round me. I used to read at that period, with a curious feeling of fascination, Blair's poem, *The Grave*. But I never dreamed of telling anybody about these thoughts. I believe that thoughtful children keep most of their thoughts to themselves; and in respect of the things of which they think most, are as profoundly alone as the Ancient Mariner in the Pacific. I have heard of a parent, an important member of a very strait sect of the Pharisees, whose child, when dying, begged to be buried not in a certain foul old hideous churchyard, but in a certain cheerful cemetery. This request the poor little creature made with all the energy of terror and despair. But the strait Pharisee refused the dying request; and pointed out with polemical bitterness to the child that he must be very wicked indeed to care at such a time where he was to be buried or what might be done with his body after death. How I should enjoy the spectacle of that unnatural, heartless, stupid wretch, tarred and feathered! The dying child was caring for a thing about which Shakspeare cared; and it was not in mere human weakness, but 'by faith,' that 'Joseph, when he was a dying, gave commandment concerning his bones.'

I believe that real depression of spirits, usually the sad heritage of after years, is often felt in very early youth. It sometimes comes of the child's belief that he must be very bad, because he is so frequently told that he is so. It sometimes comes of the child's fears, early felt, as to what is to become of him. His parents, possibly, with the good sense and kind feeling which distinguish various parents, have taken pains to drive it into the child that if his father should die, he will certainly starve, and may very probably have to become a wandering beggar. And these sayings have sunk deep into the little heart. I remember how a friend told me that his constant wonder when he was twelve or thirteen years old was *this*: If life was such a burden already, and so miserable to look back upon, how could he ever bear it when he had grown older!

But now, my reader, I am going to stop. I have a greal deal more marked down to say; but the subject is growing so thoroughly distressing to me as I go on, that I shall go on no farther. It would make me sour and wretched for the next week, if I were to state and illustrate the varied sorrows of childhood of which I intended yet to speak: and if I were to talk out my heart to you about the people who cause these, I fear my character for goodnature would be gone with you for ever. 'This genial writer,' as the newspapers call me, would show but little geniality: I am aware, indeed, that I have already been writing in a style which, to say the least, is snappish. So I shall say nothing of the first death that comes in the family in our childish days: its hurry, its confusion, its awe-struck mystery, its wonderfully vivid recalling of the words and looks of the dead. Nor of the terrible trial to a little child of being sent away from home to school: the heart-sickness, and the weary counting of the weeks and days before the time of returning home again. But let me say to every reader who has it in his power directly or indirectly to do so: Oh, do what you can to make children happy: oh seek to give that great enduring blessing of a happy youth! Whatever after-life may prove, let there be something bright to look back upon in the horizon of our early time! You may sour the human spirit for ever by cruelty and injustice in youth. There is a past suffering which exalts and purifies; but *this* leaves only an evil result: it darkens all the world, and all our views of it. Let us try to make every little child happy. The most selfish person might try to please a little child, if it were only to see the fresh expression of unblunted feeling, and a liveliness of pleasurable emotion which in after years we shall never know. I do not believe a great English barrister is so happy when he has the Great Seal committed to him, as two little and rather ragged urchins whom I saw this very afternoon. I was walking along a country road, and overtook them. They were about five years old. I walked slower, and talked to them for a few minutes, and found that they were good boys, and went to school every day. Then I produced two coins of the copper coinage of Britain: one a large penny of ancient days, another a small penny of the present age. 'There is a penny for each of you,' I said with some solemnity: 'one is large, you see, and the other small; but they are each worth exactly the same. Go and get something good.' I wish you had seen them go off! It is a cheap and easy thing to make a little heart happy. May this hand never write another essay if it ever wilfully miss the chance of doing so! It is all quite right in after years to be careworn and sad. We understand these matters ourselves. Let others bear the burden which we ourselves bear, and which is doubtless good for us. But the poor little things! I can enter into the feeling of a kindhearted man who told me that he never could look at a number of little children but the tears came into his eyes. How much these young creatures have to bear yet! I think you can, as you look at them, in some degree understand and sympathize with the Redeemer, who, when He 'saw a great multitude, was moved with compassion towards them!' Ah, you smooth little face (you may think), I know what years will make of you, if they find you in this world. And you, light little heart, will know your weight of care!

And I remember, as I write these concluding lines, who they were that the Best and Kindest this world ever saw, liked to have near Him; and what the reason was He gave why He felt most in his element when they were by His side. He wished to have little children round Him, and would not have them chidden away; and this because there was something about them that reminded Him of the Place from which He came. He liked the little faces and the little voices;—He to whom the wisest are in understanding as children. And oftentimes, I believe, these little ones still do His work. Oftentimes, I believe, when the worn Man is led to Him in childlike confidence, it is by the hand of a little child.

CHAPTER IV.

CONCERNING ATMOSPHERES;

WITH SOME THOUGHTS ON CURRENTS.

I AM not going to write an essay on Ventilation, important as that subject unquestionably is ; nor am I about to enter into any discussion of the various elements of which the air we breathe is made up. I am aware, indeed, that for the maintenance of animal and intellectual energy in their best state, it is expedient that the atmosphere should contain a certain amount of ozone; but what ozone is I do not know, and neither, I believe, does any one else. And on the matter of material currents, whether ocean currents, atmospheric currents, or river currents, I am not competent to afford the scientific reader much information. I know, indeed, as most people know, that it is well for Britain that the warm Gulf Stream sets upon our shores. I read in the newspapers how bottles thrown into the sea turn up in distant and surprising places. I am aware that the Trade Winds blow steadily from west to east. And I have sat tranquilly, and looked intently at the onward flow of streams; from the slow and smooth canal-like river that silently steals on through the rich level English landscape, to the wild Highland torrent that tears down its rocky bed, in white foam and thunder.

But what I wish, my reader, that you and I should do at present, is to take a large view of the case, not needing any special knowledge of physical science. Let us remember just this, that the atmosphere in which we live is something that touches and affects us at every inch of our superficies, and at every moment of our life. It is not to say merely that we breathe it; but that it exerts upon every part of us, inner and outer, an influence which never ceases, and which, though possibly not much marked at the time, produces in the long-run a very great and decided effect. You draw in the air from ague-laden fens, and you do not find anything very particular in each breath you draw. But breathe *that*, and live in *that*, for a few weeks or months, and see what will come to you. Or you go in the autumn, weak and weary with the season's work and worry, jaded and nervous, to the seaside, and the bracing atmosphere in a little while insensibly does its work; your limbs grow strong and active again, and your mind grows energetic and hopeful. And you have doubtless felt for yourself how the heavy, smoky air of a large city makes you dull and stupid, and how the sparkling draughts you draw in of the keen, un-breathed air of the mountains, exhilarate and nerve anew. And as for currents, without going into details, we know this general fact: If you cast a floating thing upon a current, it will insensibly go along with the current. There may not be a stronger or a more perceptible push at one moment than at another; but there is an influence which in the main is unceasing, and there is a general drifting away. Slowly, slowly, the log cast into the sea, out in the middle of the Atlantic, comes eastward, week by week, till it is thrown somewhere on the outer coast of Ireland or of the Hebrides. And when the thing cast upon the current is more energetic than a log, still the current affects it none the less really. The Mississippi steamer breasts that great turbid stream, and makes way against it; but it makes way slowly. Let the engines cease to work, and the steamer drifts as the log drifted. Or let the engines work as before, and the vessel's head be turned down the stream; and then, going with the current, its speed is doubled.

Now, the atmosphere I mean in this essay is the atmosphere in which the soul lives and breathes; and the currents, those which carry along the moral and spiritual nature to developments better or worse. Shall we say it, for the most part to worse? In this world, in a moral sense, we generally drift towards evil, if we drift at all. You must warp up the stream if you would advance towards good. It seems to be God's purpose that anything good must be attained by effort: if you slothfully go with the current, it will be only to ill.

Concerning Atmospheres.

I am not able, just now, to give you a definition of either moral atmospheres or moral currents which satisfies me. You will gradually see my meaning, if you do not see it yet. Let it be said, generally, that to follow inclination within, or to yield to the vague influence of the things and people around you, is to drift with the moral current. And sensitively to feel the moral influences amid which you live—the moral influences arising from external nature, or from the dwelling in which you live, or from the people with whom you associate, or from the books, and newspapers, and magazines, and reviews you read—is to feel the moral atmosphere. And a very great part of the influence which moulds human character, and decides human destiny, is of this vague, yet pervading kind. A tree, I am told, draws the chief part of its nourishment from the air: very much more than it draws from the earth through its roots. The tree must have roots, or it would not live or grow at all: yet the multitude of leaves draw in *that* by which it mainly lives and grows. And it seems to me to be so with human beings. We must be morally rooted and grounded, as it were, by direct education, and by directly getting principles fixed in our minds. But after this is done, we mainly take our tone from the moral atmosphere. We are mainly affected by moral currents; and just as really when we strive against them as when we yield to them.

I am sure you know that a great many of the things

we read—books, periodicals, and the like—affect us not so much by the ideas they convey, as by the general atmosphere with which they surround us. If you read, week by week, a clever, polished, cynical, heartless publication, it will do you harm insensibly; it will mould and colour your ways of thinking and feeling much more than you would think. You like its talent, you know: but you disapprove, sometimes very keenly, its general character and tone; and you think you are so on your guard against these, inwardly protesting against them each time you feel them, that no effect will be produced by them upon you. You are mistaken in thinking so. You breathe and live in a moral atmosphere, which is quite sure to tell on you. You are cast on a current; and it needs constant pulling against it to keep you from drifting with it. And your moral nature is not (so to speak) ever on the stretch with the oars; ever in an attitude of resistance to the malaria. Yes; that clever, heartless, cynical paper will leave its impress on you by degrees. And on the other side, you know that the influence of writings which are not obtrusively instructive, may sink gently into our nature and do us much good. There is not much formal teaching in them; but as you read them, you feel you are breathing a general healthy atmosphere; you are aware of a quiet but decided and powerful current, setting steadily towards what is good, and magnanimous, and true.

No doubt, friendly reader, you feel that what I have

said is just. In talking to people, in living in places, in reading books, you feel the atmosphere; you are aware of the current. I do not speak to people whose moral nature is callous as the hide of the rhinoceros, and who never feel the moral atmosphere at all. You might endeavour to prick a rhinoceros with a pin for some time without awakening any sensation in that animal. And there are human beings who, it is quite evident from their conversation and their doings on various occasions, are as little sensitive to the moral atmosphere, and the laws and proprieties which arise out of it, as the rhinoceros is to the very bluntest pin. They are not aware of any influence weaker than a physical push; as you remember the man who would take no hint less marked than a kicking. But *you* know, my friend, that in talking to different people, you insensibly take your tone from them; and you talk in a way accommodated to the particular case. There are people to whom, unawares, and without purpose prepense, you find yourself talking in a loud, lively manner, which is far from your usual one. There are others to whom you insensibly speak in a quiet, thoughtful way. And you cannot help this; it is just that you feel the atmosphere, and yield to it. It is as when you go out on a crisp, frosty day, and without any special intention to that effect, find yourself walking smartly and briskly along. But if it be a still, sunshiny October afternoon, amid the brown and golden woods, you will unconsciously accommodate yourself to the surroundings: you will (if there be no special call for haste) walk pensively and slow. Now, some may unjustly fancy, as they remark how different your demeanour is in the society of different people, that you are an impostor,—a hypocrite,—not to say a humbug; that you are falsely assuming a manner foreign to your own, that you may suit the different people with whom you converse. It is not so. There is no design in what you do. You are not desiring to please the loud man by assuming a loud manner, reflecting his; as I have heard of some one who was regarded as having paid a delicate but effective compliment to a great man who wore a very odd waistcoat, by presenting himself in the presence of the great man, clad in a waistcoat exactly like his own. There is nothing of that kind; nothing insincere; nothing flunkeyish. It is only that you have a sensitive nature, which feels the atmosphere in which it is placed for the time. You know how mercury in frost feels the cold, and shrinks; it cannot help it. Then in warm weather it expands by the necessity of its nature. It always appeared to me in my childhood that Dr. Watts effectually justifies the most offensive deportment on the part of dogs, by suggesting that it is their Maker's intention that they should exhibit such a deportment. There is a passage, not much known, in a lyric by that poet, which runs to the effect: 'Let dogs delight to bark and bite, for God has made them so.' If the fact be admitted, the principle is sound; but as judicious discipline can greatly diminish the tendency of these animals to bark and bite, I doubt whether the words of Dr. Watts are to be construed in their full meaning. But there can be no question that mercury, which is a substance not accessible to moral considerations, deserves neither blame nor praise for expanding and shrinking according to its nature. And while I admit that any doings of human beings, partaking of a moral element, are (in the main) so under the control of the will, that the human beings may justly be held responsible for them, I hold that this sensitiveness to the moral atmosphere is very much a matter of original constitution, and that the man who feels it may fairly plead that his Maker 'made him so.' And very many people—shall we say the most exquisitely constituted of the race?—discern the moral atmosphere which surrounds some men by a delicate and unerring intuition. There are men who bring with them a frosty atmosphere; there are men who bring a sunshiny. You know people whose stiffness of manner freezes up the frankest and most genial. You know there are people to whom you would no more think of talking of the things which interest you most, than you would think of talking to a horse; or, let us say, to a donkey. Do you suppose that I should show my marked copy of *In Memoriam* to either my friend Dr. Log, or my friend Mr. Snarling?

I daresay some of my readers, going to see an acquaintance, have walked into his study, and found themselves, physically, in a choky, confined, hot-house atmosphere. And on entering into conversation with the man in the study they have found, morally, the same thing repeated. The moral atmosphere was just the physical over again. You remember the morbid views, the uncharitable judgments, the despondency of tone. And I think your inward exclamation was, Oh, for fresh air, physically and morally! And, indeed, I can hardly believe that sound and healthy judgments are ever come to, or that manly and truthful thoughts are produced, except when the physical atmosphere is pure and healthful. I would not attach much importance to the vote, upon some grave matter of principle, which is come to by an excited mob of even educated men, at four o'clock in the morning, in an atmosphere so thoroughly pestilential that it might knock a man down. And there are houses, on entering which you feel directly the peculiar moral atmosphere. It is oppressive. It catches your throat; it gets into your lungs; it (morally) puts a bad taste into your mouth. There are dwellings which, even in a physical sense, seem never to have fresh air thoroughly admitted; never to have the lurking malaria that hangs in corners and about window-curtains thoroughly cleared out, and the pure fresh air of heaven let in to fill every inch of space. There are more dwellings where this is so in a moral sense. You enter such a dwelling; you talk to the people in it. You at once feel oppressed. You feel stupid; worse than that, you feel sore and cantankerous. You feel you are growing low-minded. Anything like magnanimity or generosity goes out of you. You listen to wretched sneers against everything that is good or elevating. You find a series of miserable little doings and misdoings dwelt upon with weary iteration and bitter exaggeration. You hear base motives suggested as having really prompted the best people you know to their best doings. Did you ever spend an evening in the society of a cynical, sneering man, with some measure of talent and energy? You remember how you heard anything noble or disinterested laughed at; how you heard selfish motives ascribed to everybody; how some degrading association was linked with everything pure and excellent. Did you not feel deteriorated by that evening? Did you not feel that (morally) you were breathing the atmosphere of a sewer or a pigsty? And even when the atmosphere was not so bad as that, you have known the houses of really excellent folk, which were pervaded by such a stiffness, such an unnatural repression of all natural feeling, such a sense of constraint of soul, that when you fairly got out of the house at last, you would have liked to express your relief, and to give way to your pent-up energies, by wildly dancing on the pavement before the door like a Red Indian. And, indeed, you might very probably have done so, but for the dread of the police; and for the fear that, even through the dark, you might be discerned by the eyes of Mrs. Grundy.

Some people are so energetic and so much in earnest, that they diffuse about them an atmosphere which is keenly felt by most men. And it often happens that you are very much affected by the moral influence of people, from almost all whose opinions you differ. I have no doubt that human beings who differ from Dr. Arnold and Mr. Hughes on almost every point of belief, have been greatly influenced, and influenced for the better, by these good men. There is something in the atmosphere that breathes from both of them that tends to higher and purer ways of thinking and feeling; that tends to make you act more constantly from principle, and to make you feel the solemnity of this life. And without supposing any special good fortune in the case of the reader, I may take for granted that you have known two or three persons whose presence you felt like a constant rebuke to anything mean or wrong in thought or deed, and like a constant stimulus to things good and worthy. You have known people, in the atmosphere of whose influence the evil in your nature seemed cowed and abashed. It seemed to die out like a nettle in frost; that clear, brisk, healthy atmosphere seemed to kill it. And you may have known men, after reading whose pages, or listening to whose talk, you felt more of kindly charity towards all your brethren in the helplessness and sinfulness of humanity.

Of course, to diffuse a powerful influence, whether towards evil or good, a man must possess great force and earnestness of character. Ordinary mortals are like the chameleon, which takes something of the colour of any strong-coloured object it is placed near. They take their tone very much from the more energetic folk with whom they are placed in contact. I daresay you have known a man who powerfully influences for good the whole circle of men that surrounds him. Such a one must have a vast stock of vital and moral energy. Most people are like the electric eel, very much exhausted after having given forth their influence. A few are like an electric battery, of resources so vast that it can be pouring out its energy without cease. There are certain physical characteristics which often, though not always, go with this moral characteristic. It is generally found in connexion with a loud, manly voice, a burly figure, a very frank address. Not always, indeed; there have been puny, shrinking, silent men, who mightily swayed their fellow-men, whether to evil or to good. But in the presence of the stronger physical nature, you feel something tending to make you feel cheerful, hopeful, energetic. I have known men who seemed always surrounded by a healthy, bracing atmosphere. When with such, I defy you to feel down-hearted, or desponding, or slothful. They put new energy, hopefulness, and life into you. Yes, my reader, perhaps you have found it for yourself, that to gain the friendship of even one energetic, thoughtful, good man, may suffice to give a new and healthier tone to your whole life. Yes, the influence of such a one may insensibly reach through all you think, feel, and do; as the material atmosphere pervades all material things. And such an influence may be exerted either through a fiery energy, or by an undefinable, gentle fascination. I believe that most men felt the first of these, who knew much of Dr. Chalmers. I believe that many have felt the second of these, in their intercourse with Dr. Newman or Mr. Jowett. Possibly, we might classify mankind under two divisions: the little band whose pith or whose fascination is such that they give the tone, good or bad; that they diffuse the atmosphere; and the larger host, whose soul is receptive rather than diffusive; the great multitude of human beings who take the tone, feel the atmosphere, and go with the current. It is probable that a third class ought to be added, including those who never felt anything, particularly, at all.

When you first enter a new moral atmosphere, you feel it very keenly. But you grow less sensitive to it daily, as you become accustomed to it. It may be producing its moral effect as really; but you are not so much aware of its presence. Did you ever go to a place new to you, of very unusual and striking aspect; and did you wonder if people there live just as they do in the commonplace scenes amid which you live? Let me confess that I cannot look at the pictures of the quaint old towns of Belgium, without vaguely asking myself that question. In a lesser degree, the fancy steals in, even as one walks the streets of Oxford or of Chester. You feel how fresh and marked an atmosphere you breathe, in a visit of a few days' length to either town. But of course, if you live in the strangest place for a long time, you will find that life there is very much what life is elsewhere. I have often thought that I should like to do my in-door work in a room whose window opened upon the sea; so close to the sea that looking out you might have the waves lapping on the rock fifteen feet below you; and that when you threw the window up, the salt breeze might come into the chamber, a little feverish perhaps with several toiling hours. Surely, I think, some influence from the scene would mingle itself with all that one's mind would there produce. And it would be curious to look out, before going to bed, far over the level surface in the moonlight: to see the spectral sails passing in the distance; and to hear the never-ceasing sound, old as Creation. I do not know that the reader will sympathize with me; but I should like very much to live for a week or two at the Eddystone Lighthouse. There would be a delightful sense of quiet. There would be no worry. There would be plenty of time to think. It would be absolutely certain that the door-bell would never ring. And though there would be but limited space for exercise, there would unquestionably be the freshest and purest of air. No doubt if the wind rose at evening, you might through the night feel the lighthouse vibrate with the blow of the waves; but you could recall all you had read of the magnificent engineering of Smeaton; and feel no more than the slight sense of danger which adds a zest. I am aware that in a little while one would get accustomed to the whole mode of life. The flavour of all things goes with custom. When you go back to the seaside, how salt the breeze tastes, which you never remarked while you were living there! And sometimes, looking back, you will wish you could revive the freshness and vividness of first impressions.

We have been thinking of the atmosphere diffused by books and by persons: let it be said that the thing about a book which affects your mind and character most, is not its views or arguments: it is its atmosphere. And it is so also with persons. It is not what people expressly advise you that really sways you; it is the general influence that breathes from all their life. A book may, for instance, set out sound religious views; but in such a hard cold way that the book will repel from religion. That is to say, the arguments may push one way, and the atmosphere the opposite way: and the atmosphere will neutralize the arguments and something more. And you will find people, too, whose advices and counsels are good; who often counsel their children or their friends to duty, and to earnestness in religion; but who neutralize and reverse the bearing of all these good counsels by the entire tone of their life. The words of some people say, Choose the good part, Ask for the best of all guidance and influence day by day; but their atmosphere says, Anything for money—for social standing—for spitefulness—for general unpleasantness. You will find various Pharisees now-a-days who loudly exclaim, 'God be merciful to me a sinner:' but woe betide you if you venture to hint to such that anything they can do is wrong!

Let me say, that you may read and you may hear religious instruction, which without asserting anything expressly wrong, still deteriorates you. It lowers you; you are the worse for it. There is an undefinable, but strongly-felt lack of the Christian spirit about it. Its views are mainly right; but somehow its atmosphere is wrong. I do not say this in any narrow spirit: it is not against one party of religionists more than another that I should bring this charge. Perhaps the teaching which is soundest in doctrine, is sometimes the most useless, through its want of the true Christian life; or through merely giving you the metaphysics of Christianity, without any real bringing of the vital truths of Christianity home to the heart, and to the actual case of those to whom they are told. I have read a book— a polished, scholarly tale, the leading character in which was a clergyman—but in reading the book you felt a strong smack of heathenism. I do not mean the savage, cannibal heathenism which still exists in the islands of the South Pacific; but the polished heathenism which was many centuries since in Greece and Rome. The clergyman was sound in dogma, I daresay, if you had asked him for a confession of his faith; but his Christianity was an outside garment, while his whole nature was saturated with the old literature and mythology of that ancient day. Then you may find a book, a religious book, containing nothing on which you could well put your finger as wrong: yet you were left with a general impression of scepticism. *That* was the atmosphere. The views and arguments are as the solid ground: but you touch the solid ground but at a single point—the circumambient ether is all around you, and within you. I have read pages setting out somewhat sad and discouraging views; yet as you turned the pages you were aware of a general atmosphere of hopefulness and energy. And I have listened to what might have made pages, if it had been printed (pages which assuredly I should not have read), setting out the sublimest and most glorious hopes of humanity, in a way so dreary, dull, wearisome, and stupid, that the atmosphere was most depressing. You felt as though you were environed by a damp, thick fog.

It would be an endless task to reckon up the moral atmospheres in which human beings live; or even the moral atmospheres which you yourself, my friend, have breathed. But there are some that one remembers vividly; they did not come often enough, or continue long enough, to lose their freshness. Such is the atmosphere which surrounds all operations relating to the sale and purchase of horses. You remember how, when you went to buy one of those noble animals, you found yourself surrounded by a new and strongly-flavoured phase of life. Was there not a general atmosphere as of swindling? You were surprised to hear lies, the grossest, told, even though they were sure to be instantly detected. You felt that your ignorance and capacity of being cheated were being gauged with great skill. It is a singular thing, indeed, that one of the most useful and beautiful of God's creatures should diffuse around him a most unhealthy moral atmosphere. You may have remarked that the noble steed is not merely surrounded by an ether filled with falsehoods; but that a less irritating, though still remarkable, ingredient, mingles with it, like ozone—it is the element of slang. I have remarked this with great interest, and mused much on it without succeeding in satisfactorily accounting for it. Why is it that to say a horse is a good horse should stamp you as a green hand; but that to say the animal is no bad nag, or a fairish style of hack, should convey the idea that you know various things? And wherefore should it be, that a shallow nature should be indicated by your saying you were willing to pay fifty pounds for the horse, while untold depth and craft shall be held to be implied by the statement that your tether was half a hundred?

A very disagreeable atmosphere, diffused by various persons, is that of suspicion. Some one has done you a kind turn, and your heart warms to the doer of it. But Mr. Snarling comes in; and you tell him, in hearty tones, of the kind turn, and of your warm feeling towards the man that did it. Mr. Snarling doubts; hints; insinuates; suggests a deep and traitorous design under that kind act: perhaps succeeds in chilling or souring your warm feeling; till, on the withdrawal of the unhealthy atmosphere, your better nature gets the upperhand again. And when next you meet the kind, open face of the friend who did you the kind turn, your heart smites you as you think what a wicked suspicious creature you were while within the baneful atmosphere of Snarling. You have seen, I daresay, very shallow and empty individuals, who fancied that it made them look deep and knowing, to say that beggars, for the most part, live in great luxury, and have money in the bank. *That* may be so in rare cases; but I KNOW that the want of the poor is often very real. It comes, doubtless, in some measure, from their own sin or improvidence; and as, of course, you and I never do wrong, let us throw a very large stone at the poor creature who is starving to-day, because she took a full meal of bread and butter and tea four days since. I have heard a man, with great depth of look, state that a certain cripple known to me could walk quite well. I asked the man for his authority. He had none, but vague suspicion. I told the man, with some acerbity (which I do not at all regret), that I knew the poor man well, and that I knew he was as crippled as he seemed. It looks knowing to declare of some poor starved creature that he is more rogue than fool. Whenever you hear *that* said, my reader, always ask what is the precise charge intended to be conveyed, and ask the ground on which the charge is made. In most cases you will get no answer to the second question; in very many no intelligible answer to the first. It would be a pleasant world to live in, if the people who dwell in it were such as they are represented by several persons known to me. I remember an outspoken old Scotch lady, to whom I was offering some Christian comfort after a great loss. I remember how she said, with a look as if she meant it, 'If I did not believe all *that*, I should take a knife and cut my throat!' It was an honest confession of her faith, though made in unusually energetic terms. And I might say for myself, if I had not some faith in my race, it would be better to be off to the wilderness at once, or, like Timon, to the desolate shore. The wants of beggars, even of the least deserving, are, for the most part, very real. As for their luxuries, they are generally tea and buttered toast. Sometimes fried ham may also be found. Poor creatures! These things are the only enjoyments they have; and I, for one, am not ready with my anathema maranatha. I have known very suspicious and uncharitable persons who were extremely fat; doubtless they lived entirely on parched peas. And *all* the sufferings of the poor are not shams paraded to the end of obtaining pence. I look back now, over a good many years, to the time when I was a youth at college. I remember coming home one night, between eleven and twelve o'clock, along a quiet street in a certain great city. I remember two poor girls standing in the shelter of the wall of a house, leaning against the wall, from the drenching rain. Neither noticed me. I see yet the deadly white face of one,—the haggard, sick look, as she crouched by the wall, and leant on the other's shoulder, as if just recovering from a faint. I hear yet the anxious, despairing voice with which the other said to her, 'Are you better now?' The words were not spoken at me, or spoken for the ear of any passer-by. All this was on the dark midnight street, amid the drenching rain. It was a little thing; but it brought home to one the suffering that is quietly undergone in thousands of places over Europe each day and night.

Probably you have known people who were placed in a sphere where the atmosphere, moral and physical, was awfully depressing. They did their work poorly enough; and many blamed them severely. For myself, I was inclined to wonder that they did so well. Who could be a good preacher in certain churches of which I have known? I think there are few men more sensitive to the moral atmosphere than the preacher. There are churches in which there is a hearty atmosphere; others, in which there is a chilly atmosphere; others, with a bitter, narrow-minded, Pharisaic; others, with an atmosphere which combines the pragmatic, critical, and self-sufficient, with the densely stupid. But passing from this, I say that most men, even of those who do their work in life decently well, have only energy enough to do well if you give them a fair chance. And many have not a fair chance: some have no chance at all. There are human beings set in a moral atmosphere in which moral energy and alacrity could no more exist than physical life in the choke-damp of the mine. Be thankful, my friend, if you are placed in a fairly healthful atmosphere. You are doing fairly in it; but in a different one, you might have pined and died. You are leading a quiet Christian life, free from great sin or shame. Well, be thankful; but do not be conceited: above all, do not be uncharitable to those for whom the race and the warfare have been too much.

I have said that it is the more energetic of the race that diffuse a moral atmosphere; the ordinary members of the race feel it. The energetic give the tone; the ordinary take it. There are minds whose nature is to give out; and minds whose nature is to take in. But most men have energy enough, if rightly directed, to affect the air somewhat; and though the moral ingredient they yield may not be much in quantity, it may be able to supply just the precious ozone. Let us try to be like the sunshiny member of the family, who has the inestimable art to make all duty seem pleasant; all self-denial and exertion, easy and desirable; even disappointment not so blank and crushing; who is like a bracing, crisp, frosty atmosphere throughout the home, without a suspicion of the element that chills and pinches. You have known people within whose influence you felt cheerful, amiable, hopeful, equal to anything! Oh, for that blessed power, and for God's grace to exercise it rightly! I do not know a more enviable gift than the energy to sway others to good; to diffuse around us an atmosphere of cheerfulness, piety, truthfulness, generosity, magnanimity. It is not a matter of great talent; not entirely a matter of great energy; but rather of earnestness and honesty, —and of that quiet, constant energy which is like soft rain gently penetrating the soil. It is rather a grace than a gift; and we all know where all grace is to be had freely for the asking.

You see, my reader, I have spoken of atmospheres and currents together. For every moral atmosphere is of the nature of a moral current. As you breathe the atmosphere, you feel that there is an active force in it: that you are beginning to drift away. It is not merely a present sense of something that comes over you; but you know that it sets you floating onward to something beyond your present feeling. The more frequent tendency of a moral atmosphere is to assimilate your moral nature to itself. Perhaps all atmospheres, if you live in them long enough, tend to this. But there are some atmospheres which, just at first, are so very disagreeable, that their effect is repellent; they tend to make you wish to be just as different from themselves as you can. But the refined person, at first revolted by a rude and coarse atmosphere, will, in years, grow subdued to it; and the pure young soul, shocked and disgusted at the first approach of gross sin, comes at last to bear it and to exceed it. Yes, the ultimate tendency of all moral atmospheres upon all ordinary people, is to assimilate them to the element in which they live. Let men breathe any atmosphere long enough, and this will follow; save in the case of an exceptional man here and there. It is a very bad thing for a young person to be much among thoroughly worldly people, or among mere money-making people. Let us not cry down money; it is a great and powerful thing. You remember, it was not money, but the over love of money, that was 'the root of all evil.' But it is most unhappy to live among those from whose entire ways of thinking and talking you get the general impression, that money is the first and best thing; and that the great end of life is to obtain it; and that almost any means may be resorted to for that end. All this is not said in so many words, but it pervades you unseen; you breathe it like an unwholesome malaria. You take it in, not merely at every breath, but at every pore. And the result of years of this is, that the warm-hearted, generous youth grows into the sordid, heartless old man; and that the enthusiastic young Christian is sometimes debased into a very chilly, lifeless, and worldly middle age.

And now, before I end, you must let me say this. And when I say it upon this page (which never formed any part of a sermon) you will know that I say it not because I think I must, but because I honestly believe it. There is a certain blessed influence which can mingle itself with every moral atmosphere that a human being can honestly breathe; and which can make every such atmosphere healthful. You know what I mean. It is the influence of that Holy Spirit, whose presence the Redeemer said was more valuable and profitable than even His own; and who is promised without reservation to all who heartily ask his presence. And you know, too, that we have a sure promise, that if we build on the right foundation, the current of our whole life will tend towards what is happy and good. There may be a little eddy backwards here and there, and sometimes what seems a pause, but it is in the direction of these things that the whole current sets; it is towards these that 'all things work together.' I firmly believe that the natural tendency of all moral currents, apart from God's grace, is downwards. Apart from *that*, we shall always grow worse; with it, we shall always grow better. Believe me, my reader, when I say, that if all our life and all our lot be not hallowed by the presence in all of the Blessed Spirit, we may be sure that we are breathing a moral atmosphere which wants just the precious ozone that is needful to true health and life. And if we have not, penitently and humbly, confided ourselves to our Saviour, we may know that we are drifting with a current which is certainly bearing us on towards all that is evil and all that is woful. It is sad to see the poor little pale and sickly children of some dark, stifling close in a large city; poor little things who never breathe the free country air; who are living in an unwholesome atmosphere within doors and without, in which they are pining, and growing up weak and nerveless: but it is more sad to see the immortal soul stunted, emaciated, and distorted, through the unhealthy moral air it breathes. It must have been a miserable sight, the little boat with the man in it asleep, drifting smoothly and swiftly along, beyond human reach, towards the tremendous cataract: but it is more miserable, if we saw it rightly, to see a human soul, in spiritual sleep, drifting day by day towards the fearful plunge into final woe. Let us pray, my reader, for both of us; that God would be with us by His Spirit, and keep us in all ways that we go; that in all our life we may breathe the Atmosphere of His presence; and by the Current of all our life be brought nearer to Himself!

CHAPTER V.

CONCERNING BEGINNINGS AND ENDS.

EVERYTHING in this world has a Beginning and an End.

After writing that sentence, which (as you see) sets forth a great general principle, I stopped for some time, to consider whether it holds always true. As one grows older, one grows always more cautious as to general principles. My young friend, when you are arguing any question with an acute opponent, you should, as a rule, never assent to any general principle which he may state. He may ask you, with an indignant air, Don't you admit that two and two make four? Let your answer be, No, I admit nothing, till I see how it touches the matter which concerns us at present. You do not know what may be involved in the admission sought; or what may follow from it. The most innocent-looking general principle may lead to the most appalling consequences. The general principle which appears most unquestionably true, may prove glaringly false in some very ordinary case.

You should request time for consideration before you admit any axiom in morals, metaphysics, or politics: or you should ask your adversary what he means to build upon it, before you can say either yes or no to it. Do as the Scotch judges do when a difficult case has been argued before them. I discover from the newspapers that they are wont to say, that they will take such a case to *avizandum*: which I suppose (no one ever told me) means that they must think twice, or even oftener, before deciding a matter like *that*.

I have taken the general principle, already stated, to *avizandum*. It seems all right. But I remember, in thinking of it, at how great advantage a judge is placed, in trying to come to a sound decision. Very clever and well-informed men state the arguments on either side. And all the judge has to do, is to say which arguments seem to him the strongest. He has no fear that any have been overlooked. But a human being, weighing a general principle, must act as counsel on each side, as well as judge. He must call up before his mind, all that is to be said for and against it; as well as say whether the weightiest reasons make for or against. And he may quite overlook some important reason, on one side or other. He may quite forget something so obvious and familiar, that a child might have remembered it. Or he may fail to discern that some consideration which mainly decides his judgment, is open to a fatal objection, which every one can see is fatal the instant it is stated.

Was it not Sir Isaac Newton, who had a pet cat and kitten? And did not these animals annoy him while busy in his study, by frequently expressing their desire to be let out and in? The happy thought struck him, that he might save himself the trouble of often rising to open his study door for their passage, by providing a way that should always be practicable for their exit or entrance. And accordingly the great man cut in his door, a large hole for the cat to go out and in; and a small hole for the kitten. He failed to remember, what the stupidest bumpkin would have remembered, that the large hole through which the cat passed, might be made use of by the kitten too. And the illustrious philosopher discerned the error into which he had fallen, and the fatal objection to the principle on which he had acted, only when taught it by the logic of facts. Having provided the holes already mentioned, he waited with pride to see the creatures pass through them for the first time. And as they arose from the rug before the fire, where they had been lying, and evinced a disposition to roam to other scenes, the great mind stopped in some sublime calculation: the pen was laid down: and all but the greatest man watched them intently. They approached the door; and discerned the provision made for their comfort. The cat went through the door by the large hole provided for her; and instantly the kitten followed her THROUGH THE SAME HOLE! How the great man must have felt his error! There was no resisting the

Beginnings and Ends. 119

objection to the course he had pursued, that was brought forward by the act of the kitten. And it appears almost certain that if Newton, before committing himself by action, had argued the case : if he had stated the arguments in favour of the two holes ; and if he had heard the housemaid on the other side ; the error would have been averted. But then Newton had not the advantage which the Chancellor has; he had not the matter argued before him. He argued the matter on either side, for himself: and he overlooked a very obvious and irrefragable consideration.

You and I, my reader, have many a time done what was perfectly analogous to the doing of Sir Isaac Newton. We have formed opinions and expressed them: and we have done things, thinking we were doing wisely and right : just because we forgot something so plain that you would have said no mortal could forget it—something which showed that the opinion was idiotic, and the doing that of a fool. You know, more particularly, how men who have committed great crimes, such as murder, seem by some infatuation to have been able to discern only the one obvious reason that seemed to make the commission of that crime a thing tending to their advantage ; and to have been incapable of looking just a handbreadth farther on, so as to see the fatal, crushing objection to the course they took ;—the absolute ruin and destruction that must of necessity follow. And the opinion of many men upon any subject, may often be likened to a table which the art of the upholsterer has fashioned to stand upon a single leg. They hold the opinion for just one reason; and that reason an unsound one. Give that reason a blow with the fatal, unanswerable objection; down comes the opinion: even as down would come the table, whose single leg was knocked away.

I am well aware that the severe critic who has read the lines which have been written, may feel disposed to accuse the writer of a disposition to wander from his path. A great deal of what has been said, is as when you take a look over the stile at a footpath running away from the beaten highway you are to traverse; and end by getting over the stile, and walking a little way along the footpath: intending, no doubt, ultimately to return to the beaten highway, and to plod steadily along it. All this discussion of general principles ought to have been despatched in a line or two, analogous to the glance over the stile. But let the critic take into account the fact, that since the writer last sat down to write an essay, he has written a great many serious pages, which it cost hard work to write, and in which nothing in the nature of an intellectual frisk could be permitted. And thus it is, that with a great sense of relief, he finds himself writing a page whereon he may mildly disport himself; casting logical and other trammels aside; and enjoying a little mental recreation. And now, going back from the path, and getting over the stile, we are in the highway again. We turned out of the highway, you remember, at the point where it was said, that EVERYTHING IN THIS WORLD HAS A BEGINNING AND AN END: and that, upon reflection, it seemed that the general principle might be accepted as true. No doubt, in our early days, we have heard sermons which we thought would never end; yet ultimately, and after the expiration of long time, they did. And even those things within our recollection, which seem as exceptions to the great principle, are probably exceptions rather in appearance than in reality. I remember, indeed, an aged clergyman whom in my youth I occasionally heard preach; who always began the first sentence of his sermon, but who never ended it; at least not till the close of the sermon: and no human being could know when that sentence ended, or say at what point (if any point in particular) it ceased to be. Still even that first sentence of each discourse of that good man, came to a close somehow. It stopped, if it was not finished; because the sermon stopped. So you see that even that indefinite sentence can hardly be regarded as an exception to the rule that all things in this world have a beginning and an end.

And now, my friend, having laid down the broad principle with which this dissertation sets out; let me proceed to say, that it is one of the greatest blessings of this life, as well as one of the saddest things in this life, that there are such things as beginnings and ends.

We cannot bear a very long, uniform look-out. You may remember Miss Jane Taylor's pleasantly-told story concerning a certain clock. The pendulum of that clock began to calculate how often it would have to swing backwards and forwards in the week and the month to come: then, looking still farther into futurity, it calculated, by a pretty hard exercise of mental arithmetic, how often it would have to swing in a year. And it got so frightened at the awful prospect, that it determined at once to stop. There was something crushing in that long look-out. It was killing, to take in at once that unvaried way; on, and on, and on. The pendulum forgot the blessed fact of beginnings and ends: forgot that to our feeling there are beginnings and ends even in the duration, the expanse, the employment, which in fact is most unvarying. It is an unspeakable blessing that we can stop, and start again, in everything: and that we can fancy we do so, even when we do not. The pendulum was not afraid of a hundred beats, or of a thousand: but the prospect of millions terrified it. Yet millions are just an aggregate of many hundreds: and the pendulum could without fatigue do the hundred; and then set off again upon another hundred, and do that without fatigue. The journey, that crushes us down when we contemplate it as one long weary thing, can be borne when we divide it into stages. And one great lesson of practical wisdom is to train ourselves to mentally divide everything into stages: in short, to cling habitually to the invaluable doctrine and fact, of beginnings and ends.

Beginnings and Ends.

There was a poor cabman at Paris who committed suicide, not long ago. He left behind him a letter, explaining his reasons for the miserable deed. His letter expressed no violent feeling: spoke of no great blow that had befallen him. It said that he ended his life, because he was 'weary of doing the same things over and over again every day.' The poor man's mind was doubtless unhinged. Yet you see what he did; and how he nursed his insanity. He looked too far ahead. He saw all life as one expanse. He forgot that life is broken into many stages: that it is made up of beginnings and endings. He could not bring himself, for the time, to see it so. Each separate day he might have stood: but a thousand days held in prospect at once, beat him. It was as the bundle of rods was so impossible to break, though each single rod might easily enough be broken. It was the fallacy, which tells so heavily upon most public speakers: that you stand in great awe of a crowd of a thousand or two thousand men, each of whom individually would inspire you with no awe at all.

Now, my readers, I know perfectly well that you have all known a feeling of weariness and almost of despair arise, when you looked far forward, and saw the long weary way that seemed to stretch on and on before you in life. I believe that it is not so much what we are actually enduring at the time, that prompts the cry, 'Now I can bear this no longer!' as some sudden vivid glimpse of all this, lasting on, and on, and on. There are few lives in which it is not expedient to 'take short views:' few minds that without weariness and depression can take in at one view any very great part of their life at once. Sometimes there comes on us the poor Frenchman's feeling: Here is this same round over, and over, and over: the occupations of each day are a circle, and we are just going round and round it, like a horse in a mill. To-morrow will be like to-day: and then to-morrow; and the day after that: and so on, on, on. The feeling is a morbid one; and a wrong one: but it is a common one. A little of the sea in a tumbler is colourless; but a vast deal of the sea, seen in its ocean bed, is green. With life the case is reversed. In the commonplace course of life, the path we are actually treading may look rather green—green, I mean, like the cheerful verdure of grass; but if you take in too great a prospect, the whole tract is apt to take the aspect of a desert waste, with only a green spot here and there. You will not add to the cheerfulness and hopefulness of man or of child, by drilling into him: This morning you will do such and such things: and all day such other things: and in the evening such other things: then you will sleep. To-morrow morning you will rise: and then the same things over and over: and so, on, on. I have known a malignant person who enjoyed the work of presenting to others such disheartening views of life. Let me, my reader, counsel the opposite course. Let us not look too far on. Let us not look at life as one

Beginnings and Ends.

unvaried expanse: although we may justly do so. Let us discipline our minds to look at life as a series of beginnings and ends. It is a succession of stages: and we shall think of one stage at a time. 'Sufficient unto the day is the evil thereof.' Most people can bear one day's evil: the thing that breaks men down, is the trying to bear on one day the evil of two days, twenty days, a hundred days. We can bear a day of pain: followed by a night of pain: and that again by a day of pain: and thus onward. But we can bear each day and night of pain, only by taking each by itself. We can break each rod: but not the bundle. And the sufferer, in real great suffering, turns to the wall in blank despair, when he looks too far on: and takes in a uniform dreary expanse of suffering, unrelieved by the blessed relief of even fanciful beginnings and ends.

I remember a poor woman whom I used often to visit and pray with, in my first parish. She died of cancer: and the excruciating disease took eight months to run its course, after having reached the point at which the pain became almost intolerable. In all that long time, the poor woman told me that she was never aware that she had slept; it seemed to her that the time never came in which she ceased to be conscious of agony. Her sufferings formed an unbroken duration, undivided by beginnings and ends. She was a good Christian woman: and had a blessed hope in another world. But I can never cease to remember her despairing face, as she seemed to look onward to weeks of agony, always growing worse and worse, till it should wear her down to her grave.

The power and habit of taking comprehensive views, is not in every case a desirable thing. It is well for us that we should look at our work in life in its parts, rather than as a whole. Of course you understand what I mean. I am far from saying that we ought not oftentimes to consider what is the drift and bearing of all our life, and of all we are doing in it. I mean that to avoid a fatiguing and disheartening result, we should for certain purposes, look not at the entire chain, but at each successive link of it. Of course, we know each link will be succeeded by the next: but let us think of them one at a time. Let us be thankful for Saturday night, and let us enjoy it: and let us hold at arm's length the intruding thought of Monday morning, when the shoulder must be put to the collar again. No doubt, in the work of life, every end is also a beginning. We rest for a little, perhaps only in thought and feeling; and then we go at our work again. But it is a convenient thing, and it helps to carry us on in our way, to mark out a number of successive ends, and thus to divide our journey into successive stages. It is well for us that when we start, we cannot see how far we have to go. We should give up all effort in despair, if from the beginning we held in view all the interminable length of way, whose length we shall hardly feel when we are wiled away along it gradually, step by step. It has always appeared to me extremely bad policy in any preacher, who desires to keep up the interest of his congregation, to announce at the beginning of the sermon, that in the first place he will do so and so ; and in the second place such another thing ; and in the third place something else; and finally close with some practical remarks. I can say for myself, that whenever I hear any preacher say anything like that, an instant feeling of irksomeness and weariness possesses me. You cannot help thinking of the long tiresome way that is to be got over, before happily reaching the end. You check off each head of the sermon as it closes : but your relief at thinking it is done, is dashed by the thought of what a deal more is yet to come. No : the skilful preacher will not thus map out his subject, telling his hearers so exactly what a long way they have to go. He will wile them along, step by step. He will never let them have a long out-look. Let each head of discourse be announced as it is arrived at. People can bear one at a time, who would break down in the simultaneous prospect of three, not to say of seven or eight. And then, when the sermon is nearly done, you may, in a sentence, give a connected view of all you have said : and your skill will be shown if people think to themselves, what a long way they have been brought without the least sense of weariness. I lately heard a sermon, which was divided into seven heads. If the preacher had named them all at the beginning, the congregation would have ceased to listen : or would have listened under the oppressive thought of what a vast deal awaited them before they would be free. But each head was announced just as it was arrived at : the congregation was wiled along insensibly : and the sermon was listened to with breathless attention from the first sentence to the last.

Let it be so with life, and the work of life. It would crush down any man's resolution, if he saw in one glance the whole enormous bulk of labour, which he will get through in a lifetime : without feeling it so very much at each successive stage. It is well to break up our journey into separate portions : to take it bit by bit : to set ourselves a number of successive ends : even though we know that we are practising a sort of deception on ourselves ; and that when the end we have immediately in view is reached, our work will be just as far from being done, as ever. Your little boy has before him the mighty task of his education. You do not tell the little thing at once, the whole extent of toil that is included in *that*. No: you fix on a small part of the work that is to be done : you show the little man *that* as his first end. *That* is the first thing to be done; and then we shall see what is to come next. And yet you know, and the little child knows just as well, that after he has conquered that tremendous alphabet, he must just begin again with something else; that by a hundred steps, each set out at first as an end to be attained; and each indeed an end, but likewise a beginning; he must mount from his first little book onwards and upwards into the fields of knowledge and learning. Let us, if we are wise men, hold by the grand principle of STEP BY STEP : let us be thankful that God, knowing that weariness is a thing that must be felt at intervals by the minds and bodies of all His creatures, has appointed that they shall live in a world of Beginnings and Ends. Yes : we can stand a day at a time; but if we forget the law of beginnings and ends, we shall come to be bearing the weight of a hundred days together. And *that* will crush the strongest.

Many people of an anxious temperament are like the pendulum already mentioned. The pendulum looked ahead to the incalculable multitude of ticks, forgetting that there would always be a moment to tick in. And you can easily see that many human beings plod heavily and dully through their work in life, because instead of giving their mind mainly to the present tick, they are thinking of the innumerable ticks that are coming. You know quite well that the work of life is done by most animals that have to work, in a dull, spiritless way. Few go through their work in a cheerful, lively way. Even inferior animals are coming to imitate their rational fellow-creatures. The other day, I was driving in a cab along a certain broad and ugly highway, which unites Athens with the Piræus. I overtook and passed various drays, drawn by fine large horses. I carefully remarked the expression of the countenance of each successive horse. All of them had a very gloomy and melancholy look. They seemed as though they were enduring. They could stand it; and that was all. And I thought, here is an example of the way in which this world mainly goes on. It goes on: it gets through: but not cheerfully. You could know, even if you had no better means of knowing, that there is something wrong. And the working bees of the human race, do, for the most part, go through their work like the dull, down-looking horse. The horses were plump and sleek: they were plainly well fed and well groomed: yet their expression was sorrowful, or at least apathetic. It would have struck you less, to have seen that dull look on the face of some poor, half-starved screw. And you know that it is generally the human beings whose material advantages are the greatest, who have the most unsatisfied and unhappy expression of countenance. Look at the portraits of cabinet-ministers and the like. Few work with a light heart, and with enjoyment in their work. Many forebodings, and many cares, sit heavily upon the heart and brain of most. Oh for more practical belief in Beginnings and Ends!

It is characteristic of those things which possess a Beginning and an End, that they also possess a Middle, of greater or less extent. But we do not mind about the middle nearly so much. The middle is much less affecting and striking. It is the first start, and then the close, that we mainly feel. You know the peculiar interest with which we look at the setting sun of summer, in his last minutes above the horizon. Of course he was going on just as fast through all the day: but at mid-day, we did not know the value of each minute, as we do when he is fast going down. I have been touched by the sight of human life, ebbing almost visibly away: and you could not but think of the sun in his last little space above the mountains, or above the sea. I remember two old gentlemen, great friends: both on the extreme verge of life. One was above ninety: the other above eighty. But their wits were sound and clear; and, better still, their hearts were right. They confessed that they were no more than strangers and pilgrims on the earth: they declared plainly that they sought a country, far away, where most of those they had cared for were waiting for them. But the body was very nearly worn out: and though the face of each was pleasant to look at, paralysis had laid its grasp upon the aged machinery of limb and muscle which had played so long. I used, for a few weeks, to go one evening in the week and sit with them, and take tea. They always had tea in large breakfast cups: other cups would not have done. I remember how the two paralytic hands shook about, as they tried to drink their tea. There they were, the two old friends: they had been friends from boyhood, and they had been over the world together. You could not have looked, my friend, but with eyes somewhat wet, at the large tea-cups, shaking about; as the old men with difficulty raised them to their lips. And there was a thing that particularly struck me. There was a large old-fashioned watch, always on a little stand on the tea-table, ticking on and on. You seemed to feel it measuring out the last minutes, running fast away. It always awed me to look at it and hear it. Only for a few weeks did I thus visit those old friends, till one died: and the other soon followed him, where there are no palsied hands or aged hearts. No doubt, through all the years the old-fashioned watch had gone about in the old gentleman's pocket, life had been ebbing as really and as fast as then. And the sands were running as quickly for me, as for the aged pilgrims. But then with me it was the middle; and to them it was the end. And I always felt it very solemn and touching, to look at the two old men on the confines of life; and at the watch loudly ticking off their last hours. One seemed to feel time ebbing; as you see the setting sun go down.

Beginnings are difficult. It is very hard to begin rightly in a new work or office of any kind. And I am thinking not merely of the inertia to be overcome, in taking to work: though that is a great fact. In writing a sermon or an essay, the first page is much the hardest. You know, it costs a locomotive engine a great effort to start its train: once the train is off, the engine keeps it going at great speed with a tenth, or less, of the first heavy pull. But I am thinking now of the many foolish things which you are sure to say and do in your ignorance, and in the novelty of the situation. Even a Lord Chancellor has behaved very absurdly in his first experience of his great elevation. It would be a great blessing to many men to be taken elsewhere, and have a fresh start. As a general rule, a clergyman should not stay all his life in his first parish. His parishioners will never forget the foolish things he did at his first coming, in his inexperienced youth. There, he cannot get over these: but elsewhere he would have the good of them, without the ill. He would have the experience, dearly bought: while the story of the blunders and troubles by which it was bought, would be forgotten. I daresay there are people, miserable and useless where they are; who if they could only get away to a new place, and begin again, would be all right. In that new place they would avoid the errors and follies by which they have made their present place too hot to hold them. Give them a new start: give them another chance: and taught by their experience of the scrapes and unhappiness into which they got by their hasty words, their ill temper, their suspicion and impatience, their domineering spirit, and their determination in little things to have their own way; you would find them do excellently. Yes, there is something admirable about a Beginning! There is something cheering to the poor fellow who has got the page on which he is writing, hopelessly blotted and befouled, when you turn over a new leaf, and give him the fresh unsullied expanse to commence anew! It is like wiping out a debt that never can be paid, and that keeps the poor struggling head under water: but wipe it out; and oh with what new life will the relieved man go through all his duty! It is a terrible thing to drag a lengthening chain: to know that, do what you may, the old blot remains, and cannot be got rid of. I know various people, soured, useless, and unhappy, who (I am sure) would be set right for ever, if they could but be taken away from the muddle into which they have got themselves, and allowed to begin again somewhere else. I wish I were the patron of six livings in the Church. I think I could make something good and happy of six men who are turned to poor account now. But alas, that in many things there is no second chance! You take the wrong turning; and you are compelled to go on in it, long after you have found that it is wrong. You have made your bed, and you must lie on it. And it is sad to think how early in life, all life may be marred. A mere boy or girl may get into the dismal lane which has no turning: and out of which they never can get, to start afresh in a better track. How many of us, my readers, would be infinitely better and happier, if we could but begin again!

An End is sometimes a very great blessing. I have no doubt, my readers, that in your childhood you have often felt this when a sermon was brought to a close. Perhaps in maturer years you have experienced a like emotion of relief under the like circumstances. I can say deliberately that never in my youth did I once wish that such a discourse should be longer than it was. Yet we all remember how we have shrunk from Ends. You may have read a fairy tale by Mr. Thackeray, with illustrations by its author. One of these is a cartoon, representing a boy eating a bun, apparently of superior quality; and at the same time expressing a sentiment common to early youth. He eats: and as he eats, he speaks as follows: 'Oh what fun! Nice plum-bun! How I wish it never was done!' I remember the mental state. I have known it well. In my mind it is linked with the thought of plum-pudding and of other luxuries and dainties. It was sad to see the object lessen, as it was enjoyed: to see it melt away, like a summer sunset! And about Christmas-time, one had sometimes a like feeling as to the appetite and relish for plum-pudding and the like. Would it were unceasing! I mean the appetite. But you remember how it flagged. And though you stimulated it with cold water, yet the fourth supply beat you: and had to be taken away. And you remember, too, how you shrunk from the end of your holiday season: and wished that time would stand still. You may have read the awful scene in Christopher Marlowe's *Faustus*, where the hapless philosopher, on the verge of his appointed season, seems to cling to each moment as it passes away from him. And oh my reader, if the great work of life have not been done while the day lasted, think how awful it will be to feel that the end of the day of grace is here! Think of poor Queen Elizabeth in her dying hour, offering all the wealth of her kingdom for another day of life! We cannot, in the commonplace days of ordinary health and occupation, rightly realize the tremendous fact: but think of the End of this life, to the man who has no hope beyond it! To feel that all in the world you have toiled for and loved is going from you: to feel your feeble hand losing its grasp of all: to see the faces around grow dim through the mists of death: to feel the weary heart pausing, and the last chill creeping upwards: to feel that you are driven irresistibly to the edge of the awful gulf,—and no hope beyond! But remember, reader, it will be your own fault if you come to *that*.

It is the end of a career that gives the character to it all. We feel as if a life, however honourable and happy, were blighted by a sorry ending. The thought of Napoleon at St. Helena squabbling about the thickness of his camp soup, and the number of clean shirts to be allowed him, casts back an impression of pettiness upon the man even in his mid-career. There is a graver consideration. If a man had lived many years in usefulness and honour, but finally fell into grievous sin and shame, we should think of his life as on the whole a shameful one. But if a man end his career nobly: if his last years are honourable and happy: we should think of his life on the whole as one of happiness and honour, though its beginning were ever so lowly and sad. You remember how a great king of ancient days asked a philosopher to name some of the happiest of the race. The philosopher named several men, all of whom were dead. The king asked him why he did not think of men still living : 'Look at all my splendour,' he said to the philosopher : ' why do you not think of *me* ?' ' Ah,' said the wise man ; ' who knows what your life and your lot may be yet? I call no man happy before he dies !' [Distinguished classical scholar, I am not telling the story for you.] And, sure enough, that monarch was reduced to captivity and misery ; and died a miserable captive : and so you would not say that his life was a happy or a prosperous one on the whole. But in the most important of all our concerns, my friend, the End is far more important than that. You know that though the monarch, vanquished and uncrowned, died in a dungeon, *that* could not blot out the years of royalty he had actually lived. He had been a king, once ; however fallen now. The man who sits by his lonely fireside, silent and deserted, can yet remember the days when that quiet dwelling was noisy and gladsome with young voices: they were real days, when his children were round him ; and it does him good yet to look back on them,—though now the little things are in their graves. But the fearful thing about the christian who ends in sin and shame, is this : He dare not comfort himself under the present wretchedness, by looking back to better days, when he thought he was safe. The fearful thing is that this present end of sin has power to blot out those better days : if a man, however fair his profession, end at last manifestly not a christian, this proves that he never was a christian at all ! You see what tremendous issues depend upon the christian life ending well ! It is little to say that ending ill is a sad thing at the time : it is that ending ill flings back a baleful light on all the days that went before ! If the end be bad, then there was something amiss all along, however little suspected it may have been. It is only when the end is well over, that you can be perfectly sure you are safe. You remember Mr. Moultrie's beautiful poem, about his living children and his dead child. The living children were good : were all he could wish: but God only knew how temptation might prevail against them as years went on : but as for the dead one *he* was safe. ' It may be that the Tempter's wiles *their* souls from bliss may sever: But if our own poor faith fail not, *he* must be ours for ever ! ' Yes : that little one had passed the End : no evil nor peril could touch *him* more.

I daresay you have sometimes found that for a day or two, a line of poetry or some short sentence of prose would keep constantly recurring to your memory.

Beginnings and Ends.

I find it so; and the line is sometimes Shakspere's; sometimes Tennyson's: often it is from a certain Volume (the Best Volume) of which it is my duty to think a great deal. And I remember how, not long since, for about a week, the line that was always recurring was one by Solomon, king and philosopher (and something more): it was 'Better is the end of a thing than the beginning.' And at first I thought that the words sounded sad: and more heathen-like than christian. Has it come to this, that God's Word tells us concerning the life God gave us, that the best thing that can happen to us is soonest to get rid of that sad gift; and that each thing that comes our way, is something concerning which we may be glad when it is over? I thought of Mr. Kingsley, and wondered if the sum of the matter, after all, is 'The sooner it's over, the sooner to sleep:' and of Sophocles, and how he said 'Not to be, is best of all: but when one hath come to this world, then to return with quickest step to whence he came, is next.' But then I saw, gradually, that the words are neither cynical nor hopeless; that they do but remind us of the great truth, that God would have our life here one of constant progress from good to better, and so the End best of all. We are to be 'forgetting those things which are behind, and reaching forth unto those which are before,' because the best things are still before us. If things in this world go as God intended they should, then everything is a step to something else; something farther: which ought to be an advance on what went before it; which ought to be better than what went before it. And above all, the End of our life here (if it end well), so safe and so happy, is far better than its Beginning, with all the perils of the voyage yet to come.

I thought of these things the other Sunday afternoon, seeing the Beginning and the End almost side by side. At that service I did not preach: and I was sitting in a square seat in a certain church, listening to a very good sermon preached by a friend. A certain little boy, just four years old, came and sat beside me, leaning his head on me as a pillow: and soon after the beginning of the sermon, the little man (very properly) fell sound asleep. And (attending to the sermon all the while) I could not but look down at the fat rosy little face, and the abundance of curly hair; the fresh, clear complexion, the cheerful, innocent expression; and think how fair and pleasing a thing is early youth;—how beautiful and hopeful is our life's Beginning. And after service was over, on my way home, I went to see a revered friend, who, at the end of a long christian life, was dying. There was the worn, ghastly face, with its sharp features: the weary, worn-out frame; the weakened, wandering mind, so changed from what it used to be. And standing by that good christian's bed, and thinking of the little child, I said to myself, There is the Beginning of life: Here is the End: what shall we say in the view of that sad contrast? And I thought, there and then, that ' Better is the end of a thing than the beginning!' Yes: better is the end of a dangerous voyage than its outset. You have seen a ship sailing away upon a long, perilous voyage over the ocean: the day was fair and sunshiny, and the ship looked gay and trim, with her white sails and her freshly painted sides. And you have seen a ship coming safe into port at the end of her thousands of miles over the deep, under a gloomy, stormy sky, and with hull and masts battered by winds and waves. And you have thought, I dare say, that better far was this ending, safe and sure, than even that sunshiny beginning, with all the risks before it. And here, in the worn figure on the weary bed, here is the safe end of the voyage of life! Oh what perils are yet before the merry little child! Who can say if that little one is to end in glory? But to the dying christian all these perils are over. He is safe, safe! And then, remember, *this* is not yet the end, you see. It is NOT the end, that weary figure, lying on that bed of pain. It is only the last step before the end. A very little: and how glorious and happy that sufferer will be! You would not wish to keep him here, when you think of all the blessedness into which the next step from this pain will bear him. Nay: but you may take up, in a sublimer significance than that of deliverance from mere earthly ill, the beautiful words of the greatest poet:

> Vex not his soul: oh let him pass! He hates him,
> That would, upon the rack of this rough world,
> Stretch him out longer!

CHAPTER VI.

GOING ON.

THERE are many things of which you have a much more vivid perception at some times than at others. The thing is before you; but sometimes you can grasp it firmly, sometimes it eludes you mistily. You are walking along a country path, just within hearing of distant bells. You hear them faintly; but all of a sudden, by some caprice of the wind, the sound is borne to you with startling clearness. There is something analogous to that in our perceptions and feelings of many great facts and truths. Commonly, we perceive them and feel them faintly; but sometimes they are borne in upon us we cannot say how. Sometimes we get vivid glimpses of things which we had often talked of, but which we had never truly discerned and realized before. And for many days it has been so with me. I have seemed to feel the lapse of time with startling clearness. I have no doubt, my reader, that you have sometimes done the like. You have seemed to actually perceive the great current with which we are all gliding steadily away and away.

Rapid movement is a thing which has a certain power to disguise itself from the person who is involved in it. Every one knows that if you are travelling in an express train at sixty miles an hour, you do not feel the speed nearly so much as the man does who stands beside the track and sees the great mass sweep by like a hurricane. Have you ever thought it would be curious if we could for a few minutes be made sensible of the world's motion? Here we are, tearing on through space at an inconceivable speed. We do not feel it, of course; we could not stand it. I should like to feel it for half a minute—not for more.

But it is not *that* motion we are to think of at present. No special illumination has been accorded to me, making me feel that fact which we all know without feeling. But there is another rapid motion, common to all of us as is the motion of the earth which bears us all. There is a great current bearing us along and all things about us, which is commonly not much felt. But it seems to me that for several weeks I have been actually feeling it. I have been excessively busy; living in a great pressure and hurry of occupations. In that state, my reader, you feel Sunday after Sunday return with a rapidity which takes away your breath; and let me say that if you have to provide one sermon, and still more if you have to provide two, against the return of each, you will in that fever of work and haste come to look from one Sunday to the next till you will come to find them flying past you like the quarter-mile posts on a railway. You will find that you can hardly believe, walking into church on Sunday morning, that a week has gone since the last Sunday. And in such a time you will realize much more distinctly than you usually do, that all things are going on—drifting away—all in company. These April days are taking life away from you, from me—from prince and peasant. There is one thing at least which all human beings are using up at exactly the same rate. We can all get out of the day just twenty-four hours, neither more nor less. One man may live at the rate of a hundred pounds a year, and another at the rate of a hundred thousand; but each expends his time at the rate of three hundred and sixty-five days a year. Whatever other differences there may be between the lots of human beings, we are all drifting on with the current of time, and drifting at the same rate exactly. And we are certainly drifting. We are never quite the same in two successive weeks. One Sunday is not like the last. Look closely, and you will see that there is a difference—slight perhaps, but real. Each time you sit down to your *Saturday Review* you feel there is a difference since the last time. Still more do you feel it as you read the returning *Fraser*, coming at the longer interval of a month. Things never come back again quite the same. And indeed in Nature there is a singular dislike to uniformity. If to-day be a fine day, look back; it is almost certain that this day last year was rainy. If to-day you are in very cheerful spirits, it is probable that on the corresponding day in the year that is gone you were very dull and anxious. No doubt human beings sometimes successfully resist Nature's love of variety. Some men have an especial love for having and doing things always in the same way. They walk on special days always on the same side of the street; perhaps they put their feet, like Dr. Johnson, on the same stones in the pavement. They dress in the same way year after year. They maintain anniversaries, and try to bring the old party around the table once more, and to have the old time back. But we cannot have things exactly over again. There is a difference in the feeling, even if you are able precisely to reproduce the fact. And indeed the wonder is that things are so much like, as they are to-day, to what they were a year ago, when we think of the innumerable possibilities of change that hang over us. Yes, we are drifting on and on, down to the great sea. Sit down, my friend, to write your article. You have written many. The paper is the same; the table on which you write is the same; the inkstand is the same; and the pen is made by the same mender that made all the rest. And it is possible enough that when the article is printed at last, your readers will say that it is just the same thing over again; but it is not. To your feeling this day's work is quite different from the work of all preceding days.

There is an undefinable variation from what ever was before. And as weeks and months go on, there come to be differences which some may think more real than any in the comparatively fanciful respect of feeling. The hair is turning thin and gray; the old spirit is subdued. There are changes in taste, in judgment, in feeling, in many ways. Yes, we are all Going On.

I wish to stop. There is something awful in this perpetual progression. If the current would slacken its speed, at least, and let one quietly think for a little while. Let us sit down, my friend, by the wayside. We are old enough now to look back, as well as to look round; and to think how life is going with us, and with those we know. We are now in the middle passage: perhaps farther on. And if we are half-way in fact, assuredly we are far more in feeling. Though a man live to seventy, his first thirty-five years are by far the longer portion of his life.

Let us think to-day, my reader, of ourselves and of our friends; and of how it is faring with us as we go on.

It is a curious thing now, when we have settled to our stride, and are going on (in most cases) very much as we probably shall go on as long as we live, to compare what we are, with what we promised at our entrance on life to be. You remember people who began with a tremendous flourish of trumpets: people of whom there was a vague impression, more or less general, that they were to do great things. Sometimes this impression was confined to the man himself. Not unfrequently it was shared by his mother and his sisters. It occasionally extended to his father and his brothers. And in a few cases, generally in these cases not without some reason, it prevailed in the mind of his fellow-students. And it may be said, that a belief that some young lad is destined to do considerable things, if it be anything like universal among his college companions, must have some foundation. A belief to the same effect with regard to any young man, if confined to two or three of his intimate companions, is generally quite groundless; and if it exist only in the heart of his mother and of himself, it is quite sure to be absurd and idiotic. We can all, probably, remember individuals who, without any reason apparent to onlookers, cherished a most extraordinarily high opinion of themselves; and one which was not at all taken down by frequently being beaten, and even distanced, in the competitions of College life. Such individuals, for the most part, indulged a very bitter and malicious spirit towards students more able and successful than themselves. I wish I could believe that modesty always goes with merit. I fear no rule can be laid down. I have beheld inordinate self-conceit in very clever fellows, as well as in very stupid ones. And I have beheld self-conceit developed in a degree which could hardly be exceeded, in individuals who were neither very clever nor very stupid, but remarkably ordinary in every way. Let me here remark, that I have known the most enthusiastic admiration excited in the breasts of one or two individuals by a very commonplace man. I mean admiration of his talents. And I beheld the spectacle with great wonder, not unmixed with indignation. I can quite understand man or woman feeling enthusiastic admiration for a great and wonderful genius. I can feel that warm admiration myself. And I can imagine its existing in youthful minds, even when the genius is dashed with great failings, or is of a very irregular nature. But the thing I wonder at, and cannot understand, is enthusiastic admiration professed and felt for dreary commonplace. I am not in the least surprised when I hear a young person, or indeed an old one, speaking in hyperbolical terms of the preaching of Bishop Wilberforce. I have heard it myself, and I know how brilliant and effective it is. But I really look with wonder at the young woman who professes equally enthusiastic admiration of the sermons of Dr. Log. I nave heard Dr. Log preach. I could not for my life attend to his sermon. It was horribly tiresome. There was not in it a trace of pith or of beauty. It approached to the nature of twaddle. I was awe-stricken when I heard it described in rapturous phrases. I recognised a superior intelligence. I thought to myself, reversing Mr. Tickell's lines, ' You hear a voice I cannot hear; you see a hand I cannot see.' It is right to add, that the enthusiastic appreciators of Dr. Log were very few in number, and that they appeared to me nearly as stupid as Dr. Log himself.

But leaving Dr. Log and his admirers, let me say that very clever fellows, very stupid fellows, and very commonplace fellows, have started in life with a great flourish of trumpets. The vanity of many lads, leaving the University, is enormous. They expect to set the Thames on fire: to turn the world upside down. A few takings-down bring the best of them to modesty and sense. And the men for whom the flourish was loudest do sometimes, when all find their level, have to rest at a very low one. Many painful mortifications and struggles bring them to it. Oh! if talent and ambition could always be in a man, in just proportion! But I have known the most commonplace of men, with ambition that would have given enough to do to the abilities of Shakspeare. And we may perhaps say, that no one who begins with a great flourish ever fails to disappoint himself and his friends. He may do very well: he may do magnificently; but he does not come up to the great expectations formed of him. I was startled the other day to hear a certain man named as a failure, who has attained supreme eminence in his own walk in life, and that a conspicuous one. I said No: he is anything but a failure: he has attained extraordinary eminence: he is a great man. But the reply was, 'Ah, we expected far more! We thought he would leave an impression on the age, and he has certainly not done that; while it seems certain he has done the best he is ever to do.' But look round, my friend, and think how the world goes with those who set out with you. They are generally, I suppose, jogging on humbly and respectably. The present writer did not in his youth live among those from whom the famous of the earth are likely to be taken. One or two of the number have risen to no small eminence; but the lot of most has circumscribed their ambition. It is not in the senate that he can look to find many of the names of his old companions. It is not likely that any will be buried in Westminster Abbey. The life of two or three may perhaps be written, if they leave behind them a warm friend who is not very busy. It does not matter. The nonsense has been taken out of us by the work of life. And on the whole, we are going creditably on.

It is worthy of notice, that things which at the beginning were very bad, may be made good by a very small change wrought upon them. You see this in human beings, as they go on through life. You remember, I have no doubt, how various passages in the earlier writings of Mr. Tennyson, on which the *Quarterly Review* savagely fixed at their first publication, and which Mr. Tennyson's warmest admirers must admit to have been in truth very weak, affected, and ridiculous, have by alterations of wonderfully small amount been brought to a state in which the most fastidious critic could find no fault in them. Just a touch from the master-hand did it all. You have in a homelier degree felt the same yourself, in correcting and re-writing your own crude and immature compositions. Often a very small matter takes away the mark of that Beast whose name shall not be mentioned here. I know a very distinguished preacher, really a pulpit orator, whose manner at his outset was remarkably awkward. No doubt he has devoted much pains to his manner since: though his art is high enough to conceal any trace of art. I heard him preach not long since: and his manner was singularly graceful; while yet there was no great change materially. You have remarked how the features of a girl's face, very plain at fourteen, have at twenty grown remarkably pretty. And yet the years have wrought no very great change. The face is unquestionably and quite recognisably the same: yet it has passed from plainness into beauty. And so, as we go on in life, you will find a man has got rid of some little intrusive folly which just makes the difference between his being very good and his being very bad. The man whose tendency to boast, or to exaggerate, or to talk thoughtlessly of others, made him appear a fool in his youth, has corrected that one evil tendency, and lo! he is quite altered—he is all right; he is a wise and good man. You would not have believed what a change for the better would be made by that little thing. You know, I dare say, how poor and bad are the first crude thoughts for your sermon or your article, thrown at random on the page. Yet when you have arranged and rounded them into a symmetrical, and accurate, and well-considered composition, it is wonderful how little change there is from the first rude sketch. Look at the waste scraps of paper before you throw them into the fire, and you will find some of your most careful and best sentences there, word for word. You have not been able to improve upon the way in which you first dashed them down.

There is a sad thing which we are all made to feel, as we are going on. It is, that we are growing out of things which we are sorry to outgrow. The firmest conviction that we are going on to what is better, cannot suppress some feeling of regret at the thought of what we are leaving behind. When I was a country parson, I used to feel very sorry to see a laurel or a yew growing out of the shape in which I remembered it; and which was associated with pleasant days. There was a dull pang at the sight. I remember well a little yew I planted with my own hand. It looks like yesterday since I held its top, while a certain man filled in the earth, and put the sod round its stem. For some time it appeared doubtful if that yew would live and grow; at last it was fairly established, and it began to grow vigorously the second year. For a year or two more, it was a neat, shaggy little thing; but then it began to put out tremendous shoots, and to grow out of my acquaintance. I felt I was losing an old friend. Many a time I had stood and looked at the little yew; I knew every branch of it; and always went to look at it when I had been a few days away. No doubt it was growing better; it was progressing with a yew's progress; I was getting a new friend better than the old one; yet I sighed for the old one that was gradually leaving me. You do not like to think that your little child must grow into something quite different from what it is now; must die into the grown up man or woman; must grow hardened to the world, and cease to be loveable as now. You would like to keep the little thing as it is; when it climbs on your knee, and lays a little soft cheek against your own. Even in the big girl of seven, that goes to school, you regret the wee child of three that you used to run after on the little green before your door; and in the dawn of cleverness and thought, though pleasant to see, still you feel there is something gone which you would have liked to keep. But it is an inevitable law, that you cannot have two inconsistent good things together. You cannot at once have your field green as it is in spring, and golden as it is in autumn. You cannot at once live in the little dwelling which was long your home, and which is surrounded by the memories of many years; and in the more beautiful and commodious mansion which your increasing wealth has been able to buy. You cannot at once be the merchant prince, wealthy, influential, esteemed by all, though gouty, ageing, and careworn; and the hopeful, light-hearted lad that came in from the country to push his way, and on whose early aspirations and struggles you look back with a confused feeling as though he were another being. You cannot at the same time be a country parson, leisurely and quiet, living among green fields and trees, and knowing the concerns of every soul in your parish; and have the privilege and the stimulus of preaching to a congregation of educated folk in town. Yet you would look round in silence and regret, when you look for the last time upon the scenes amid which you passed some considerable part of your life; even though you felt that the new place of your labours and your lot were ever so much better. And though you know it is well that your children should grow up into men and women, still you will sometimes be sorry that their happy childhood must pass so swiftly and so completely away; that it must be so entirely lost in that which is to come after it; that even in the healthy maturity of body and of mind, there is so little that recalls to you the merry little boy or girl you used to know. Yes; we may have got on to something that is unquestionably better; but still we miss the dear old time and way. It is as with the emigrant, who has risen to wealth and position in the new world across the sea; but who often thinks, with fond regret, of the hills of his native land; and who, through all these years, has never forgotten the cottage where he drew his first breath, and the little churchyard where his father and mother are sleeping. Yes; you little man with the very curly hair, standing at that sofa turning over the leaves of a large Bible with pictures; stay as you are, as long as you can! For I may live to see you grow into something far less pleasant to see; but I shall never live to see you Lord Chancellor; though that distinguished post (it is well known) is the natural destination of a Scotch clergyman's son.

There is something rather awful implied in going on. Its possibilities are vast; you may yet have greatly to modify your opinion of any man who is still going on. The page is not finished yet; and it may be terribly blotted before it is done with. But the man who is no longer going on; the man who has finished his page and handed it in; is fixed and statuesque. There he is, for ever. You may finally make up your mind about *him*. He can never do anything to disappoint you now. But very many men do live on, just to disappoint. They have done their best already; and they are going on producing work very inferior to what they once did, and to what we might expect of them. You go and hear a great preacher; not upon a special occasion, but in his own church upon a common Sunday. You have read his published sermons, and thought them very fine; some sentences from them still linger on your ear. Unhappily, he did not stop with these fine things. He is going on still; and what he is turning off now is quite different. There is little to remind you of what he was. Your lofty idea of that

great and good man is sadly shattered. No doubt, this
is not always so. There are men who go on through
life; and go on without deterioration. There are men
who are always themselves; always up to the mark.
But for the most part, going on implies a great falling
off. Think of Sir Walter Scott's last novels. Think
of Byron's last poetry. Compare *The Virgin Widow*
with *Philip Van Artevelde*. Think of the latter productions of the author of *Festus*. Think of the last
squeezings from the mind of Dr. Chalmers. Think
of the recent appearances, intellectual and moral, of
Mr. Walter Savage Landor. Think how roaring Irish
patriots have become the pensioners of the Saxon,
after having publicly sworn never to touch the alien
coin. Think how men who bearded the tyrant in their
youth, have ended in contented toadyism. We are
never perfectly safe in forming a judgment of any man
who is still going on; that is, of any living man. We
shall not call him good, any more than happy, till we
have seen the last of him. His very ending may be
enough to blight all his past life. You cannot as yet
settle the mark of a man who is still painting pictures,
still publishing poems, still writing books, still speaking in parliament, still taking a prominent part in
public business. He may possibly rise far above anything he has yet done. He may possibly sink so far
below it, as to lower the general average of his entire
life. As regards fame, the right thing is an end like
Nelson's. *He* ended at his best; and ended defini-

tively. Even Trafalgar would have been overclouded, if the hero had still kept going on. Think of him perhaps coming back; being made a duke; evincing great vanity; trying to become a leader among the Peers, and showing his lack of business aptitude and of sound judgment in politics; coming to be occasionally hissed about the streets of London: getting involved in discreditable tricks to gain office. Now, Nelson might have done none of these things. But I believe any one who reads his life will feel that he might have done them all. And was it not far better that the weak, but great man; the true hero; the warm-hearted, loveable, brave, honest admiral; should be taken away from the petty and sordid possibilities of Going On; that it should be made sure he should never vex or disappoint us; that he should die in a blaze of glory, and leave a name for every Briton to cherish and to love? There are living men, concerning whom we might regret that they are still going on. They cannot rise above their present estimation; they may well sink below it. It would be a great thing if some means could be devised, by which a man might stop, without dying. A man might say, after having done some difficult and honourable work, reaching over a large portion of his life, 'Now, I stop here. I take my stand on what I have done; judge of me by that. I must still go on breathing the air as before; but I fear I shall let myself down; so don't inquire about me any farther.' We all know that great and good men have sometimes, in the latter chapters of their life, done things on which we can but shut our eyes, and which we can but strive to forget. It seems quite certain that Solomon, albeit the wisest of men, became a weak old fool in his latter days; nor does the only reliable history say anything of final repentance and amendment. And silly or evil doings early in life, may be effaced from remembrance by wise and good doings afterwards; while silly and evil doings in the last stage of life, appear to stamp the character of it all.

It is this thought which sometimes makes the recollection that we are still going on, weigh heavily on one. There is no saying how the page of our life may be blotted before it is finished : and you must let me say, my friend, that the wise man will stand in great fear and suspicion of himself; and will very earnestly apply for that sacred influence which alone can hold him right to the end, where alone it is to be found. There are many things to make one thoughtful, as we remember how we are going on; but the great thing (as regards oneself) is, after all, the sight of the gloom before us, into which we are advancing day by day; not seeing even a step a-head. And to *that* may be added the occasional examples which are pressed upon us in the case of others, who once seemed very much like ourselves, of what human beings may come to be. And that which man has done, man may do. I see various things that are worthy of note, as I look round on the procession

Going On.

of the human beings I know and remember, and think what comes as we go on. I see some who are rather battered and travel-stained. The greatness of the way is beginning to tell. I see some who look somewhat worn and jaded. There are little physical symptoms of the wear of the machine. The hair of certain men is going, or even gone. The teeth of some are not complete, as of yore. On the whole, I trust, we are gaining. I do not think there is any period of life that one would wish to live over again; no period, at least, of more than a very few days. There are wrecks, no doubt: some who broke down early, and have quite disappeared, one does not know where; and among these, more than one or two whose promise was of the best.

Thinking of this one day, I was walking along a certain street, and came to a place where it was needful to cross. A carriage stopped the way, if that indeed can be called a carriage which was no more than a cab. And my attention was attracted by the cab-horse, which was standing close by the pavement. He was a sorry creature; but, as you looked at him, there was no mistaking the thoroughbred. There was the light head, once so graceful: the dilated, sensitive nostrils were still there, and the slender legs. But the poor legs were bent and shaky; the neck was cut into by the collar; the hair was rubbed off the skin in many places; and the sides were going with that peculiar motion which indicates broken wind.

Here was what the poor horse had come to. At first doubtless he was a graceful, cheerful creature, petted and made much of in his youth. Probably he proved not worth training for a race-horse; and a thoroughbred without sufficient bone and muscle is very useless for practical purposes; though it may be remarked that a thoroughbred with sufficient bone and muscle is the best horse for every kind of work except drawing coals or beer. So the poor thing became a riding-hack, and having fallen a few times, was sold for a cab-horse. And it was plain that for many days he had been poorly fed, and hardly worked; and that now the cab-proprietor was taking all he could out of him, before giving him over to the knacker, to be made into sausages. It is a popular delusion that the last stage in a horse's existence is to go to the dogs. There are some districts in which he goes to the pigs; and others in which he ends by affording nutriment, in a disguised form, to human beings. I am no alarmist, and I believe horse-flesh is quite salutary. All I have to add is, that persons having an antipathy to that article of food, had better inquire where their bacon was fed, and had better keep a sharp eye upon their sausages.

This, however, is a digression from a sad reflection. That poor cab-horse suggested various human beings whom I once knew. We have all known clever and promising youths who became drunken wrecks, and who deviated into various paths of sin, shame, and ruin. I laid down my pen when I had written that sentence, and thought of four, five, six, who had ended so, thinking of them not without a tear. Some were the very last you would have expected to come to this. There are indeed men whose career as youths is quite of a piece with their after career of shame; but my early friends were not such as these. I can think of some, cheerful, amiable, facile in the hand of companions good or bad, who bade fair for goodness and happiness, yet who went astray, and who were wrecked very soon. I knew of one, once a man of high character and good standing, who had to become as one dead, and who was long afterwards traced, a sailor in distant seas. He had a beautiful voice; and I have heard that it was fine to hear him singing on the deck by moonlight as he kept his watch. Poor wretch, with what a heavy heart!

The change that passes upon one's self, as we go on through life, comes so gradually through the wear of successive days, that we are hardly conscious how perceptibly we are getting through all that we have to get through here. We fancy, quite honestly, that we do not look any older in the last ten years, and that we are now just the same as we were ten years since. We fancy that, intellectually and morally, we are better; and physically, just the same. People whose character and history are commonplace at least fancy this in their more cheerful hours. But sometimes it comes home to us what a change has passed on us, perhaps in not a very long time. You will feel this especially in reading old letters and diaries; the letters you wrote and the diary you kept long ago. You probably thought that your present handwriting is exactly the same as your handwriting of ten years since; but when you put the two side by side, you will see how different they are. And in the perusal of these ancient documents, it will be borne in upon you how completely changed are the things you care for. The cares and interests, the fears and hopes, of the old days, are mainly gone. You have arrived at quite different estimates of people and of things; and if you be a wiser, you are doubtless a sadder man. And when you go back to the schoolboy spot, or to the house where you lived when you were ten years old, it will be a curious thing to contrast the little fellow of that time, with your own grave and sobered self. And you will do so the more vividly in the presence of some well-remembered object, which has hardly changed at all in the years which have changed you so much. It is a commonplace; but commend me to commonplaces for reaching the common heart: the picture of the aged man, or even the man in middle age, standing beside the tree or the river by which he played when he was a little child. The hills, the fields, the trees around, are the same; and there is he, so changed ! You remember Wordsworth's beautiful ballad, in which the old schoolmaster is lying beside the fountain, by which he was used to lie in his days of youthful strength: you remember the same old man, looking back, from a bright April morning, to another April morning exactly like it, but past for forty years. We may well believe, that there is not a human being but knows the feeling. It is some little thing in our own history that we remember; but it has touched the electric chain of association, and wakened up the past. There is a rude song current among the coal-miners of the north of England, in which an old man is standing by an old oak tree, and speaking to that unchanged friend of the change that has passed upon himself; and though the chorus, recurring at the end of each verse, is not so graceful as the lines which Wordsworth gives to Matthew, the thought is exactly the same. The words are, 'Sair failed, hinny, sair failed now: sair failed, hinny, sin I kenned thou.' But of all the poems which contrast the much-changed man and the little-changed tree, I know of none more touching than one I lately read in an American magazine. It is called *The Name in the Bark*. Here is a part of the poem:—

   The self of so long ago,
   And the self I struggle to know,
I sometimes think we are two,—or are we shadows of one?
   To-day the shadow I am,
   Comes back in the sweet summer calm,
To trace where the earlier shadow flitted awhile in the sun.

   Once more in the dewy morn,
   I trod through the whispering corn:
Cool to my fevered cheek soft breezy kisses were blown;

The ribboned and tasselled grass
Leaned over the flattering glass;
And the sunny waters trilled the same low musical tone.

To the gray old birch I came,
Where I whittled my schoolboy name:
The nimble squirrel once more ran skippingly over the rail:
The blackbirds down among
The alders noisily sung,
And under the blackberry-trees whistled the serious quail.

I came, remembering well,
How my little shadow fell,
As I painfully reached and wrote to leave to the future a sign:
There, stooping a little, I found
A half-healed, curious wound;—
An ancient scar in the bark, but no initial of mine!

I shall not add the verses in which the poet wisely moralizes on this instance how fast the traces we leave behind us pass away. Is it because I can remember how *my* little shadow fell, many years since, that the last-quoted verse touches me as it does? We cast a different shadow now, my friend, from that little one we remember well; and it will not be very long till the shadows that fell and the substance that cast them shall have left here an equal trace.

Yes, my readers, we are all changed, as we are going on, from what we used to be. And it is no wonder we are changed. The wonder is that we are not changed a great deal more. How much hard work we have done; how much care, trouble, anxiety, disappointment, we have come through! What painful lessons we have been obliged to learn, every one of us! A great deal of the work we do is merely to serve the purposes of the time, and it leaves no trace; but when the work done leaves its tangible memorial, it often strikes us much; and we wonder to see how fresh and unwearied the man looks who did it all. I have seen the accumulated stock of sermons of a clergyman of more than forty years in the Church. It was awful to see what a vast mass they were. And even when we look not at the work of a lifetime, but at the results of what was no more than part of the work of a few years, we do so with a feeling of surprise that the man who did it was not at the end of his work much changed to appearance from what he was when he began it. Some time since I got back for a short time the prize essays I wrote while at college. They filled a whole shelf, and not a very small shelf. It was awful to look at them. They were all written before the writer was twenty-two. They were great heavy volumes—heavy physically; and intellectually and æsthetically still heavier. I tried to read one, but could not, because it was so tiresome; and I may therefore fairly conclude that no one will ever read them. Yet let me confess, that having arranged them on a lower shelf, I sat down on a rocking-chair immediately in front of them, and looked at them with great interest and wonder. In such a prospect, what could one do but shake one's head and sigh? The essays were all successful, Mr. Snarling. Every one of those prize essays got its prize.

It is not in mortification that one sighs, but vaguely in the view of such an immense deal of hard work done to so very small purpose. And when you look at a man advanced in life, whose whole life has been one of hard work, you cannot but confusedly wonder to see him looking as he does. To see Lord Campbell walking about at Hartrigge, when he had reached the highest place that a British subject can reach—to see the benignant and cheerful face of that remarkable man—and then to think of the tremendous amount of mental labour he had gone through in his long life, was a most perplexing and bewildering sight. When you are shown a ship that has come back from an Arctic voyage, you will generally remark that the ship looks like it; it has a weatherbeaten and battered aspect, suggestive of crunching against icebergs and the like. But when you are shown a man whose voyage in life has been a long and laborious one, you are sometimes surprised to find that he looks as fresh and unwearied as if he had done nothing all his life but amuse himself.

I have already said that it is a great blessing that in this world there are such things as *Beginnings and Ends*. It is a blessing that we can divide our way, as we go on, into stages—that we are saved the wearying and depressing effect of a very long uniform look-out. We begin a succession of tasks: we end them; and then we begin afresh. And even those things in which, in fact, there are no beginnings nor ends, have them in our feeling. The unvarying advance of time is broken into days and weeks; and we feel a most decided end on Saturday night, and we make a new start on Monday morning. It must be dreadful for a man to work straight on, Sunday and all other days. I believe it is impossible that any man should do so long. The man who refuses to observe a weekly day of rest will knock his head against the whole system of things, to the detriment of his head.

But even more valuable than this obvious result of the existence of Beginnings and Ends is another. It is an unspeakable blessing that a man who has got himself thoroughly into a mess anywhere or in any occupation, should be able to get away somewhere else and begin again. If Mr. Snarling, who has quarrelled with all his parishioners in his present charge, were removed to another a hundred miles off, I think he would take great pains to avoid those acts of folly and ill-temper which have made him so unhappy where he is. And let me say in addition, that most of us, as we go on, are always in our hearts admitting the imperfection and unsatisfactoriness of our past life. We are every now and then, in thought and feeling, beginning again. Men are every now and then cutting off the past; and acknowledging that they must start, or (more commonly) that a little while back they *did* start, anew. You occasionally avow to yourself, my reader, though not to the world, that you were a blockhead even two or three years ago. You occasionally say to yourself that your real life begins from this day three years. From that date you think you have been a great deal wiser and better. That course of conduct five years ago; those opinions you held then; that poem, essay, or book you wrote then; you are willing to give up. You have not a word to say for them. But *that* was in a former stage — in a different life. You have begun again since that; you have cut connexion with it. You say to yourself, 'It may be thirty years since I came into the world; but my real life—the part of my life I am willing to avow and to answer for—began on the 1st of January, 1860. I cut off all that preceded. I began again then; and as for what I have said and done since then, I am ready (as Scotch folk say) to *stand on the head of it*. It is only in a limited sense that I admit my identity with the individual who before that date bore my name and wore my aspect. I disavow the individual. I condemn him as severely as you can do.' Tell me, my reader, have you not many a time done that? Have you not given up one leaf as hopelessly blotted, and tried to turn over a new one—cut off (in short) the preceding days of life and resolved to begin again? Do so, my friend. You may make something of the new leaf, but you will never make anything of the old one. And whenever you find any human being anxious to begin again, always let him do it, always help him to do it. Don't do as some malicious wretches do, try to make it as difficult and humiliating as possible for him to turn over the new leaf. Don't try to compel him to a formal declaration in words that he sees his former life was wrong, and wants to break away from it; it was bitter enough for him to make that avowal to himself. You will find malicious animals who, if man or child has done wrong, and is sorry for it, and wishes to turn into a better way, will do all they can to prevent the poor creature from quietly turning away from the blurred page and beginning the clean one. If there be joy in heaven over the repenting sinner, it cannot be denied that there is vicious spite over the repenting sinner in certain hearts upon earth. Let us not seek to make repentance harder than it is by its nature. Unhappily there are cases in which neither in fact nor in feeling is it possible to begin again—at least upon an unsullied page. There are many people who never have a second chance. They must go deeper and deeper; they took the wrong turning, and they can never go back. Such is generally the result of crime. There is one sex, at least, with which the one wrong step is irretraceable. And even with the ruder half of mankind, there are some deeds which, being done, shut you in like the spring-lock in poor Ginevra's oak-chest. There is no repassing; and often the irreversible turning into the wrong track was not the result of anything like crime; often the cause was no more than ill-luck, or some foolish word or doing. What disproportionate punishment often follows on little acts of haste or folly! In the order of Providence folly is often punished much more severely than sin. A young fellow, foolishly thinking to gain the favour of a sporting patron by exhibiting an extraordinary knowledge of the turf and the chase, cuts himself off from the living on which his heart was set. A flippant word, hardly spoken till it was repented, has prejudicially affected a man's whole after career. Various men, in pique and haste, have made marriages which blighted all their life, and which brought an actual sorer punishment than that with which the law visits aggravated burglary or manslaughter. It is well in most cases to keep a way of retreat. It is well that before entering in you should see if you can get out, should it prove desirable. You must be very confident or very desperate if you cut off the bridge behind you, when in front there is but to do or to die. No doubt a habit of keeping the retreat open is fatal to decision of action and character. There is good, in one view, in feeling that we have crossed the Rubicon and are *in for it*; then we shall hold stoutly on; otherwise, we may be advancing with only half a heart. And there are important cases in which the difference between half a heart and a whole one makes just the difference between signal defeat and splendid victory.

It is to be admitted, my friends, that as we go on, the nonsense is being taken out of us. You have seen a horse start upon its journey in a very frisky condition, kicking about and prancing; but after a few miles it settles into doing its work steadily. That is the image which to my mind represents our career, going on. The romance has mainly departed. We look for homely things, and are content with them. Once, too, we expected to do great achievements, but not now. We know, generally, our humble mark. Indeed, the question as to the earning of bread and butter has utterly crowded out of our hearts the question as to the attainment of fame. We would not give one pound six and eightpence for wide renown. We would not give the eightpence for posthumous celebrity. We know our humble mark, I have said. I mean intellectually. And it is a great comfort to know it. It saves us much fever of competition, of suspense, of disappointment. We cannot possibly be beaten in the race of ambition; we cannot even injure our lungs or our heart in the race of ambition; because we shall not run it at all. A wise man may be very glad, and very thankful, that he does not think himself a great genius, and that he does not think what he can do very splendid. For if a man thought himself a great genius, he would be bitterly mortified that he was not recognised as such. And if a man thought his sermons or his books very fine, he would be mortified that his church was not crammed to suffocation, instead of being quite pleased when it is respectably filled; and he would be disappointed that his books do not sell by scores of thousands of copies, instead of being joyful that about half the first edition sells, leaving his publishers or himself only a little out of pocket, besides all their time and trouble. I know a man of highly respectable talents, who once published a theological book. Nobody ever bought a copy except himself. But he bought a good many, which he gave to his friends. And then he was extremely pleased that so many copies were sold. Was he not a wise and modest man?

Among other follies, I think that in going on, men, if they have any sense at all, get rid of Affectation. Few middle-aged men, unless they be by nature incurably silly and conceited, try to walk along the street in a dignified and effective way. They wish to get quickly and quietly along; and they have utterly discarded the idea that any passer-by thinks it worth while to look at them. Generally speaking, they sign their names in a natural handwriting. They do not, as a rule, look very cheerful. They seem, when silent, to fall into calculations, the result of which is not satisfactory. The great tamer of men is, doubtless, the want of money. *That* is the thing that brings people down from their airy flights and romantic imaginations; especially when there are some dependent on them. You may dismiss the very rich, who never need think and scheme about money, and how it is to be got, and how far it can be made to go, as an inappreciable fraction of the human race. Care sits heavy upon the great majority of those who are going on. You know the anxious look, and the inelastic step, of most middle-aged people who have children. All these things are the result of the want of money. Probably the want of money serves great ends in the economy of things. Probably it is a needful and essential spur to work; and a useful teacher of modesty, humility, moderation. No man will be blown up with a sense of his own consequence, or walk about fancying that he is being pointed out with the finger as the illustrious Smith, when (like poor Leigh Hunt) the fears lest the baker should refuse to send him bread, or that the washerwoman should impound his shirts. It is a lamentable story that is set out in the latter portions of the *Correspondence* of that amiable but unwise man. And human vanity needs a strong pressure to keep it within moderate limits. Even the wise man, with all his unsparing efforts to keep self-conceit down, has latent in him more of it than he would like to confess. I lately heard of an outburst of the vanity latent in a decent farmer of moderate means. One market day he got somewhat drunk, unhappily. And walking home, on the country road, he fell into a ditch, wherein he remained. Some of his friends found him there, and proceeded to rescue him. On approaching him, they found he was praying. For though drunk that day, he was really a worthy man: it was quite an exceptional case; I suppose he never got drunk again. They caught a sentence of his prayer. It was, '*Lord, as Thou hast made me great, so do Thou make me good!*' His friends had no idea of the high estimation in which the man held himself. He was, in the matter of greatness, exactly on the same footing with the other people round him. But he did not think so. In his secret soul he fancied himself a very superior man. And when his self-restraint was removed by whisky, the fancy came out.

But he must have been at least a well-to-do man, who had this idea of his own importance. Many men are burdened far too heavily for that. Very many men in this world are bearing just as much as they can. A little more would break them down, as the last pound breaks the camel's back. When a man is loaded with as much work, or suffering, or disappointment, as he can bear, a very trifling addition will make his burden greater than he can bear. I remember how a friend told me of a time when he was passing through the greatest trouble of his life. He had met a very heavy trial, but was bearing up wonderfully. One day, only a day or two after the stroke had fallen, he was walking along a lonely and rocky path, when he tripped and fell down, giving his knee a severe stunning blow against a rock. He had been able to bear up before, though his heart was full. But that was the drop too much: and he broke down and cried like a child, though before *that* he had not shed a tear.

There are various conclusions at which men arrive as they go on, which at an earlier part of their journey they would have rejected with indignation. One thing you will learn, my reader, as you advance, is, what you may expect. I mean, in particular, how much you may expect from the kindness of your friends; how much they are likely to do for you; how much they are likely to put themselves about to serve you. I do not say it in the way of finding fault; but the ordinary men of this world are so completely occupied in looking to their own concerns, that they have no time or strength to spare for those of others. And, accordingly, if you stick in the mud, you had much better, in all ordinary cases, try to get out yourself. Nobody is likely to help you particularly. Good Samaritans, in modern society, are rare; priests and Levites are frequent. I lately came to know a man who had faithfully and effectually served a certain cause for many years. He came at last to a point in his life at which those interested in the cause he had served might have greatly helped him. He made sure they would. But they simply did nothing. Nobody moved a finger to aid that meritorious man. He was mortified; but after waiting a little, he proceeded to help himself; which he did effectually. I do not think he will trust to his friends any more. The truth is, that beyond the closest circle of relationship, men in general care very little indeed for each other. I know men, indeed—and I say it with pride and thankfulness —with whom the case is very different: I remember one who loved his friends as himself, and who stood up for them everywhere with a noble devotion: I think a good many of them caught from him the impulse that would have made them do as much for *him*; but *he* was one of the truest friends and the noblest-hearted men on this earth. Many months are gone since he was laid in his grave; but how many of those who will read this page cherish more warmly than ever, the memory of John Parker! 'If I forget thee,' my beloved friend,—you remember David's solemn words. But, compared with the chance acquaintances whom every one knows, *he* was a Man among Gorillas. And I recur to my principle, that beyond closest ties of blood, men in general care very little for one another. You have known, I dare say, an old gentleman, dying in great suffering through many weeks; but his old club friends did not care at all; at most, very little. His suffering and death caused them not the slightest appreciable concern. You may expect certain of your friends to be extremely lively and amusing at a dinner party, on the day of your funeral. I remember, a good many years ago, feeling very indignant at learning about a gay entertainment, where was much music and dancing, attended by a number of young people, on the evening of the day on which a fair young companion of them all was laid in her last resting-place. I am so many years older; yet I confess I have not succeeded in schooling myself to feel none of the indignation I then felt; though I have thoroughly got rid of the slightest tendency to the surprise I felt in that inexperienced time. For, since then, I have seen a young fellow of six-and-twenty engaged in a lively flirtation with two girls who were in a railway carriage while he was standing on the platform, just the day after his mother's funeral. I have beheld two young ladies decked to go out to a ball. Their dresses happily combined a most becoming aspect with the expression of a modified degree of mourning. They had recently lost a relative. The relative was their father. I have witnessed the gaiety and the flirtations of a newly-made widow. It appeared to me a sorry sight. There are human beings, it cannot be denied, whose main characteristics are selfishness and heartlessness. For it is unquestionably true, that the most thorough disregard for the feelings, and wishes, and interests of others, may coexist with the keenest concern for one's self. You will find people who bear with a heroic constancy the sufferings and trials of others; but who make a frightful howling about their own. And singularly, those who never gave sympathy to another mortal, expect that other mortals shall evince lively sympathy with them. Commend me to a thoroughly selfish person, for loud complaints of the selfishness of others.

As you go on, you will come to understand how well you can be spared from this world. You remember Napoleon's axiom, that No man is necessary. There is no man in the world whom the world could not do without. There are many men who, if they were taken away, would be missed ; would be very much missed, perhaps, by more or fewer human beings. But there is no man but what we may say of him that, useful and valuable as he may be, we might, sooner or later, with more or less difficulty, come to do without him. The country got over the loss of Sir Robert Peel and the Duke of Wellington; it misses Prince Albert yet, but it is getting over his absence. I do not mean to say that there are not hearts in which a worthy human being is always remembered, and always missed; in which his absence is felt as an irreparable loss, making all life different from what it used to be. But in the case of each, these hearts are few. And it is quite fit that they should be few. If our sympathy with others were as keen as our feeling for ourselves, we should get poorly through life: with many persons, sympathy is only too keen and real as it is. But though you quite easily see and admit that human beings can be spared without much inconvenience, when you think how the State comes to do without its lost political chief, and the country without its departed hero, you are somewhat apt, till growing years have taught you, to cherish some lurking belief that you yourself will be missed, and kindly remembered, longer and by more people than you are ever likely to be. A great many clergymen, seeing the strong marks of grief evinced by their congregation as they preach their farewell sermon before going to another parish, can hardly think how quickly the congregation will get over its loss; and how soon it will come to assemble Sunday by Sunday with no remembrance at all of the familiar face that used to look at it from the pulpit, or of the voice which once was pleasant to hear. Let no man wilfully withdraw from his place in life, thinking that he will be missed so much that he will be eagerly sought again. If you step out of the ranks, the crowd may pass on; the vacant space may be occupied; and you may never be able to find your place any more. There are far more men than there are holes, and all the holes get filled up. Who hastily resigned a bishopric? who in dudgeon threw up an Attorney-Generalship? who (thinking he could not be spared) abdicated the Chancellorship? And did not each of these men find out his mistake? The holes were filled up, and the men remained outsiders ever afterwards. There is a very striking story of Hawthorne's analysing the motives and feelings of a man who, in some whim, went away from his house and his wife, but went no farther than the next street, and lived there in disguise for many years, all his relatives fancying him dead. And the eminent American shows, with wonderful power, how a human being so acting may make himself the outlaw of the universe. It needs all your presence, all your energy, all your present services, to hold you in your place in life, my friend. There are certain things whose value is felt through their absence; but I think that, as a general rule, a man can make his value felt only by his presence.

A friend of mine, who is a successful author, told me how, when he published his first book, he made quite sure that all his friends would read it, and more particularly that all his cousins, to whom he sent copies of his book, would do so. But he confided to me, as one of the lessons he had arrived at in going on, that it is with total strangers that any writer must hope for whatever success he may reach. Your cousins, thinking to mortify you, will diligently refrain from reading your volume. At least they will profess that they do so; though you will find them extremely well coached up in all the weak and foolish passages with which the reviewers have found fault. And these passages they will hasten to point out to your father and mother, also to your wife; at the same time expressing their anxious hope that these foolish passages may not do you harm. My friend told me how in his first book there was a sentence which his cousins feared would give offence to a certain eminent person who had shown him kindness; and the promptitude with which they could always turn up the passage, and the vigorous and fluent manner in which they could point out how offensive it must prove to the eminent person, testified to the amount of pains they had bestowed upon the discussion of the subject. Among the six hundred pages, how easily and swiftly they could always find this unlucky page! My friend told me that in a rather popular book of his, there was a passage of a few pages in length which had been severely criticised. Possibly it was weak; possibly it was absurd. I confess that I read it, and it did not strike me as remarkable. However, the critics generally attacked it; and probably they were right. A few weeks ago, my friend told me he met a very pretty young cousin, of twenty years, for the first time. With a radiant smile, the fair cousin began to talk to my friend about his efforts in authorship. 'Oh, Mr. Smith,' said she, 'do you know, the only thing I ever read in your book was that part where you said'—no matter what. 'It was so funny! Do you know, Cousin Dick showed it to me the moment I arrived at Ananias-street!' I have not the faintest doubt that Cousin Dick did. I have myself heard Dick quote a sentence from his relative's work, which sounded very flippant and presumptuous. I turned up the page, and requested Dick to observe that he was (unintentionally, but) grossly misrepresenting the passage. It was not the least like what he quoted; and the version given by him was altered greatly for the worse. Dick saw he was wrong. But several times since have I heard him give the incorrect quotation, just as before. Of course, his purpose was not to represent his relative as a man of taste and sense.

I think that as we go on we come to have a great charity for the misdoings of our fellow-men. There are, indeed, flagrant crimes, whose authors can never be thought of but with a burning abhorrence. I have heard of the doings of men whom I should be happy to help to hang. But I am thinking of the little misdoings of social life in a civilized country. As for deliberate cruelty and oppression, as for lying and cheating to make money, I never have learned to think of them but with a bitterness approaching the ferocious. Nor have I grown a bit more charitable with advancing years in my estimate of the liar, cheat, and blackguard (of whatever rank), who will mislead some poor girl to her ruin. I should be glad to burn such a one, with this hand, with a red-hot iron, upon the forehead with the word LIAR. And something of the emotion I feel in the thought of him extends to the thought of the young ladies who waltz with him, knowing perfectly what he is; and to the thought of the parsons who toady him, in hope of a presentation to the wealthy living of Soapy-cum-Sneaky. But, setting these extreme cases aside, you will come, as you go on through life, to see some excuse for various little misdoings, towards which you felt somewhat bitterly in earlier years. You will come to frankly recognise the truth, which at first you are slow to admit, that there are certain positions which are too much for human nature. I mean too much for human nature to hold without exhibiting a good deal of pettiness, envy, spitefulness, and malevolence; unless, indeed, with very fine and amiable natures. There is an ecclesiastical arrangement peculiar to Scotland; it is what is termed a *Collegiate Charge*. It means that a parish church shall have two incumbents of authority, dignity, and eminence, exactly similar. The incumbents, in many cases, quarrel outright; in many more they do not work cordially together. In a smaller number, indeed, they have been known to be as brothers, or as father and son. There is something trying in the position of a parish clergyman who has a curate, or assistant, who is more popular than himself. You may sometimes find a church poorly attended when the clergyman preaches, but crowded when the curate does so. Even in such a case, if the rector be a good man, and the curate another, perfect kindliness may exist between the rector and the curate; but I doubt whether that kindliness is much to be expected from the rector's wife. And when the curate at length gets a parish of his own, he need not expect that his old principal will often ask him back to preach. Now, many people will be found ready to speak with much severity of the principal who acts thus; and to blame the clergyman who, not being able to fill his church himself, prefers having it empty to seeing it filled by any one else. Such people are unquestionably wrong. They expect from the poor clergyman more than ought to be looked for from average human nature. The clergyman's conduct is very natural. Put yourself in his place: look at the matter from his point of view. You would not like yourself the thing he does not like. You would very possibly do exactly what he does. And you might do it all quite conscientiously. You might fancy you had high and pure reasons for what you did, and that there was no intrusion of jealousy. The young curate's sermons were, very likely, very crude and extravagant; and you may honestly think it your duty to prevent your people from being presented with spiritual food so immature. And rely upon it, those men who carefully exclude from their pulpits all interesting and attractive preachers, and put there (in their own absence) the dullest and poorest preachers they can find, though doubtless actuated in great measure by a determination that they themselves shall not be eclipsed, but shall rather shine by comparison, are quite able to persuade themselves that they act from the purest motives. But even while you pity the men (let us hope there are very few) in whose mind such unworthy considerations have weight, do not blame them severely. They are in a difficult position. No doubt they would find it happier as well as worthier to spurn the first suggestion of petty jealousy; no doubt the magnanimous man would do so; but there are men who are not magnanimous, and who could no more be magnanimous than they could be six feet high, or than they could write *King Lear*. Now, my friend, as you go on, you come to understand all these things. You learn to make great allowances for the pettiness of human nature. You come to be able to treat with cordiality people to whom in your hot and hasty youth you could not have spoken without giving them a bit of your mind which they would not have liked to hear. And when I say that with advancing years you come to excuse human misdoings, I do not mean that as we grow older we come to think more lightly of the difference between right and wrong, or between the generous and the mean. I hope we know better than that. It is another principle that comes into play—the principle, to wit, that not being without sin yourself, you should be slow to cast a stone at an erring brother. It has been already said that there are cases as to which we shall not reason thus. Of heartless and deliberate cruelty and treachery we shall never think but with fury; and we do not wish ever to think but with fury. Give me the knout, and lead out one of several human beings of whom I have heard, and I will warrant you you should hear extensive howling! I am not afraid to plead the highest of all precedents, for the permission of the bitterest wrath and for the dealing of the sharpest blows. But I humbly and firmly trust, my friendly reader, that in you and me there is nothing like heartless deliberate cruelty and treachery. We have no sympathy at all with these, any more than with the peculiar taste which makes worms like filth. But as to very much of human error and weakness, do you not feel in yourself the capacities which (though restrained by God's grace) might have brought you to all that? The thing we can least forgive is that which we cannot imagine how any one could do—that which we think we have in us nothing like.

In your earlier days, you were perpetually getting into scrapes, by speaking hastily and acting hastily. As you go on, you learn by experience to avoid these things in great measure; and you learn to be very cautious as to the people you will take into your confidence. It is a sorrowful lesson of experience, but it *is* a lesson of experience, that there are many people to whom you should never say a sentence, without first calculating whether that sentence can be repeated, or can be misrepresented, to your disadvantage. Like a skilful chess-player, you need to consider what may be the result of this move. It is to be admitted, that much of worldly wisdom is far from being a pleasing or noble thing. You learn by experience a great deal which it is right you should know and act upon, yet which does not ennoble you. It is a fine sight, after all, a warm-hearted, outspoken, injudicious man of more than middle age! I know well an eminent professor in a certain university, who is a very clever and learned man, and a very injudicious one. I admire his talents and his learning; but I feel a warm affection for his outspoken and injudicious honesty and truthfulness. I am quite sure that if he thought a neighbouring marquis a humbug, he would call him one. I have the strongest ground for believing that if he thought a bishop a fool, he would say so. Let us ever try to hold our prudence free from the suspicion of baseness. I trust that as we go on, we are not coming to practice sneaky arts to the end of getting on. Sneakiness, and underhand dealing, are doubtless to be reckoned among the arts of self-advancement. Honesty is, in many cases, unquestionably, the very worst policy. But though honesty be so, honesty is the right thing, after all! But honest men sometimes think to possess, together, two inconsistent things. They think to possess the high sense of scrupulous integrity; and at the same time the favour, patronage, and profit, which can be had only by parting with *that*.

We are all going on: a man here and there is also getting on. As you look round upon the people who started with you, you will discern that even those who are doing well in life, for the most part reached their utmost elevation before very many years were gone; and for a large tract of time past have not been gaining. They are going on, in short: Time makes sure that we shall all do *that*; but they are not getting on. Their income is just the same now that it was five or ten years since; and the estimation in which they are held by those who know them has neither grown nor lessened. But there is a man here and there who is growing bigger as well as growing older. He is coming, yearly, to be better known: he is gaining in wealth, in influence, in reputation. Every walk of life has its rising men. There are country gentlemen who gradually elbow their way forward among the members of their class, till they stand conspicuously apart from them. So with painters, authors, barristers, preachers. Who are they, among those whom I know, who are making way, and rising in the world? And what is the secret of their success? I must stop and think.

CHAPTER VII.

CONCERNING DISAGREEABLE PEOPLE.

'ON the whole, it was very disagreeable.'

Thus wrote a certain great traveller and hunter, summing up an account of his position as he composed himself to rest upon a certain evening after a hard day's work. And no doubt it must have been very disagreeable. The night was cold and dark: and the intrepid traveller had to lie down to sleep in the open air, without even a tree to shelter him. A heavy shower of hail was falling; each hailstone about the size of an egg. The dark air was occasionally illuminated by forked lightning, of the most appalling aspect: and the thunder was deafening. By various sounds, heard in the intervals of the peals, it seemed evident that the vicinity was pervaded by wolves, tigers, elephants, wild boars, and serpents. A peculiar motion, perceptible under a horsecloth which was wrapped up to serve as a pillow, appeared to indicate that a snake was wriggling about underneath it. The hunter had some ground for thinking that it was a very venomous one; as indeed in the morning it proved to be: but he was too tired to look. And speaking of the general condition of matters upon that evening, the hunter stated, with great mildness of language, that 'it was very disagreeable.'

Most readers would be disposed to say, that disagreeable was hardly the right word. No doubt, all things that are perilous, horrible, awful, ghastly, deadly, and the like, are disagreeable too. But when we use the word *disagreeable* by itself, our meaning is understood to be, that in calling the thing disagreeable, we have said the worst of it. A long and tiresome sermon is disagreeable: but a venomous snake under your pillow passes beyond being disagreeable. To have a tooth stopped, is disagreeable: to be broken on the wheel (though nobody could like it): transcends *that*. If a thing be horrible and awful, you would not say it was disagreeable. The greater includes the less: as when a human being becomes entitled to write D.D. after his name, he drops all mention of the M.A. borne in preceding years.

Let this truth be remembered, by such as shall read the following pages. We are to think about Disagreeable People. Let it be understood that (speaking generally) we are to think of people who are no worse than disagreeable. It cannot be denied, even by the most prejudiced, that murderers, pirates, slave-drivers, and burglars, are disagreeable. The cut-throat: the poisoner: the sneaking blackguard who shoots his landlord from behind a hedge: are no doubt disagreeable people; so very disagreeable that in this country the common consent of mankind removes them from human society by the instrumentality of a halter. But disagreeable is too mild a word. Such people are all that, and a great deal more. And accordingly, they stand beyond the range of this dissertation. We are to treat of folk who are disagreeable; and not worse than disagreeable. We may sometimes, indeed, overstep the boundary line. But it is to be remembered, that there are people who in the main are good people, who yet are extremely disagreeable. And a further complication is introduced into the subject by the fact, that some people who are far from good, are yet unquestionably agreeable. You disapprove them; but you cannot help liking them. Others, again, are substantially good; yet you are angry with yourself to find that you cannot like them.

I take for granted that all observant human beings will admit that in this world there are disagreeable people. Probably the distinction which presses itself most strongly upon our attention as we mingle in the society of our fellow-men, is the distinction between agreeable people and disagreeable. There are various tests, more or less important, which put all mankind to right and left. A familiar division is into rich and poor. Thomas Paine, with great vehemence, denied the propriety of that classification; and declared that

Concerning Disagreeable People. 191

the only true and essential classification of mankind is into male and female. I have read a story whose author maintained that to his mind, by far the most interesting and thorough division of our race, is into such as have been hanged and such as have not been hanged: he himself belonging to the former class. But we all, more or less, recognise and act upon the great classification of all human beings into the agreeable and the disagreeable. And we begin very early to recognise and act upon it. Very early in life, the little child understands and feels the vast difference between people who are nice, and people who are not nice. In schoolboy days, the first thing settled as to any new acquaintance, man or boy, is on which side he stands of the great boundary line. It is not genius, not scholarship, not wisdom, not strength nor speed, that fixes the man's place. None of these things is chiefly looked to: the question is, Is he agreeable or disagreeable? And according as that question is decided, the man is described, in the forcible language of youth, as 'a brick,' or as 'a beast.'

Yet it is to be remembered, that the division between the agreeable and disagreeable of mankind, is one which may be transcended. It is a scratch on the earth: not a ten-foot wall. And you will find men who pass from one side of it to the other; and back again; probably several times in a week, or even in a day. There are people whom you never know where to have. They are constantly skipping from side to side of that line of demarcation: or they even walk along with a foot on each side of it. There are people who are always disagreeable; and disagreeable to all men. There are people who are agreeable at some times, and disagreeable at others. There are people who are agreeable to some men and disagreeable to other men. I do not intend by the last-named class, people who intentionally make themselves agreeable to a certain portion of the race, to which they think it worth while to make themselves agreeable; and who do not take that trouble in the case of the remainder of humankind. What I mean is this: that there are people who have such an affinity and sympathy with certain other people: who so *suit* certain other people: that they are agreeable to these other people: though perhaps not particularly so to the race at large. And exceptional tastes and likings are often the strongest. The thing you like enthusiastically, another man absolutely loathes. The thing which all men like, is for the most part liked with a mild and subdued liking. Everybody likes good and well-made bread: but nobody goes into raptures over it. Few persons like caviare: but those who like it are very fond of it. I never knew but one being who liked mustard with apple-pie: but that solitary man ate it with avidity, and praised the flavour with enthusiasm.

But it is impossible to legislate for every individual case. Every rule must have exceptions from it; but it would be foolish to resolve to lay down no more rules.

Concerning Disagreeable People. 193

There may be, somewhere, the man who likes Mr. Snarling: and to that man Mr. Snarling would doubtless be agreeable. But for practical purposes, Mr. Snarling may justly be described as a disagreeable man, if he be disagreeable to nine hundred and ninety-nine mortals out of every thousand. And with precision sufficient for the ordinary business of life, we may say that there are people who are essentially disagreeable.

There are people who go through life, leaving an unpleasant influence on all whom they come near. You are not at your ease in their society. You feel awkward and constrained while with them. *That* is probably the mildest degree in the scale of unpleasantness. There are people who disseminate a much worse influence. As the upas-tree was said to blight all the country round it, so do these disagreeable folk prejudicially affect the whole surrounding moral atmosphere. They chill all warmth of heart in those near them: they put down anything generous or magnanimous: they suggest unpleasant thoughts and associations: they excite a diverse and numerous array of bad tempers. The great evil of disagreeable people lies in this: that they tend powerfully to make other people disagreeable too. And these people are not necessarily bad people, though they produce a bad effect. It is not certain that they design to be disagreeable. There are those who do entertain that design; and they always succeed in carrying it out. Nobody ever tried diligently to be disagreeable; and failed. Such persons may indeed inflict much less annoyance than they wished: they may even fail of inflicting any pain whatever on others: but they make themselves as disgusting as they could desire. And in many cases, they succeed in inflicting a good deal of pain. A very low, vulgar, petty, and uncultivated nature, may cause much suffering to a lofty, noble, and refined one: particularly if the latter be in a position of dependence or subjection. A wretched hornet may madden a noble horse: a contemptible mosquito may destroy the night's rest which would have recruited a noble brain. But without any evil intention: sometimes with the very kindest intention: there are those who worry and torment you. It is through want of perception: want of tact: coarseness of nature: utter lack of power to understand you. Were you ever sitting in a considerable company, a good deal saddened by something you did not choose to tell to any one, and probably looking dull and dispirited enough: and did a fussy host or hostess draw the attention of the entire party upon you, by earnestly and repeatedly asking if you were ill, if you had a headache, because you seemed so dull and so unlike yourself? And did that person time after time return to the charge, till you would have liked to poison him? There is nothing more disagreeable, and few things more mischievous, than a well-meaning meddling fool. And where there was no special intention, good or bad, towards yourself, you have known people make you uncomfortable through the simple exhibition to you,

Concerning Disagreeable People. 195

and pressure upon you, of their own inherent disagreeableness. You have known people after talking to whom for awhile, you felt disgusted with everything: and above all, with those people themselves. Talking to them, you felt your moral nature being rubbed against the grain: being stung all over with nettles. You showed your new house and furniture to such a man: and with eagle eye he traced out and pointed out every scratch on your fine fresh paint, and every flaw in your oak and walnut. He showed you that there were corners of your big mirrors that distort your face: that there were bits of your grand marble mantlepieces that might be expected soon to scale away. Or you have known a man who, with no evil intention, made it his practice to talk of you before your face, as your other friends are accustomed to talk of you behind your back. It need not be said that the result is anything but pleasant. 'What a fool you were, Smith, in saying *that* at Snooks's last night,' your friend exclaims when you meet him next morning. You were quite aware, by this time, that what you said was foolish: but there is something grating in hearing your name connected with the unpleasant name. I would strongly advise any man, who does not wish to be set down as disagreeable, entirely to break off the habit (if he has such a habit) of addressing to even his best friends any sentence beginning with 'What a fool you were.' Let me offer the like advice as to sentences which set out as follows: 'I say, Smith, I think your brother is the greatest fool on the face of the earth.' Stop that kind of thing, my friend; or you may come to be classed with Mr. Snarling. You are probably a manly fellow, and a sincere friend: and for the sake of your substantial good qualities, one would stand a great deal. But over-frankness is disagreeable: and if you make over-frankness your leading characteristic, of course your entire character will come to be a disagreeable one: and you will be a disagreeable person.

Besides the people who are disagreeable through malignant intention, and through deficiency of sensitiveness, there are other people who are disagreeable through pure ill-luck. It is quite certain that there are people whom evil fortune dogs through all their life: who are thoroughly and hopelessly unlucky. And in no respect have we beheld a man's ill-luck so persecute him, as in the matter of making him (without the slightest evil purpose, and even when he is most anxious to render himself agreeable) render himself extremely disagreeable. Of course there must be some measure of thoughtlessness and forgetfulness: some lack of that social caution so indispensable in the complication of modern society, which teaches a man (so to speak) to try if the ice will bear him before venturing his entire weight upon it: about people who are unlucky in the way of which I am speaking. But doubtless you have known persons who were always saying disagreeable things, or putting disagreeable questions; either through forgetfulness of things which they ought to have remembered, or through unhappily chancing on forbidden ground. You will find a man, a thoughtless but quite good-natured man, begin at a dinner table to relate a succession of stories very much to the prejudice of somebody : while somebody's daughter is sitting opposite him. And you will find the man quite obtuse to all the hints by which the host or hostess tries to stop him ; and going on to particulars worse and worse : till in terror of what all this might grow to, the hostess has to exclaim, ' Mr. Smith, you won't take a hint: *that* is Mr. Somebody's daughter sitting opposite you.' It is quite essential that any man, whose conversation consists mainly of observations not at all to the advantage of some absent acquaintance, should carefully feel his way before giving full scope to his malice and his invention, in the presence of any general company. And before making any playful reference to halters, you should be clear that you are not talking to a man whose grandfather was hanged. Nor should you venture any depreciatory remarks upon men who have risen from the ranks, unless you are tolerably versed in the family history of those to whom you are talking. You may have heard a man very jocular upon lunatic asylums, to another who had several brothers and sisters in one. And though in some cases, human beings may render themselves disagreeable through a combination of circumstances which really absolves them from all blame : yet, as a general rule, the man who is disagreeable through ill-luck is at least guilty of culpable carelessness.

You have probably, my reader, known people who had the faculty of making themselves extremely agreeable. You have known one or two men who, whenever you met them, conveyed to you by a remarkably frank and genial manner, an impression that they esteemed you as one of their best and dearest friends. A vague idea took possession of your mind, that they had been longing to see you ever since they saw you last: which in all probability was six or twelve months previously. And during all that period it may be regarded as quite certain, that the thought of you had never once entered their mind. Such a manner has a vast effect upon young and inexperienced folk. The inexperienced man fancies that this manner, so wonderfully frank and friendly, is reserved specially for himself; and is a recognition of his own special excellences. But the man of greater experience has come to suspect this manner, and to see through it. He has discovered that it is the same to everybody: at least, to everybody to whom it is thought worth while to put it on. And he no more thinks of arguing the existence of any particular liking for himself, or of any particular merit in himself, from that friendly manner; than he thinks of believing, on a warm summer day, that the sun has a special liking for himself, and is looking so beautiful and bright all for himself. It is perhaps unjust to accuse the man, always overflowing in geniality upon everybody he meets, of being an impostor or humbug. Perhaps he does feel an irrepressible gush of love to all his race: but why convey to each individual of the race that he loves *him* more than all the others?

Yet it is to be admitted, that it is always well that a man should be agreeable. Pleasantness is always a pleasing thing. And a sensible man, seeking by honest means to make himself agreeable, will generally succeed in making himself agreeable to sensible men. But although there is an implied compliment, to your power if not to your personality, in the fact of a man's taking pains to make himself agreeable to you; it is certain that he may try to make himself so by means of which the upshot will be, to make him intensely disagreeable. You know the fawning, sneaking manner which an occasional shopkeeper adopts. It is most disagreeable to right-thinking people. Let him remember that he is also a man: and let his manner be manly as well as civil. It is an awful and humiliating sight, a man who is always squeezing himself together like a whipped dog whenever you speak to him: grinning and bowing: and (in a moral sense) wriggling about before you on the earth, and begging you to wipe your feet on his head. You cannot help thinking that the sneak would be a tyrant if he had the opportunity. It is pleasant to find people in the humblest position, blending a manly independence of demeanour with the regard justly due to those placed by Providence farther up the social scale. Yet doubtless there are persons to whom the sneakiest manner is agreeable: who enjoy the flattery and the humiliation of the wretched toady who is always ready to tell them that they are the most beautiful, graceful, witty, well-informed, aristocratic-looking, and generally-beloved, of the human race. You must remember that it depends very much upon the nature of a man himself, whether any particular demeanour shall be agreeable to him or not. And you know well that a cringing, toadying manner, which would be thoroughly disgusting to a person of sense, may be extremely agreeable and delightful to a self-conceited idiot. Was there not an idiotic monarch, who was greatly pleased when his courtiers, in speaking to him, affected to veil their eyes with their hands, as unable to bear the insufferable effulgence of his countenance? And would not a monarch of sense have been ready to kick the people who thus treated him like a fool? And every one has observed that there are silly women who are much gratified by coarse and fulsome compliments upon their personal appearance, which would be regarded as grossly insulting by a woman of sense. You may have heard of country gentlemen, of Radical politics, who had seldom wandered beyond their paternal acres (by their paternal acres I mean the acres they had recently bought), and who had there grown into a fixed belief that they were among the noblest and mightiest of the earth; who thought their parish clergyman an agreeable man if he voted at the county election for the candidate they supported, though that candidate's politics were directly opposed to those of the parson. These individuals, of course, would hold their clergyman as a disagreeable man, if he held by his own principles: and quite declined to take their wishes into account in exercising the trust of the franchise. Now of course a nobleman or gentleman of right feeling, would regard the parson as a turncoat and sneak, who should thus deny his convictions. Yes: there is no doubt that you may make yourself agreeable to unworthy folk, by unworthy means. A late notorious Marquis declared on his dying bed, that a two-legged animal of human pretensions, who had acted as his valet, and had aided that hoary reprobate in the gratification of his peculiar tastes, was ' an excellent man.' And you may remember how Burke said that as we learn that a certain Mr. Russell made himself very agreeable to Henry the Eighth, we may reasonably suppose that Mr. Russell was himself (in a humble degree) something like his master. Probably to most right-minded men, the fact that a man was agreeable to Henry the Eighth, or to the Marquis in question, or to Belial, Beelzebub, or Apollyon, would tend to make that man remarkably disagreeable. And let the reader remember the guarded way in which the writer laid down his general principle as to pleasantness of character and demeanour. I said that a sensible man, seeking by honest means to make himself agreeable, will generally succeed in making himself agreeable to sensible men. I exclude from the class of men to be esteemed agreeable, those who would disgust all but fools or blackguards. I exclude parsons who express heretical views in theology, in the presence of a patron known to be a free-thinker. I exclude men who do great folk's dirty work. I exclude all toad-eaters, sneaks, flatterers, and fawning impostors: from the schoolboy who thinks to gain his master's favour by voluntarily bearing tales of his companions, up to the bishop who declared that he regarded it not merely as a constitutional principle but as an ethical fact, that the King could do no wrong: and the other bishop who declared that the reason why George the Second died, was that this world was not good enough for him, and it was necessary to transfer him to heaven that he might be the right man in the right place. Such persons may succeed in making themselves agreeable to the man with whom they desire to ingratiate themselves, provided that man be a fool or a knave; but they assuredly render themselves disagreeable, not to say revolting, to all human beings whose good opinion is worth the possessing. And though any one who is not a fool will generally make himself agreeable to people of ordinary temper and nervous system if he wishes to do so; it is to be remembered that too intrusive attempts to be agreeable often make a man very disagreeable: and likewise, that a man is the reverse of agreeable if you see that he is trying by managing and humouring you to make himself agreeable to you. I mean, if you can see that he is smoothing you down, and agreeing with you, and trying to get you on your blind side, as if he thought you a baby or a lunatic. And there is all the difference in the world, between the frank hearty wish in man or woman to be agreeable; and this diplomatic and indirect way. No man likes to think that he is being managed as Mr. Rarey might manage an unbroken colt. And though many human beings must in fact be thus managed: though a person of a violent or a sullen temper, or of a wrong head, or of outrageous vanity, or of invincible prejudices, must be managed very much as you would manage a lunatic (being, in fact, removed from perfect sanity upon these points): still, they must never be allowed to discern that they *are* being managed; or the charm will fail at once. I confess, for myself, that I am no believer in the efficacy of diplomacy and indirect ways in dealing with one's fellow-creatures. I believe that a manly, candid, straightforward course is always the best. Treat people in a perfectly frank manner: with frankness not put on, but real: and you will be agreeable to most of those to whom you would desire to be so.

My reader, I am now about to tell you of certain sorts of human beings, who appear to me as worthy of being ranked among disagreeable people. I do not pretend to give you an exhaustive catalogue of such.

Doubtless you have your own black beasts, your own special aversions, which have for you a disagreeableness beyond the understanding or sympathy of others. Nor do I make quite sure that you will agree with me in all the views which I am going to set forth. It is not impossible that you may regard as very nice people, or even as quite fascinating and enthralling people, certain people whom I regard as intensely disagreeable. Let me begin with an order of human beings, as to which I do not expect every one who reads this page to go along with me: though I do not know any opinion which I hold more resolutely than that which I am about to express.

We all understand the kind of thing which is meant by people who talk of *Muscular Christianity*. It is certainly a noble and excellent thing to make people discern that a good Christian need not be a muff (pardon the slang term: there is no other that would bring out my meaning). It is a fine thing to make it plain that manliness and dash may co-exist with pure morality and sincere piety. It is a fine thing to make young fellows comprehend that there is nothing fine and manly in being bad; and nothing unmanly in being good. And in this view, it is impossible to value too highly such characters and such biographies as those of Hodson of Hodson's Horse and of Captain Hedley Vicars. It is a splendid combination, pluck and daring in their highest degree, with an unaffected and earnest regard to religion and religious duties: in short, muscularity with Christianity. A man consists of body and soul: and both would be in their ideal perfection, if the soul were decidedly Christian, and the body decidedly muscular.

But there are folk whose admiration of the muscularity is very great; but whose regard for the Christianity is very small. They are captivated by the dash and glitter of physical pluck: they are quite content to accept it without any Christianity; and even without the most ordinary morality and decency. They appear, indeed, to think that the grandeur of the character is increased, by the combination of thorough blackguardism with high physical qualifications: their gospel, in short, may be said to be that of *Unchristian Muscularity*. And you will find various books in which the hero is such a man: and while the writer of the book frankly admits that he is in strict morality an extremely bad man, the writer still recals his doings with such manifest gusto and sympathy, and takes such pains to make him agreeable on the whole, and relates with such approval the admiration which empty-headed idiots express for him when he has jumped his horse over some very perilous fence or thrashed some insolent farmer, that it is painfully apparent what is the writer's ideal of a grand and imposing character. You know the kind of man who is the hero of some novels: the muscular blackguard: and you remember what are his unfailing characteristics. He has a deep chest. He has huge arms and limbs: the muscles being knotted. He has an immense moustache. He has (God knows why) a serene contempt for ordinary mortals. He is always growing black with fury, and bullying weak men. On such occasions, his lips may be observed to be twisted into an evil sneer. He is a seducer and liar: he has ruined various women, and had special facilities for becoming acquainted with the rottenness of society: and occasionally he expresses, in language of the most profane, not to say blasphemous character, a momentary regret for having done so much harm; such as the Devil might sentimentally have expressed when he had succeeded in misleading our first parents. Of course, he never pays tradesmen for the things with which they supply him. He can drink an enormous quantity of wine without his head becoming affected. He looks down with entire disregard on the laws of God and man, as made for inferior beings. As for any worthy moral quality: as for anything beyond a certain picturesque brutality and bull-dog disregard of danger: not a trace of such a thing can be found about him.

We all know, of course, that such a person, though not uncommon in novels, very rarely occurs in real life: and if he occur at all, it is with his ideal perfections very much toned down. In actual life, such a hero would become known in the Insolvent Court, and would frequently appear before the police magistrates. He would eventually become a billiard-marker; and might ultimately be hanged, with general approval.

If the man, in his unclipped proportions, did actually exist, it would be right that a combination should be formed to wipe him out of creation. He should be put down: as you would put down a tiger or a rattlesnake if found at liberty somewhere in the Midland Counties. A more hateful character, to all who possess a grain of moral discernment, could not even be imagined. And it need not be shown, that the conception of such a character is worthy only of a baby. However many years the man who deliberately and admiringly delineates such a person may have lived in this world, intellectually he cannot be more than about seven years old. And none but calves the most immature can possibly sympathize with him. Yet if there were not many silly persons to whom such a character is agreeable, such a character would not be portrayed. And it seems certain that a single exhibition of strength or daring will to some minds be the compendium of all good qualities: or (more accurately speaking) the equivalent for them. A muscular blackguard clears a high fence: he does precisely that, neither more nor less. And upon the strength of that single achievement, the servants at the house where he is visiting declare that they would follow him over the world. And you may find various young women, and various women who wish to pass for young, who would profess, and perhaps actually feel, a like enthusiasm for the muscular blackguard. I confess that I cannot find words strong enough to express my contempt and abhorrence for the theory of life and character which is assumed by the writers who describe such blackguards, and by the fools who admire them. And though very far from saying or thinking that the kind of human being who has been described, is no worse than disagreeable, I assert with entire confidence that to all right-thinking men, he is more disagreeable than almost any other kind of human being. And I do not know any single lesson you could instil into a youthful mind, which would be so mischievous, as the lesson that the muscular blackguard should be regarded with any other feeling than that of pure loathing and disgust. But let us have done with him. I cannot think of the books which delineate him, and ask you to admire him, without indignation more bitter than I wish to feel in writing such a page.

And passing to the consideration of human beings who though disagreeable, are good in the main; it may be laid down, as a general principle, that any person, however good, is disagreeable, from whom you feel it a relief to get away. We have all known people, thoroughly estimable, and whom you could not but respect, in whose presence it was impossible to feel at ease; and whose absence was felt as the withdrawal of a sense of constraint of the most oppressive kind. And this vague, uncomfortable influence, which breathes from some men, is produced in various ways. Sometimes it is the result of mere stiffness and awkwardness of manner: and there are men whose stiffness and awkwardness of manner are such as would freeze the most genial and silence the frankest. Sometimes it arises from ignorance of social rules and proprieties: sometimes from incapacity to take, or even to comprehend, a joke. Sometimes it proceeds from a pettedness of nature, which keeps you ever in fear that offence may be taken at the most innocent word or act. Sometimes it comes of a preposterous sense of his own standing and importance, existing in a man whose standing and importance are very small. It is quite wonderful what very great folk, very little folk will sometimes fancy themselves to be. The present writer has had little opportunity of conversing with men of great rank and power. Yet he has conversed with certain men of the very greatest: and he can say sincerely that he has found head-stewards to be much more dignified men than dukes: and parsons of no earthly reputation, and of very limited means, to be infinitely more stuck-up than archbishops. And though at first the airs of stuck-up small men are amazingly ridiculous, and so rather amusing; they speedily become so irritating, that the men who exhibit them cannot be classed otherwise than with the disagreeable of the earth.

Few people are more disagreeable than the man who (you know) is, while you are conversing with him, taking a mental estimate of you; more particularly of the soundness of your doctrinal views: with the intention of showing you up if you be wrong, and of inventing or misrepresenting something to your prejudice if you be right. Whenever you find any man trying (in a moral sense) to trot you out, and examine your paces, and pronounce upon your general soundness; there are two courses you may follow. The one is, severely to shut him up; and sternly make him understand that you don't choose to be inspected by him. Show him that you will not exhibit for his approval your particular views about the Papacy, or about Moral Inability, or about Pelagianism or the Patripassian heresy. Indicate that you will not be pumped: and you may convey, in a kindly and polite way, that you really don't care a rush what he thinks of you. The other course is, with deep solemnity and an unchanged countenance, to horrify your inspector by avowing the most fearful views. Tell him that on long reflection, you are prepared to advocate the revival of Cannibalism. Say that probably something may be said for Polygamy. Defend the Thugs, and say something for Mumbo Jumbo. End by saying that no doubt black is white, and twice ten are fifty. Or a third way of meeting such a man, is suddenly to turn upon him, and ask him to give you a brief and lucid account of the views he is condemning. Ask him to tell you what are the theological peculiarities of Bunsen; and what is the exact teaching of Mr. Maurice He does not know, you may be tolerably sure. In the case of the latter eminent man, I never met anybody who did know: and I have the firmest belief that he does not know himself. I was told, lately, of an eminent foreigner, who came to Britain to promote a certain public end. For its promotion, the eminent man wished to conciliate the sympathies of a certain small class of religionists. He procured an introduction to a leading man among them; a good, but very stupid and self-conceited man. This man entered into talk with the eminent foreigner; and ranged over a multitude of topics, political and religious. And at an hour's end the foreigner was astonished by the good but stupid man suddenly exclaiming: 'Now, sir, I have been reckoning you up; you won't do: you are a'—no matter what. It was something that had nothing earthly to do with the end to be promoted. The religious demagogue had been trotting out the foreigner; and he had found him unsound. The religious demagogue belonged to a petty sect, no doubt: and he was trying for his wretched little Shibboleth. But you may have seen the like, even with leading men in National Churches. And I have seen a pert little whippersnapper ask a venerable clergyman what he thought of a certain outrageous lay-preacher; and receive the clergyman's reply that he thought most unfavourably of many of the lay-preacher's doings, with a self-conceited smirk that seemed to say to the venerable clergyman, 'I have been reckoning *you* up: you won't do.'

People whom you cannot get to attend to you when

you talk to them, are disagreeable. There are men whom you feel it is vain to speak to; whether you are mentioning facts, or stating arguments. All the while you are speaking, they are thinking of what they are themselves to say next. There is a strong current, as it were, setting outward from their minds; and it prevents what you say from getting in. You know, if a pipe be full of water, running strongly one way, it is vain to think to push in a stream running the other way. You cannot get at their attention. You cannot get at the quick of their mental sensorium. It is not the dull of hearing whom it is hardest to get to hear; it is rather the man who is roaring out himself, and so who cannot attend to anything else. Now this is provoking. It is a mortifying indication of the little importance that is attached to what we are saying: and there is something of the irritation that is produced in the living being by contending with the passive resistance of inert matter. And there is something provoking even in the outward signs that the mind is in a non-receptive state. You remember the eye that is looking beyond you: the grin that is not at anything funny in what you say: the occasional inarticulate sounds that are put in at the close of your sentences, as if to delude you with a show of attention. The non-receptive mind is occasionally found in clever men: but the men who exhibit it are invariably very conceited. They can think of nothing but themselves. And you may find the last-named characteristic strongly developed, even in men with gray hair, who ought to have learned better through the experience of a pretty long life. There are other minds which are very receptive. They seem to have a strong power of suction. They take in, very decidedly, all that is said to them. The best mind, of course, is that which combines both characteristics: which is strongly receptive when it ought to be receiving; and which gives out strongly when it ought to be giving out. The power of receptivity is greatly increased by habit. I remember feeling awe-stricken by the intense attention with which a very great Judge was wont, in ordinary conversation, to listen to all that was said to him. It was the habit of the judgment seat, acquired through many years of listening, with every faculty awake, to the arguments addressed to him. But when you began to make some statement to him, it was positively alarming to see him look you full in the face, and listen with inconceivable fixedness of attention to all you said. You could not help feeling that really the small remark you had to make was not worth that great mind's grasping it so intently, as he might have grasped an argument by Follett. The mind was intensely receptive, when it was receiving at all. But I remember, too, that when the great Judge began to speak, then his mind was (so to speak) streaming out: and he was particularly impatient of inattention or interruption: and particularly non-receptive of anything that might be suggested to him.

It is extremely disagreeable when a vulgar fellow, whom you hardly know, addresses you by your surname with great familiarity of manner. And such a person will take no hint that he is disagreeable: however stiff, and however formally polite, you may take pains to be to him. It is disagreeable when persons, with whom you have no desire to be on terms of intimacy, persist in putting many questions to you as to your private concerns: such as your annual income and expenditure, and the like. No doubt, it is both pleasant and profitable for people who are not rich, to compare notes on these matters with some frank and hearty friend, whose means and outgoings are much the same as their own. I do not think of such a case: but of the prying curiosity of persons who have no right to pry: and who, very generally, while diligently prying into your affairs, take special care not to take you into their confidence. Such people, too, while making a pretence of revealing to you all their secrets, will often tell a very small portion of them, and make various statements which you at the time are quite aware are not true. There are not many things more disagreeable than a very stupid and ill-set old woman, who, quite unaware what her opinion is worth, expresses it with entire confidence upon many subjects of which she knows nothing whatever, and as to which she is wholly in-

Concerning Disagreeable People. 215

capable of judging. And the self-satisfied and confident air with which she settles the most difficult questions, and pronounces unfavourable judgment upon people ten thousand times wiser and better than herself, is an insufferably irritating phenomenon. It is a singular fact, that the people I have in view invariably combine extreme ugliness with spitefulness and self-conceit. Such a person will make particular inquiries of you as to some near relative of your own : and will add, with a malicious and horribly ugly expression of face, that she is glad to hear how *very much improved* your relative now is. She will repeat the sentence several times, laying great emphasis and significance upon the *very much improved*. Of course, the notion conveyed to any stranger who may be present, is that your relative must in former days have been an extremely bad fellow. The fact probably is, that he has always, man and boy, been particularly well-behaved; and that really you were not aware that he needed any special improvement: save indeed in the sense that every human being might be and ought to be a great deal better than he is.

People who are always vapouring about their own importance, and the value of their own possessions, are disagreeable. We all know such people; and they are made more irritating by the fact, that their boasting is almost invariably absurd and false. I do not mean ethically false, but logically false. For doubtless, in many cases, human beings honestly think themselves and their possessions as much better than other men and their possessions; as they say they do. If thirty families compose the best society of a little country town, you may be sure that each of the thirty families in its secret soul looks down upon the other twenty-nine; and fancies that it stands on a totally different level. And it is a kind arrangement of Providence, that a man's own children, horses, house, and other possessions, are so much more interesting to himself than are the children, horses, and houses of other men, that he can readily persuade himself that they are as much better in fact, as they are more interesting to his personal feeling. But it is provoking when a man is always obtruding on you how highly he estimates his own belongings, and how much better than yours he thinks them, even when this is done in all honesty and simplicity: and it is infuriating when a man keeps constantly telling you things which he knows are not true, as to the preciousness and excellence of the gifts with which fortune has endowed him. You feel angry when a man, who has lately bought a house, one in a square containing fifty, all as nearly as possible alike, tells you with an air of confidence that he has got the finest house in Scotland, or in England, as the case may be. You are irritated by the man who on all occasions tells you that he drives in his mail-phaeton 'five hundred pounds' worth of horseflesh.' You are well aware that he did not pay a quarter of that sum for the animals in question: and you assume as certain that the dealer did not give him that pair of horses for less than they were worth. It is somewhat irritating when a man, not remarkable in any way, begins to tell you that he can hardly go to any part of the world without being recognised by some one who remembers his striking aspect, or is familiar with his famous name. 'It costs me three hundred a year, having that picture to look at,' said Mr. Windbag, pointing to a picture hanging on a wall in his library. He goes on to explain that he refused six thousand pounds for that picture; which at five per cent. would yield the annual income named. You repeat Windbag's statement to an eminent artist. The artist knows the picture. He looks at you fixedly; and for all comment on Windbag's story, says (he is a Scotchman) HOOT TOOT. But the disposition to vapour is deep set in human nature. There are not very many men or women whom I would trust, to give an accurate account of their family, dwelling, influence, and general position, to people a thousand miles from home, who were not likely ever to be able to verify the picture drawn.

It is hardly necessary to mention among disagreeable people, those individuals who take pleasure in telling you that you are looking ill; that you are falling off, physically or mentally. 'Surely you have lost some of your teeth since I saw you last,' said a good man to a man of seventy-five years: 'I cannot make out a word you say, you speak so indistinctly.' And so obtuse, and so thoroughly devoid of gentlemanly feeling, was that good man, that when admonished that he ought not to speak in that fashion to a man in advanced years, he could not for his life see that he had done anything unkind or unmannerly. 'I dare say you are wearied wi' preachin' to-day: you see you're gettin' frail noo,' said a Scotch *elder*, in my hearing, to a worthy clergyman. Seldom has it cost me a greater effort than it did to refrain from turning to the elder, and saying with candour, 'What a boor and what a fool *you* must be, to say *that*!' It was as well I did not: the boor would not have known what I meant. He would not have known the provocation which led me to give him my true opinion of him. 'How very bald you are getting,' said a really goodnatured man, to a friend he was meeting for the first time in several years. Such remarks are for the most part made by men who, in good faith, have not the least idea that they are making themselves disagreeable. There is no malicious intention. It is a matter of pure obtuseness, stupidity, selfishness, and vulgarity. But an obtuse, stupid, selfish, and vulgar person is disagreeable. And your right course will be, to carefully avoid all intercourse with such a person.

But besides people who blunder into saying unpleasant things, there are a few who do so of set intention. And such people ought to be cracked. They can do a great deal of harm: inflict a great deal of suffering. I believe that human beings in general are more miserable than you think. They are very anxious: very careworn: stung by a host of worries: a good deal disappointed, in many ways. And in the case of many people, worthy and able, there is a very low estimate of themselves and their abilities; and a sad tendency to depressed spirits and gloomy views. And while a kind word said to such is a real benefit, and a great lightener of the heart; an ingenious malignant may suggest to such, things which are as a stunning blow, and as an added load on the weary frame and mind. I have seen, with burning indignation, a malignant beast (I mean man) playing upon that tendency to a terrible apprehensiveness which is born with many men. I have seen the beast vaguely suggest evil to the nervous and apprehensive man. 'This cannot end here:' 'I shall take my own measures now:' 'A higher authority shall decide between us:' I have heard the beast say; and then go away. Of course I knew well that the beast could and would do nothing: and I hastened to say so to the apprehensive man. But I knew that the poor fellow would go away home; and brood over the beast's ominous threats; and imagine a hundred terrible contingencies: and work himself into a fever of anxiety and alarm. And it is because I know that the vague threatener counted on all that; and wished it; and enjoyed the thought of the slow torment he was causing; that I choose to call him a beast rather than a man. Indeed, there is an order of beings, worse than beasts, to which that being should rather be referred. You have said or done something, which has given offence to certain of your neighbours. Mr. Snarling comes and gives you a full and particular account of the indignation they feel, and of their plans for vengeance. Mr. Snarling is happy to see you look somewhat annoyed: and he kindly says, 'Oh, never mind: this will blow over, as *other things you have said and done have blown over.*' Thus he vaguely suggests that you have given great offence on many occasions, and made many bitter enemies. He adds, in a musing voice, ' Yes, as MANY other things have blown over.' Turn the individual out; and cut his acquaintance. It would be better to have a upas tree in your neighbourhood. Of all disagreeable men, a man with his tendencies is the most disagreeable. The bitterest and longest lasting eastwind, acts less perniciously on body and soul, than does the society of Mr. Snarling.

Suspicious people are disagreeable: also people who are always taking the pet. Indeed, suspiciousness and pettedness generally go together. There are many men and women who are always imagining that some insult is designed by the most innocent words and doings of those around them: and always suspecting that some evil intention against their peace is cherished by some one or other. It is most irritating to have anything to do with such impracticable and silly mortals. But it is a delightful thing to work along with a man who never takes offence: a frank, manly man, who gives credit to others for the same generosity of nature which he feels within himself; and who if he thinks he has reason to complain, speaks out his mind and has things cleared up at once. A disagreeable person is he who frequently sends letters to you without paying the postage; leaving you to pay twopence for each penny which he has thus saved. The loss of twopence is no great matter; but there is something irritating in the feeling that your correspondent has deliberately resolved that he would save his penny at the cost of your twopence. There is a man, describing himself as a clergyman of the Church of England (I cannot think he is one) who occasionally sends me an abusive anonymous letter; and who invariably sends his letters unpaid. I do not mind about the man's abuse; but I confess I grudge my twopence. I have observed, too, that the people who send letters unpaid, do so habitually. I have known the same individual send six successive letters unpaid. And it is probably within the experience of most of my readers, that out of (say) a hundred correspondents, ninety-nine invariably pay their letters properly; while time after time the hundredth sends his with the abominable big 2 stamped upon it; and your servant walks in and worries you by the old statement that the postman is waiting. Let me advise every reader to do what I intend doing for the future: to wit, to refuse to receive any unpaid letter. You may be quite sure that by so doing you will not lose any letter that is worth having. A class of people, very closely analogous to that of the people who do not pay their letters, is that of such as are constantly borrowing small sums from their friends, which they never restore. If you should ever be thrown into the society of such, your right course will be to take care to have no money in your pocket. People are disagreeable, who are given to talking of the badness of their servants, the undutifulness of their children, the smokiness of their chimneys, and the deficiency of their digestive organs. And though with a true and close friend, it is a great relief, and a special tie, to have spoken out your heart about your burdens and sorrows; it is expedient, in conversation with ordinary acquaintances, to keep these to yourself.

It must be admitted, with great regret, that people who make a considerable profession of religion have succeeded in making themselves more thoroughly disagreeable than almost any other human beings have ever made themselves. You will find people, who not merely claim to be pious and Christian people, but to be very much more pious and Christian than others, who are extremely uncharitable, unamiable, repulsive, stupid, and narrow-minded; and intensely opinionated and self-satisfied. We know, from a very high authority, that a Christian ought to be an epistle in commendation of the blessed faith he holds. But it is beyond question, that many people who profess to be Christians, are like grim Gorgon's heads warning people off from having anything to do with Christianity. Why should a middle-aged clergyman walk about the streets with a sullen and malignant scowl always on his face, which at the best would be a very ugly one? Why should another walk with his nose in the air, and his eyes rolled up till they seem likely to roll out? And why should a third be always dabbled over with a clammy perspiration; and prolong all his vowels to twice the usual length? It is indeed a most woful thing, that people who evince a spirit in every respect the direct contrary of that of our Blessed Redeemer, should fancy that they are Christians of singular attainments: and it is more woful still, that many young people should be scared away into irreligion or unbelief by the wretched delusion that these creatures, wickedly caricaturing Christianity, are fairly representing it. I have beheld more deliberate malice, more lying and cheating, more backbiting and slandering, denser stupidity, and greater self-sufficiency, among badhearted and wrongheaded religionists; than among any other order of human beings. I have known more malignity and slander conveyed in the form of a prayer, than should have consigned any ordinary libeller to the pillory. I have known a person who made evening prayer a means of infuriating and stabbing the servants: under the pretext of confessing their sins. 'Thou knowest, Lord, how my servants have been occupied this day:'

with these words did the blasphemous mockery of prayer begin one Sunday evening in a house I could easily indicate : and then the man, under the pretext of addressing the Almighty, raked up all the misdoings of the servants (they being present, of course) in a fashion which, if he had ventured on it at any other time, would probably have led some of them to assault him. 'I went to Edinburgh,' said a Highland elder, 'and was there a Sabbath. It was an awfu' sight! There, on the Sabbath day, you would see people walking along the street, smiling AS IF THEY WERE PERFECTLY HAPPY!' There was the *gravamen* of the poor Highlander's charge. To think of people being or looking happy on the Lord's day! And indeed to think of a Christian man ever venturing to be happy at all! 'Yes, this parish was highly favoured in the days of Mr. Smith and Mr. Brown,' said a spiteful and venomous old woman; with a glance of deadly malice at a young lad who was present. That young lad was the son of the clergyman of the parish: one of the most diligent and exemplary clergymen in Britain. Mr. Smith and Mr. Brown were the clergymen who preceded him. And the spiteful old woman adopted this means of sticking a pin into the young lad : conveying the idea that there was a sad falling off now. I saw and heard her, my reader. Now when an ordinary spiteful person says a malicious thing, being quite aware that she is saying a malicious thing, and that her motive is pure malice, you are disgusted. But when a spiteful person says a malicious thing, all the while fancying herself a very pious person ; and fancying that in gratifying her spite, she is acting from Christian principle : I say the sight is to me one of the most disgusting, perplexing, and miserable, that ever human eye beheld. I have no fear of the attacks of enemies on the blessed Faith in which I live, and hope to die. But it is dismal, to see how our holy religion is misrepresented before the world, by the vile impostors who pretend to be its friends.

Among the disagreeable people who make a profession of religion, probably many are purely hypocrites. But we willingly believe that there are people, in whom Christianity appears in a wretchedly stunted and distorted form, who yet are right at the root. It does not follow that a man is a Christian, because he turns up his eyes and drawls out his words; and when asked to say grace, offers a prayer of twenty minutes' duration. But again, it does not follow that he is *not* a Christian, though he may do all these things. The bitter sectary, who distinctly says that a humble, pious man, just dead, has 'gone to hell,' because he died in the bosom of the Church,—however abhorrent that sectary may be in some respects, may be, in the main, within the Good Shepherd's fold, wherein he fancies there are very few but himself. The dissenting teacher who declared from his pulpit that the parish clergyman (newly come, and an entire stranger to him) was 'a servant of Satan,' may possibly have been a good man, after all. Grievous defects and errors may exist in a Christian character, which is a Christian character still. And the Christian, horribly disagreeable and repulsive now, will some day, we trust, have all *that* purged away. But I do not hesitate to say, that any Christian, by so far as he is disagreeable and repulsive, deviates from the right thing. Oh my reader, when my heart is sometimes sore through what I see of disagreeable traits in Christian character, what a blessed relief there is in turning to the simple pages, and seeing for the thousandth time The True Christian Character,—so different! Yes, thank God, we know where to look, to find what every pious man should be humbly aiming to be: and when we see That Face, and hear That Voice, there is something that soothes and cheers among the wretched imperfections (in one's self as in others) of the present :—something that warms the heart, and that brings a man to his knees!

The present writer has a relative, who is Professor of Theology in a certain famous University. With that theologian I recently had a conversation on the matter of which we have just been thinking. The Professor lamented bitterly the unchristian features of character which may be found in many people making a great parade of their Christianity. He mentioned various facts, which had recently come to his own knowledge; which would sustain stronger expressions of opinion than any which I have given. But he went on to say, that it would be a sad thing if no fools could get to heaven; nor any unamiable, narrow-minded, sour, and stupid people. Now, said he, with great force of reason, religion does not alter idiosyncrasy. When a fool becomes a Christian, he will be a foolish Christian. A narrow-minded man, will be a narrow-minded Christian: a stupid man, a stupid Christian. And though a malignant man will have his malignity much diminished, it by no means follows that it will be completely rooted out. 'When I would do good, evil is present with me.' 'I find a law in my members, warring against the law of my mind; and enslaving me to the law of sin.' But you are not to blame Christianity for the stupidity and unamiability of Christians. If they be disagreeable, it is not the measure of true religion they have got, that makes them so. In so far as they are disagreeable, they depart from the standard. You know, you may make water sweet or sour; you may make it red, blue, black: and it will be water still, though its purity and pleasantness are much interfered with. In like manner, Christianity may co-exist with a good deal of acid; with a great many features of character very inconsistent with itself. The cup of fair water may have a bottle of ink emptied into it, or a little verjuice, or even a little strychnine. And yet, though sadly deteriorated: though hopelessly disguised; the fair water is there: and not entirely neutralised.

And it is worth remarking, that you will find many persons who are very charitable to blackguards, but who have no charity for the weaknesses of really good people. They will hunt out the act of thoughtless liberality, done by the scapegrace who broke his mother's heart, and squandered his poor sisters' little portions: they will make much of that liberal act: such an act as tossing to some poor Magdalen a purse, filled with money which was probably not his own; and they will insist that there is hope for the blackguard yet. But these persons will tightly shut their eyes against a great many substantially good deeds, done by a man who thinks Prelacy the abomination of desolation, or who thinks that stained glass and an organ are sinful. I grant you that there is a certain fairness in trying the blackguard and the religionist by different standards. Where the pretension is higher, the test may justly be more severe. But I say it is unfair to puzzle out with diligence the one or two good things in the character of a reckless scamp: and to refuse moderate attention to the many good points about a weak, narrow-minded, and uncharitable good person. I ask for charity in the estimating of all human characters: even in estimating the character of the man who would show no charity to another. I confess freely that in the last-named case, the exercise of charity is extremely difficult.

CHAPTER VIII.

OUTSIDE.

THERE is a tremendous difference between being Inside and being Outside. The distance in space may be very small: but the distance in feeling is vast. Sometimes the outside is the better place, sometimes the inside : but I have always thought that this is a case in which there is an interruption of nature's general law of gradation. Other differences are shaded off into each other. Youth passes imperceptibly into age: the evening light melts gradually into darkness: and you may find some mineral production to mark every step in the progress from lava to granite, which (as you probably do not know) are in their elements the same thing. But it is a positive and striking fact, that you are outside or inside. There is no gradation nor shaking off between the two. I am sitting here on a green knoll : the ground slopes away steeply on three sides, down to a little river. The grass is very rich and fresh : and it is lighted up with innumerable buttercups and daisies.

You can see that the old monks, who used to worship in that lovely Gothic chapel, brought these acres under cultivation in days when what is now the fertile country round, was a desolate waste. And the warm air of one of the last days of May is just stirring the thick trees around. But all this is because I am outside. There is an inside hard by where things are very different. Down below this green knoll, but on a rock high above the little river, you may see the ruins of an old feudal castle. Last night I passed over the narrow bridge that leads to the rock on which the ruins stand: and a young fellow, moderately versed in its history, showed me all that remains of the castle. You go away down, stair after stair, and reach successive ranges of chambers, all of stone, formerly guardrooms and kitchens. These chambers are sufficiently cheerful; for though on one side far underground, on the other side they are high above the glen and the river. The setting sun was streaming into their windows: and the fresh green of beeches and pines looked over from the other side of the narrow gorge. But now the young fellow mentioned that the dungeons were still far beneath; and in a pitch-dark passage, he made me feel a small doorway, black as night, going down to the horrible dark recesses below, to which not a ray of light was admitted, and to which not a breath of the fragrant spring air without could ever come. You could not but think what it must have been, long ago, to be dragged through those dark passages, and violently thrust through that narrow door, and down to the black abyss. You felt how thoroughly hopeless escape would be: how entirely you were at the mercy of the people who put you there. And coming up from those dungeons, climbing the successive stairs, you reached the daylight again: and descending the steep walks of the garden, you reached a place just outside the dungeons: which on this side are far above ground. There was the pleasant summer sunset: there were the milk-white hawthorns and the fragrant lilacs; there was an apple-tree, whose pink-and-white blossoms were gently swayed by the warm wind against the outside of the dungeon wall. And, almost hidden by green leaves, you could hear the stream below, whose waters (it is to be confessed) had suffered somewhat from the presence, a few miles above, of various paper-mills. And here, I thought, were the outside and the inside: only six feet of wall between: but in all their aspect, and above all in the feeling of the crushed captive within, a thousand miles apart. Of course, there was no captive there now: but all this scene was the same in the days when those dungeons were fully inhabited. And doubtless, many of those who were then thrust into those dismal places, liked them just as little as you and I should; and were missed and needed by some outside, just as much as you or I could be.

In this case, you observe, it is better to be outside than to be inside. But there are many cases in which it is otherwise.

You may be outside physically: as you would be if you were to fall, unnoticed, and in the night, overboard from a ship; and it to pass on, and leave you to perish in the black waters. Many human beings have done *that*: an old school-fellow of mine did. It must be a dreadful thing. It would be better, in such a case, not to be able to swim: for then the suffering would be the sooner over; and the mind would be in such a bewildered, hurried state, that there would be less room for the agony of thought. But in warmer seas, where the chill of the water would not speedily benumb into loss of power and consciousness, the single hour through which, as Cowper tells us, an unaided swimmer might sustain himself in life, would seem like a lifetime. I know a man who supported himself for a whole night by the help of two oars, after his vessel had gone down in the Indian Ocean. His wife and child went with it: and after desperate efforts to save them, he found himself in the water, clinging to his two oars. Three times, through that awful night, he cast the oars away from him, and dived deep under the surface, hoping that he might never come up: but the instinctive clinging to life was too strong: and each time he faintly struggled back to his oars again.

Then you may be outside morally. You may somehow have turned out of the track in which those who started with you are going on in life. Perhaps through folly: perhaps through sin: you have got beyond the pale. There is a narrow passage in a certain city, a steep and narrow passage of evil odours, through which many clergymen are wont to go to a certain building, in which a great ecclesiastical council meets. In a dark recess, opening into that narrow passage, and leading to various wretched dwellings, I have beheld a deposed and degraded minister standing in the darkest shadow he could find, and watching those who were once his brethren going up by the way he once used to go : but shrinking back from their notice. Alas for the poor outsider : so near physically to the place where he used to be: but morally so far away ! Surely his case is worse than that of the castaway, swept from the deck into the boiling ocean. After that sad instance, we shall feel the less sympathy for such moral outsiders as those who suffer through the existence of lines of social cleavage : the people who chafe at being excluded from the society of the great and exclusive First Circle of a little country town ; or who complain keenly that some wealthy or perhaps noble neighbour keeps them on the outside of his dwelling. Probably you have known people feel this moral exclusion very bitterly. You may have heard a lady in some small community complain with extreme severity that she was thus made an outsider ; and that, in the festive tea-parties which went on in the halls of light around her she was permitted to have no part. At the same time she probably showed with great force of statement and argument, that she was in all respects a great deal better than the people inside that charmed circle to whose outside she was condemned. You could but sympathise with the individual in her sorrow; and advise her not to mind. Every one has known the wrath and jealousies which have arisen from thus putting people morally outside: from not sending them cards on the occasion of a marriage: from not inviting them to some entertainment. You may remember a classical instance of the wrathful spirit awakened in a human being stung by the sense of being outside. Mr. Samuel Warren describes a man as standing in Hyde Park on an afternoon in the fashionable season: seeing all that gay life going on; and feeling that he had nothing to do with it; and bestowing on the whole system of things his extremest malison. Perhaps a worthier nature might have looked on in kindly interest at a class of concerns and a mode of existence in which he had no share: and hoped that all paths through this world, however far apart in time, might yet end and meet in the same happy place together. We may wish well, my reader: and I trust we shall wish well: even to those with whom we have little in common; even to those beyond the circle of whose sympathies we stand, and beyond whose comprehension our great interests lie.

Moral outsideness may co-exist with physical insideness. This truth is well known to unpopular officers in regiments, who though physically inside are morally outside ; also to schoolboys who for some offence have been temporarily sent to Coventry by their young companions. And probably such find it a heavy trial to be placed outside the pale of society : to sit on a form at school with thirty other boys, none of whom will speak to them : to be cut off from joining in the games of the playground. There used to be a vulgar expression current among Scotch schoolboys : probably it is current still : which was founded on this principle : that a human being though physically an insider may be morally an outsider. You spoke of being *in with* such a youthful companion ; and *out with* such another. You are aware how consignment to moral outsideness often serves as a fearful punishment of offences to which laws cannot reach. To be entirely repudiated and cast off by the society amid which you live, whether lofty or lowly : to be made a social outlaw and outsider : is something not easily borne even by the most callous : something which right-thinking men could support only by the firm conviction that solemn principle prompted the conduct which brought down this reprobation. It is not nearly so lonely a thing to dwell in the wilderness, never seeing a human face : as it would be to live in the town in which you were born and brought up : and to see, as you walked its streets, scores of faces you know well, but each averted as you pass. You may have seen poor women bear this : with what crucifixion of the whole nature they only know : you may have beheld them face the unconsciousness of their presence on the part of old friends with a disdainful smile; or meet it with the look that betokened a breaking heart. I have witnessed this, my reader, more than once; and I doubt not you have done so too. As for men, they can stand all this better. *They* can always find a certain class who are content to associate with them: a class of people like themselves. And with a great injustice, not indeed without some reasons in its favour, you know how even the most reputable society passes lightly in a man what it visits with its severest reprobation in a woman. Yes: you may have witnessed a brazen outsider, who ought never to have been suffered inside again, gradually elbowing himself, by force of face, into weight in the senate of a certain moral country. You may have known an unrepenting blackguard, once cast out by the society of the town and the county, and who never afforded the faintest reason why he should be let in, step by step getting in again; till at length the aged reprobate was in high favour in families abounding in girls, and saw clergymen of great pretensions seated at his hospitable board. Yet, in the main, a man becomes an outsider by deserving it. I mean an outsider with people with whom he would wish to be an insider. With others, it may be different. I have heard of a young midshipman who was made an outsider because he read his Bible morning and evening; and because he would not get drunk when the rest did. A man would be made an outsider in certain parts of this empire, unless he helped to screen the sneaking, cowardly murderer who shoots his landlord from shelter of a tree, because asked to pay his rent. And there are parts of America in which you would become an outsider unless you spoke in praise of the biggest and blackest outrage on humanity that the sun looks down on: I mean negro slavery. Of course, among thieves you must say nothing against stealing: or they might turn you out. But in the main, in this country, people are put outside because it serves them rightly. And the punishment is a fearfully severe one: reaching to sins and to people not otherwise easily punished. You have known persons obliged, by this moral outlawry, to go away from the district or the country where all their interests lay: even great wealth and rank have not sufficed to prevent a man's feeling bitterly that he was made an outsider. You may have seen the fair mansion and the noble trees which their owner could never enjoy, because he durst not show his face where he was known. There was once a man of no small position, who was master of a pack of fox-hounds, let us say in Ethiopia. On a certain Sunday, that man chose to amuse himself by taking out his hounds, and chasing a fox which he had caught: having cut off the poor fox's feet previously to turning it out to be chased. Of course, the brute (I mean the master of hounds) was brought before the magistrates of that part of Ethiopia; and heavily fined. The law could do no more : and the punishment was most insufficient. The brute probably cared very little for that. But he probably cared a good deal when in a day or two he received a communication from all the princes and nobles of that district, in which they told him that they withdrew from his hunt and cut his acquaintance. Prompt and resolute outsiding inflicted justice in the most satisfactory way.

I have more to say of moral outsiders; but at this point I cannot help looking round, and thinking what a blessing it sometimes is to be physically outside. Not far away, there lies the great city. Inside it the writer lives; and he judges it the best of cities: but now he is beyond it : he is an outsider for three days of perfect rest in the quiet country. It is often worth while to go in, that you may fully appreciate the blessing of coming out. Did you ever, reader, live in July, on that most beautiful Frith of Clyde? After a week in that pure air, and amid that scenery that combines so wonderfully richness and magnificence, you cease fully to understand what a privilege you are enjoying. But go up for a day to the hot, choky Glasgow of July! Remain for five hours in that sweltering atmosphere, hurrying from place to place on business, and stunned by the ceaseless whirl of that hearty and energetic town: and then go back to the seaside ! Oh, how delightful to get away into the clear air and the quiet again ! And in this green place, I think of the city already spoken of; and of much work and worry there: and feel that here for a little one is outside it all. I think of a certain Gothic building, in which is now sitting an ecclesiastical council which I much revere. I think of the hot atmosphere: of the buzz: of the excitement: of the speeches so very interesting and so very long. I observe from the newspaper that yesterday two gentlemen spoke four hours each. And then I look at that rich sycamore, with foliage so thick: and at the hawthorn blossoms: and at the yellow broom: and at the green grass (for there is 'much grass in this place'): and thank God for all!

Last night, on the little village green, I saw several moral outsiders: I mean members of a class from which respectable folk would for the most part shrink away. There were four poor fellows, acrobats or tumblers: and a girl who is a rope-dancer. They had sent in advance a large bill, which was stuck on a tree, to say there was a grand entertainment coming. The entertainment hardly came up to its description. Still the men did many really wonderful gymnastic feats. They had a striking scene in which to display their ability. It was a beautiful twilight: the little green had fine large trees round it: in the distance there was a great purple hill: and close by was the gray old chapel. The only drawback was a very cold wind. There was a large assemblage of country folk, not very hearty or appreciative spectators: and all evidently regarding themselves as on a totally different level from the poor wanderers. The four men turned somersaults and the like: the poor girl, in her sorry finery, stood by: wrapped in a large shawl till the time of her performance should come. I observed that when the hat went round, the rustic audience evinced great economy in their gifts. The Fool, poor fellow, his face bedaubed with coarse red and white, and wearing a cap with two ears, simulated great spirits, and made many jokes. I looked at him with great pity; and wondered if any human being ever deliberately chooses that way of earning his bread: or whether some men are gradually hedged up to it, without having had a chance of anything else. I was specially sorry for the poor girl, standing with the cold wind blowing through her thin dress. The rustics roared with laughter, as the fool quoted Shakespere. He was evidently a man of better education than the rest. His most effective point was when he took up a small looking-glass, which was to be given as a prize in some way I did not make out: and looking into the glass, exclaimed, 'Ah, that face: that fine old face! He was a man, take him for all in all,'—and so forth. Not since I was a child have I seen such people: and I was greatly touched by the sight of them, and by thinking what kind of life they must lead. I wondered if they ever went to church; or if any clergyman cared for them when they might be sick or dying. And if I had been able, I should assuredly, in defiance of all the laws of Political Economy, have seized them, and taken them away from their sorry occupation: and set them to respectable work: and made them go regularly to church: and, in short, brought them inside!

There is a curious feeling of the difference of being inside and outside, when you are sitting in the cabin of a ship at sea. It is so, even if you be making a voyage no longer than that from Glasgow to Liverpool. It is more so, if you be sailing on distant seas. Fancy a snug little sleeping-cabin; and you lying there in a comfortable berth placed against the side of the ship. You lazily lay your head upon the end of the pillow next the ship's side: about six inches distant from you, but outside, there is a huge shark rubbing its nose against the vessel. Your head, and the horrible head of the strange monster, are but a few inches apart: happily you are inside, and the monster outside. Somehow it seems as if it were a more remarkable thing for a homely Scot, who went in his youth to a Scotch parish school, and a Scotch parish church, to be eaten by a shark in a far-away place, than it would be for almost any other human being to meet a like end. The parish school and the Shorter Catechism are things wholly inconsistent with a man's living any other than a decent life, or meeting any other than a quiet Christian close. You know how pleasant and refreshing it is, when you are walking along a dusty road in June, outside some beautiful park, to come to a spot whence you have a view into a green recess of the woods within. And probably you know a city where, as you walk the glaring summer streets, you can look in many places through iron rails into depths of cool grass and verdant leaves that gladden eyes and heart together. And if you pay a yearly subsidy for a share in such a place, you know that when the iron gate swings noisily into its place behind you, and you pass from the pavement to the neat gravelled walk or the cool turf, though it be but for a quarter of an hour at the close of a busy afternoon, you have felt that there is far more than a physical difference between the outside and the inside; you have felt that breaths of balmy country air come back to you, and the remembrance of pleasant country cares. There are human beings, the possessors of fair domains, who seek by lofty walls to keep their fellow-creatures outside their belongings: even to prevent their fellow-creatures from refreshing their weary eyes by looking upon green expanses which they are not likely to tread. It is a narrow and unworthy mind that feels it cannot fully enjoy its own possessions, unless all mankind be kept definitively outside them! But it testifies to a truly noble nature, when we see what may be seen in many places now: the possessor of a beautiful stretch of landscape around his dwelling, cordially welcoming his humbler neighbours to its paths and glades: giving up the prettiest portion of his park for a cricket-ground for the lads of the adjoining village: and judging that his charming acres look all the more charming when they cease to be a charming solitude, and are lighted up by happy faces. But a sweet country place is usually in the midst of a sweet country: and there is

Outside.

no place where you value green grass and green trees so much, as when you see them in contrast to the streets of a town; and especially to the ugliest streets of a town. I know a spot, which on a summer day, is peculiarly stifling and dusty: the dust being mainly the dust of coal. There is a suburban railway station: there are various mills: there are houses of unattractive exterior: everything is glaring in the sunshine: everything is covered with dust. But you enter by a door in a lofty wall: and you feel the difference between being outside and inside. There is a curious old fashioned house, surrounded by a pretty garden, laid out with much taste. Everything is green, fresh, cool, quiet. It would be a pleasant spot anywhere: but being where it is, it is a true feast to the eyes. You enjoy the inside so much more keenly, for the contrast with the outside. Green grass: green trees: clear water: abundant flowers and blossoms: freshness and fragrance in the air. And outside the coal-dust, the glaring pavements, the railway station!

I suppose most people like to contrast insides and outsides, that they may relish one or other the more. Did you ever, my reader, sit in your warm, cheerful library, on a cold winter night, away in the country, which in winter (it must be confessed) looks dreadfully bleak to people accustomed to the town? Your curtains are drawn, and your lamp is lit; and there are your familiar books all round, with their friendly-looking backs. There is the blazing fire: and notwithstanding the condemnation of a certain great Bishop, you do not think it wrong to possess various easy-chairs. All this is pleasant. There is an air of snugness and comfort: and you feel very thankful, it is to be hoped, to the Giver of all. But you do not know, from the survey of the mere interior, how pleasant it is. Go away out; and look at the cold wall outside your chamber. There it is, dark with the plashes of rain, which the howling blast bitterly beats against it. There are the leafless trees, shivering in the blast. There is the stormy sky, with the racking clouds; which the chilly moon is wading through. If you try to make out the landscape as a whole, there is nothing but a dense gloom, with a spectral shape here and there, which you know to be a gate or a tree. On a moonless night, the country is terribly dark. It is dark to a degree that townfolk, with their abundant street lamps, have no idea of. After beholding all these things outside, come in again: and you will understand in some measure how well off you are. You will know the distance there may be, between the two sides of a not very thick wall.

Less than a wall may make the distance. You have probably travelled in a railway carriage through a dark stormy night. If you are a quiet, stay-at-home person, who do not travel so much that all railway travelling has come to be a mere weariness to you, you will enjoy such a night with considerable freshness of interest. And especially, you will feel the distance between being outside and being inside. Inside, the thick cushions: the two great powerful lamps, which give abundant light: the warm rugs and wraps: the hot water stool for your feet: the newspapers, and the new magazine: one or two pleasant companions, who do not trouble you by talking, except at the stations: the stations forty miles apart. There you lie in luxury, with the feeling that you may honestly do nothing: that you may rest. And looking through the window, there is the bleak, dark landscape, with all kinds of strange shapes which you cannot make out: the glare cast upon cuttings through which you tear: the fearful hissing and snorting of a passing engine: the row of lighted windows of a passing train: the lurid flame of distant furnaces: the lights of sleeping towns. Yes, a night's travelling between Edinburgh and London is as wonderful a thing as anything recorded in the *Arabian Nights*, if it were not that it has grown so cheap and common!

Looking out of the carriage-window over the tracts on either side; and thinking how little parts you from them: you may call to mind a certain ghastly journey by a night-train. A deliberate and cruel murderer, who had committed (it was believed) more than one or two murders for gain, was very justly sentenced to be hanged. He was tried and sentenced in London: and then he was conveyed in a railway carriage a journey of a hundred and forty miles to the place of execution. He sat, manacled, between two officers of justice, through these hours of travelling. It must have been an extraordinary journey! It was a near glimpse of freedom for a man to have when the tightest meshes of the law had grasped him. There he was, inside: a person going to a dreadful death: and outside, stretching away and away, the free fields: and only the two or three inches between that inside and that outside! I can imagine how the poor wretch thought, Oh if I could but get into the middle of that thick wood: if I could but hide under that ivied bridge: if I could but put a hundred yards of midnight darkness between me and those terrible keepers who have me in their charge! I can imagine how, as he felt rapid mile after mile bringing him nearer the scaffold, he would wish for some terrible accident: some awful smash: nothing could come amiss to him: nothing could make *him* worse! But in such a case, of course, the little partition between the inside and the outside,—the couple of inches of timber and cloth, the eighth of an inch of glass,—was the little indication of an awful gulf, that had been making for months and perhaps years. Sometimes, indeed, the grievous moral lapse that puts a man in the cage of which he can never get out; or that puts him outside the pale through which he can never afterwards get in: may be the doing of a very short time. The hasty blow: the terribly wrong turning: may have marked a change as definite as that when the poor castaway is swept from the ship's deck into the waves of the Atlantic.

Outside.

In old days, when society was unsettled, it seems as if one would have felt, more vividly than now, the difference between being inside and being outside, in the matter of safety. There must have been a pleasant feeling of security in looking over the battlements of a great castle, and thinking that you were safe inside them. The sense of danger with which men must in those days have gone abroad, would be compensated by the special enjoyment of safety when they were fairly inside some place of strength. Human nature is so made that even though you are aware that no one desires to attack or injure you, still there is a pleasure in thinking, that even if any one had such a desire, he could not. You know how children like to imagine some outer danger, that they may enjoy the sense of safety inside. It is with real delight that your little boy, sitting on your knee, suddenly hides his face in your breast, exclaiming loudly that there is a great bear coming to eat him. He feigns a danger outside, that he may enjoy the feeling of being safe from it. So you will find a man who has been labouring hard, going away for a little rest to some remote quiet place. He tells you, no one can get at him there. The truth is, nobody wants to get at him; but like the child with the great bear, he calls up some vague picture of a great number of people coming to worry him about a great many matters, that he may have the pleasant feeling that he is safe from them where he is. You can think of a man who has committed some crime, flying from justice : and as he puts mile after mile of desolate country between him and the place from which he has fled, thinking that surely he is safe in this retreat. You can think of the forger, a few years since, who fled across the Atlantic : fled from the American seaboard and penetrated deeper and deeper into the backwoods, till he stopped in an utter solitude somewhere in the Far West. You can think how, as week after week went on, he began to feel as if he might breathe in peace at last : and think of the poor wretch, sitting one evening in his little log-house, when two London detectives walked in, having tracked him all this way!

Did you ever see a foolish duck dive at a hole made in the ice; and come up again under the ice at a hopeless distance from the opening? It is a sad thing to see even that poor creature perishing, with only an inch or two of transparent ice between it and the air. You hasten to break a hole near it to let it escape: but by the time the hole is made the duck is twenty yards off. The duck I have seen : but it must be a fearful case when a human being gets into the like position. You may have lately read how a man was at the bottom of a deep well, when the earth near the top fell together and shut him in. There were ready hands to rescue him : and he was not so shut in but that his voice could be heard hurrying his deliverers. He told them that the water was rising: that it was at his knees, at his breast, at his neck : and the workers above were too late to save him. I suppose it is quite ascertained that in those wicked and cruel ages which ignorant people call the good old times, it was not unusual to wall up a nun in a niche of a massive wall, and leave her there to perish. *Vade in pacem*, were the words that sentenced to this doom ; which the reader probably knows, mean not *Depart in peace*, but *Go to rest*. Such was the kindly repose provided in those happy days. And another dismal inside is that of which Samuel Rogers tells us the true story : the massive chest of oak in which a poor Italian girl hid herself, which closed with a spring-lock, and never chanced to be opened for fifty years. You can think of the terrible rush of confused misery in the poor creature's heart when she felt herself shut in, and heard the voices that seemed approaching her die away. But half a century after, when the chest was drawn out to the light and its lid was raised, there was no trace in the mouldering bones of the thrilling anguish which had been endured within that little space. It is a miserable story. Yet perhaps it has its moral analogies not less miserable. There are human beings who by some wrong or hasty step have committed themselves like the poor girl that perished : who have, in a moral sense, been caught, and who can never get out.

Yes : it is a great question, Outside or Inside : and now, my reader, you must let me remember, drawing these desultory thoughts to a close, that the testing question which puts all mankind to right and left, is just the question, in its most solemn significance, which may be set out in that familiar phrase. There is the Christian fold : there is the outer world : and we are either within the fold of the Good Shepherd of souls, or without it. It is not a question of degree, as it might be if it founded on our own moral character and deservings. It is the question, have we confided ourselves to the Saviour or not : are we right or wrong : are we within or without ? And the two great alternatives, we know, are carried out, without shading off between, into the unseen world. We know that there, when some have gone in to the feast, the door is shut : and others may stand without, and find no admission. Let us humbly pray, that He who came to seek and to save that which was lost, may find each reader of this page, a lost sheep by nature, a poor wanderer in the outer wilderness ; and draw all with the cords of love within his fold. And let us humbly pray that at the last, we may all, however our earthly paths have varied, find entrance into that Golden City, which has a wall great and high, whose building is of jasper, and which shall exclude all sin and sorrow: through whose gates, though not shut at all by day (and there shall be no night there), ' there shall in no wise enter into it anything that defileth :' and where the blessed inhabitants ' shall go no more out,' but be safe in their Father's house for ever !

CHAPTER IX.

GETTING ON.

EVERYBODY is Going On. We are all getting through our little span of daylight. We are spending the time that is allotted to us, at the rate of three hundred and sixty-five days a year. We are all going on through life, somehow : not very cheerfully, if one may judge by the care-worn, anxious faces of most middle-aged people you pass on the street. But some people are not merely Going On: they are also Getting On; which is a very different thing. All are growing older : a man here and there is also growing bigger. I mean bigger in a moral sense. As you and I, my reader, look round on those early companions who started with us in the race of life, we can discern that great changes have passed upon many of them. Some who started as cart-horses, of a very shaggy and uncombed appearance, have gradually assumed the aspect of thorough-bred, or at least of well-bred animals. Some who set out as horses sixteen hands high, have shrunk to the size of Shetland ponies

Certain who started as calves, have not attained maturity with advancing years: and instead of turning into consolidated oxen, they have only grown into enormous calves. But without going into such matters, I am sure you know that among your old companions there are those who are shooting ahead of the rest, or who have already shot ahead of them. There are those who are pointed at as Rising Men. They are decidedly Getting On. I do not mean that they are becoming famous, or that they are becoming great men. They have not had much chance of *that*. Their lot has circumscribed their ambition. Their hearts do not beat high for praise: but have known various perplexities as to the more substantial question of the earning of bread and butter. But they are quietly and surely progressing. They have now advanced a good deal beyond what they were five or ten years since. Every profession has its rising men. The Church, the Law, Medicine, Commerce, Literature, have their men who are Getting On: year by year Getting On. A great many men find their level rather early in life: and remain for many years much the same in standing. They are not growing richer, as they grow older. They are not coming to be better known. They are not gaining a greater place and estimation in their walk of life. Many a little shopkeeper at fifty-five is in worldly wealth much as he was at thirty-five. He has managed to rub on, sometimes with a hard struggle: it has been just enough to make the day provide for the day's wants : and there has been no accumulation of money. Many a domestic servant after many years of toil, is not a whit better off than when she was a hopeful girl. If she has been provident and self-denying, she may have a few pounds in the Savings'-bank. Many a labouring man in the country has been able each week to make the hard-earned shillings provide food and clothing for his children and their mother : but he has laid up no store : he has not advanced : he lives in the same little cottage : and his poor sticks of furniture are all the worse for their wear : and his carefully-kept Sunday suit is not so trim now as it used to be when he courted his hard-featured wife in her fresh girlhood, and was esteemed as a rustic beau. Many a faithful clergyman at sixty is a poorer man than he was at thirty ; or in any case not richer. It has cost many an anxious thought, through these years, to make the ends meet : and that hard task will cost its anxious thoughts to the end. You who wish to have an efficient clergy, who will do their work heartily and well, agitate against that wicked and idiotic notion, that a clergyman is likely to do his work best if he be crushed down by the pressure of poverty: if his wife be worn into her grave by sorry schemings to make the little means go their farthest ; and if his poor little children have to run about without shoes and stockings. There are certain opinions which I should not think of meeting by argument: but rather by the severest application of the cat of ninetails. And one of these is the opinion of the old fool (he was a Scotch Judge) who said that 'a puir church would be a pure church.'

But returning from this digression, let me repeat, that however hard it may be to explain how some men get on while others do not, there can be no question as to the fact that some men do get on while others do not. People get on in many ways : as you will understand, if you look back a few years; and compare what some of your friends were a few years since with what they are now. There is A, whom you remember in his early days at college, an ungainly cub with a shock head of red hair and a tremendous Scotch accent. That man has taken on polish: he has got on: he has seen the world: he is an accomplished gentleman. There is B, ten years since a poor curate ; now risen to the charge of an important parish. There is C : he has married a rich wife : he has a fine house : he has several horses, various dogs, and many pigs: he has made so great a rise in life, that you would say that sometimes when he comes down stairs in the morning, he must think that he is the wrong man. There is D : some years ago he tried in vain for a certain very small appointment : the other day he was offered one of the most valuable in the same profession, and declined it. There is E : he tried to write for the magazines. His early articles were ignominiously rejected. The other day he got a thousand pounds for one edition of a few of the rejected articles. You know how, in running the race of life, some one individual shows his head a little in front: gradually increases his lead; and finally distances all competition. Once upon a time, there was a staff of newspaper reporters attached to a certain London journal. One of them, not apparently cleverer than the rest, drew bit by bit ahead, till he reached the woolsack. And when he presided in the great assembly whose speeches he was wont to report, he must unquestionably have felt that he had Got On. Indeed, I have heard that homely phrase applied to him by an old Scotch lady who knew him in his youth; and so who could never speak of his success in life save in modified terms. 'Our minister,' said the old lady to me, 'had two sons. One went to India. As for John, he went to London: and he got on very well.' No doubt John had got on: for he was at that time Chief Justice of England. If you look at *The Reliques of Father Prout*, you will find a large picture, containing portraits of the contributors to a well-known London magazine, thirty years ago. There is a portrait of a comparatively unnoted man, with a glass stuck in his eye. He was an outsider then: and had given little sign of what he was to be to-day. The portrait is of Mr. Thackeray. You may have heard the name before. This very day, I was told about a man who forty years since opened a little shop, stocked chiefly with coarse towels. So my informant averred. If so, the demand for coarse towels in a certain great town must have been enormous: or the individual in question must have been most fortunate in drawing general attention to his coarse towels: for he drew ahead of other dealers in towels, and became one of the greatest merchant-princes of England. But without taking extreme cases, you know that within more modest limits, there are people who are steadily Getting On. While one man lives for thirty years in the same house, and maintains the same general appearance; his next neighbour ascends the scale of fashion: gets time after time a better house, till he attains a grand country mansion: and from the total absence of any save the conveyance common to mankind, attains to the phaeton, the brougham, and the family chariot. One preacher does his duty steadily and respectably, year after year: and no one thinks anything particular about him. Another tears like a rocket to the highest elevation of the preacher's precarious popularity. His church-doors are mobbed: his fame overspreads the land: his portrait is in the shop-windows: his sermons sell by scores of thousands.

How is it that men Get On? How is it that in every walk of life, there are those who draw ahead of their competitors? It is a very simple and primary notion, not likely to be entertained unless by youthful and unsophisticated minds in remote rural districts, that the most deserving men Get On the best. To gain any advantage or eminence, indeed, which is not bestowed by high-handed patronage, a man must have a certain amount of merit. The horse that wins the Derby must unquestionably be able to gallop at a very great pace. Of course, if the Derby prize were given by patronage, it might occasionally fall to a horse with only three legs. And there are places in the Church and the Law which are filled up by unchecked patronage; and in which a perfectly analogous state of matters may be discerned. It would be insulting some men to suggest that they were placed where they are because they were the best men eligible; or even because they were fit to be placed there at all. You may have known instances in which a man was put in a certain place, because he was the worst man, or one of the worst men, that could be found. But even in cases where the eminence is not arbitrarily given: where it is understood to be earned by the man himself, and not allotted to him by some other man: it is a simple and unsophisticated notion, that the best man gets the best place. The winner of the Derby must be able to gallop very fast: but nine times out of ten, he is by no means the best horse that starts. A bad place at starting: an unlucky push from a rival in mid career: the awkward straining of a muscle: a little nervousness or want of judgment in the jockey who rides him: and the best horse is beaten by a very inferior one, more lucky or better handled. I am obliged to say, as the result of all my observation of the way in which human beings Get On, that human beings get on mainly by Chance, or Luck. I use the words in their ordinary meaning. I mean that human beings Get On or fail to Get On, in a fashion that looks fortuitous. There must be merit, in walks where men have to make their own way: but that a man may get on, he must be seconded by Good-Luck, or at least not crossed by Ill-Luck. We must speak of things, you know, as they appear to our ignorance. I know there is a Higher Hand: and I humbly recognise *that*. I know that 'Promotion cometh neither from the East, nor from the West, nor from the South: but God is the Judge: he putteth down one, and setteth up another.' We all feel that. I believe that these words of the Psalmist give us the entire philosophy of Getting On. It is a matter of God's sovereignty: and God's sovereignty, as it affects human beings, we speak of as their Good or Ill Luck. Of course, there is no chance in the matter: everything is tightly arranged and governed: and doubtless, if we could see aright, we should see that there are wise and good reasons for all: but as we do not know the reasons, and as we cannot foresee the arrangement, we fall back on a word which expresses our ignorance; and which states the fact of the apparent arbitrariness of the government of Providence. Nothing can be more certain than the fact, that there are men who are lucky; and other men who are unlucky. The unlucky, perhaps, need it all: and the lucky can stand it all: but there is the fact. And we know that there are blessed compensations, not known to onlookers, which may make the thorn in the flesh or the crook in the lot a true blessing: which cause men thankfully to say that it was good for them that they were afflicted and disappointed; good for them that they did not Get On. The wise man Jabez, you remember, knew that God might 'bless indeed,' while to other eyes He did not seem to bless at all. And so his prayer was, not that he might absolutely Get On: but that he might Get On or fail to do so as God saw best. 'Oh that thou wouldst bless me *indeed*!' And so, speaking in ordinary language, let me say that I hold by the Psalmist. It is God's sovereignty. *Fiat Voluntas Tua!* The thing that makes men Get On in this world, is mainly their luck; and in a very subordinate degree, their merit or desert.

Life is a lottery. No doubt, there is no real chance in life; but then there is no real chance in any lottery. I do not hesitate to say that what we deserve has very little to do with our Getting On. And all human scheming and labour have very little to do with the actual result in Getting On. And for this reason, I find a great defect in all that I have seen written as to the arts of self-advancement; whether these arts be honest and commendable, or otherwise. It is easy to point out a number of honourable means which tend to help a man on; and a number of contemptible tricks and dodges which tend towards worldly wealth and influence. But the practical use of all these directions is nullified by the fact, that some fortuitous accident may come across all the hard work and self-denial of the worthy man, or all the dirty trickery of the diplomatic cheat: and make all perfectly futile. Honest industry and perseverance; also resolute selfishness, meanness, toadyism, and roguery: tend to various forms of worldly success. But you can draw no assurance from these general principles, as to what either may do for yourself. Out of a hundred men, the Insurance tables will tell you very nearly how many will live for five or ten years to come: but not the slightest assurance can be conveyed by these tables to any individual man of the hundred as to his expectations of life. I have a practical lesson to draw from all this, by and by: but here let it be repeated, that, as a general rule, it is not the most deserving who Get On, but the most lucky. My reader, if you have met success in life yourself, you know this well. The man who has succeeded knows this far better than the man who has failed. The writer states his principle the more confidently, because he knows he has himself got on infinitely better than he deserves. He looks back on the ruck with which he started: and he sees that he has drawn ahead of some who deserved at least as well: who deserved far better. The writer says earnestly that it is not the most deserving who get on the best; not because he thinks he has got less than he deserves, but because he knows he has got an immense deal more. For these things he knows Whom to thank; and he desires to be thankful.

Chance, then (which means God's Providence), advances people in many ways. A man publishes a book. It meets great success. There is no particular reason. Other books as good, and some books a great deal better, prove entire failures. A man goes to the bar: and shortly a stream of briefs begins to set in towards his chambers. Men of equal ability, and eager to excel in their profession, wait wearily on year after year. A man goes into the Church: he is put in conspicuous places, where his light is not hid under a bushel: he gets large preferments, no one can exactly say why. He fills respectably the place where he is put: but doubtless there are many who would fill it just as well. You will find a man chance upon a general reputation for great learning, of which he never gave the slightest proof. Somehow it became the fashion to speak of him as the possessor of unexplored mines of information. Then you know how a man then and there becomes a privileged person, you cannot say how. A privileged person means a man who is permitted to say and do the silliest and most insolent things: and to evince the most babyish pettedness of temper,—things for which anybody else would be kicked, or esteemed as an idiot: but when the privileged man does all this, every one sets himself to smooth the creature down if he be petted, and to applaud his silly jokes if he be jocular. I do not know any more signal instance of the arbitrary allotment of things in this world, than this. It has been truly said that one man may steal a horse, while another must not look over the gate. To a certain extent, it is a matter of natural constitution. You remember how the dog was accustomed, without rebuke, to jump upon his master's knee; while the donkey was chastised severely on endeavouring to do the same thing. You will find a man who is always being stroked down and flattered by the members of some public body, to which he never rendered any particular service. One can understand why the great Duke of Wellington, even when he had grown an extreme obstruction to army business and reform, should be deferred to by the nation for which he had done so much: but you may have known people treated with the like deference, who had never done anything through life but diligently aim at securing the greatest advantage of the greatest number; which (it is well known) is Number One. Then there are men who Get On, even to places of very great dignity, because somehow they have got into the track, and are pushed on with very little motive force of their own. It would be invidious to mention striking instances of this: but it would be very easy. Other men Get On, by being appointed, with little competition, to some position which at the time is not worth much; but which grows important and valuable. And a worthier way of Getting On, is when a man, by his doings and character, makes a position important, which in other hands would not be so.

The Chance (as already explained) which rules events in this life, never appears more decidedly than in making the diligent efforts of some men successful, and of other men futile. We can see the arts which men use, thinking to advance themselves: and no doubt these arts often tend directly to that end; but then Chance comes in to say whether these arts shall signally fail or splendidly succeed. I have known a laborious student get up many pages of Greek for an examination: all his pages most thoroughly, save two or three which were hastily read over. And upon the examination-day, sure enough he was taken upon the pages he did not know well; while his competitor was taken on his pet page, which he knew by heart. And there were scores of pages which that competitor had never looked at: but he trusted his Luck, and it did not fail him.

It may be assumed as certain, that all men would like to Get On. If you see a number of cabs upon a stand, you may be quite sure that any one of them would take a fare if it could get it. And a man, in all ordinary cases, by entering any profession, becomes as a cab upon the stand waiting for a fare. If he stand idle in the market-place all day, it may be taken for granted that it is because no man has hired him. And though we may have quite outgrown our early ambitions: though we may never have had much ambition: though we may be quite contented with our present position and circumstances; still, we should all like to Get On. We do not talk of ambition, in the case of commonplace folk like ourselves: and though the 'love of fame' has been called the 'universal passion,' I believe that it is practically confined to a very little fraction of mankind. We call it ambition when Mr. Disraeli goes in for leader of the House of Commons; or when Napoleon twists his way to a throne. We do not call it ambition when a clergyman would like a larger congregation to preach to, or another hundred or two a year of income. We do not speak of ambition in such cases: it is only that people would like to Get On a little. We like to think that we are Getting On: that we live in a better house than we used to do: that our little library is gradually growing: that our worldly means are improving: that we are a little wiser and better than we used to be. But though we may take for granted, that all men would like to Get On, we may be assured that there are many who would not take much trouble to do so. Their wishes are moderate: they have learned to be content. They will not fret themselves into a fever: they will not push. And much less will they sneak, or cheat, or wriggle. If success comes, they are pleased: but they are not vexed though it do not come. They look with interest, and with some amusement, at the diplomatic schemes of their friends, who enter themselves in the race of ambition. They see that pertinacious pushing will make a man Get On, unless he be very unlucky or very incapable. But they do not think it worth while pertinaciously to push. They see that judicious puffing, on your own part and that of your friends, is a helpful thing: but they shrink from puffing themselves, or from hearing their friends puff them. Puffing is a great power: as Mr. Barnum and others know. It is a great thing, to have friends to back you and puff you. One man publishes a book. He does not know a soul who ever printed a line. There is not a human being to say a good word of his book for friendship's sake. Another author has a host of literary friends: and when his book comes out, they raise a *sough* of applause through the press. And all this is very natural; and is not unfair. Only the unlucky man who has got no friends will probably grumble. Yet all this will not always succeed. I have known two books come out together. One was written by a man who had no writing friends; the other by a man who had many. The former was reviewed widely and favourably: the other was very little noticed by the reviewers. But you cannot always force things upon the reading public. The unreviewed book sold splendidly: the other hardly sold at all. The unreviewed book enriched its author: the other slightly impoverished its author. All this, of course, was Luck again.

I have already stated what appears to me the great defect in all treatises on the arts of self-advancement and self-help. There appears to me a fallacy at the foundation of all their instructions. They all say, in one form or other, ' Do so and so, and you will Get On.' Some of these treatises recommend fair and worthy means; as industry, self-denial, perseverance, honesty and the like. Others of them recommend unworthy means; as selfishness, unscrupulousness, impudence, toadyism, sneakiness, and the like. But they fail to allow for Chance or Providence. They fail to bring out the utter uncertainty which attends all arts for Getting On. No mortal can say how a man is to Get On. A poor Scotch lad, walking the London streets, fell into a cellar and broke his leg. *That* made his fortune. The wealthy owner of the cellar took him up, and pushed him on: and he rose to be Lord Mayor of London and an eminent member of Parliament. A certain man (and a good man too) became a Bishop through accidentally attracting the notice of a disreputable peeress who was in high favour with a disreputable monarch, who once reigned (let us say) in the centre of Africa. The likeliest arts, whether honest or dishonest, may fail utterly. And the lesson, I think, is this: Do your duty quietly and honestly: Don't push, don't puff: don't set your heart upon any worldly end; it is not worth while: if success comes, well; if it does not come, you do not mind much. 'Seekest thou great things for thyself? seek them not!'

There never were words written more worthy of being remembered and acted on by all men. There is no use in being ambitious. Being ambitious just means setting your whole heart on Getting On : and in this world people seldom get the thing on which they set their heart. And no matter how you may labour to attain your end, you cannot make sure of attaining it. You may probably see it carried away by some easy-going man who cared very little for it, and took very little trouble to get it. Read Mr. Smiles' excellent book on *Self-Help*. It will do you good to read it. It will spur you to do your best, to see what other men have done. But remember, you are in God's hands. The issue is with Him. It no more follows that if you work like George Stephenson or Lord Eldon, you will get on as they did ; than that if you eat the same thing for breakfast as the man who gets the great prize in a lottery, you will get the prize like him. Still, Mr. Smiles will do you good. Unless luck sets very greatly against you, you may, by honestly doing your best, Get On fairly. Your chance of Getting On to the highest point of success is just about the same as your chance of being smashed altogether. It is not great. And remember, my friend, that it is not worldly success that is the best thing we can get in this world. There is something far better. And perhaps it may be by forbidding that you should Get On, that God may discipline you into *that*. I should feel very great interest in reading the lives of a number of men who honestly did their best, and failed; yet who were not soured by failure; men who, like St. Paul, bore the painful weight through life, and bore it kindly and humbly: getting great good and blessing out of it all. Let us always keep it in our remembrance, that there is something far better than any amount of worldly success, which may come of worldly failure.

Still, remembering all this, it is interesting to look at the various arts and devices by which men have Got On. Judicious puffing is a great thing. But it must be very judicious. Some people irritate one by their constant stories as to their own great doings. I have known people who had really done considerable things; yet who did not get the credit they deserved, just because they were given to vapouring of what they had done. It is much better to have friends and relatives to puff you: to record what a splendid fellow you are, and what wonderful events have befallen you. Even here, if you become known as one of a set who puff each other, your laudations will do harm instead of good. It is a grand thing to have relations and friends who have the power to actually confer material success. Who would not wish to be Dowb, that so he might be 'taken care of?' You have known men at the Bar, to whom some powerful relative gave a tremendous lift at starting in their profession. Of course this would in some cases only make their failure more apparent, unless they were really equal to the work to which they were set. There is a cry against Nepotism. It will not be shared in by the *Nepotes.* It must be a fine thing to be one of them. Unhappily, they must always be a very small minority; and thus the cry against them will be the voice of a great majority. I cannot but observe that the names of men who hold canonries at cathedrals, and other valuable preferments in the Church, are frequently the same as the name of the Bishop of the diocese. I do not complain of that. It is the plain intention of Providence that the children should suffer for their fathers' sins, and gain by their fathers' rise. It is utterly impossible to start all human beings for the race of life, on equal terms. It is utterly impossible to bring all men up to a rope stretched across the course, and make all start fair. If a man be a drunken blackguard, or a heartless fool, his children *must* suffer for it: *must* start at a disadvantage. No human power can prevent *that.* And on the other hand, if a man be industrious and able, and rise to great eminence, his children gain by all this. Robert Stephenson had a splendid start, because old George his father got on so nobly. Lord Stanley entered political life at an immense advantage, because he was Lord Derby's son. And if any reader of this page had some valuable office to give away; and had a son, brother, or nephew, who deserved it as well as anybody else, and who he could easily think deserved it a great deal better than anybody else; I have little doubt that the reader would give that valuable office to the son, brother, or nephew. I have known, indeed, magnanimous men who acted otherwise : who in exercising abundant patronage suffered no nepotism : it was a positive disadvantage to be related to these men: they would not give their relatives ordinary justice. The fact of your being connected with them made it tolerably sure that you would never get anything they had to give. All honour to such men! Yet they surpass average humanity so far, that I do not severely blame those who act on lower motives. I do not find much fault with a certain Bishop who taught me theology in my youth, because I see that he has made his son a canon in his cathedral. I notice, without indignation, that the individual who holds the easy and lucrative office of Associate in certain Courts of Law, bears the same name with the Chief-Justice. You have heard how Lord Ellenborough was once out riding on horseback, when word was brought him of the death of a man who held a sinecure office with a revenue of some thousands a year. Lord Ellenborough had the right of appointment to that office. He instantly resolved to appoint his son. But the thought struck him, that he might die before reaching home : he might fall from his horse, or the like. And so the eminent Judge took from his pocket a piece of paper and a pencil: and then and there wrote upon his saddle a formal appointment of his son to that wealthy place. And as it was a place which notoriously was to be given, not to a man who should deserve it, but merely to a man who might be lucky enough to get it, I do not know that Lord Ellenborough deserved to be greatly blamed. In any case, his son, as he quarterly pocketed the large payment for doing nothing, would doubtless hold the blame of mankind as of very little account.

But whether you Get On by having friends who cry you up, or by having friends who can materially advance you, of course it is your luck to have such friends. We all know that it is ' the accident of an accident' that makes a man succeed to a peerage or an estate. And though trumpeting be a great fact and power, still your luck comes in to say whether the trumpet shall in your case be successful. One man, by judicious puffing, gets a great name: another, equally deserving, and apparently in exactly the same circumstances, fails to get it. No doubt the dog who gets an ill name, even if he deserves the ill name, deserves it no more than various other sad dogs who pass scot free. Over all events, all means and ends in this world, there rules God's inscrutable sovereignty. And to our view, that direction appears quite arbitrary. ' One shall be taken, and the other left.' ' Jacob have I loved, and Esau have I hated.' ' Hath not the potter power over the clay, of the same lump to make one vessel unto honour, and another unto dishonour?' A sarcastic London periodical lately declared that the way to attain eminence in a certain walk of life, was to ' combine mediocrity of talent with family affliction.' And it is possible that instances might be indicated in which that combination led to very considerable position. But there are many more cases in which the two things co-existed in a very high degree, without leading to any advancement whatsoever. It is all luck again.

A way in which small men sometimes Get On, is by finding ways to be helpful to bigger men. Those bigger men have occasional opportunities of helping those who have been helpful to them. If you yourself, or some near relation of yours, yield effectual support to a candidate at a keenly contested county election, you may possibly be repaid by influence in your favour brought to bear upon the Government of the day. From a bishopric down to a beadleship, I have known such means serve valuable ends. It is a great thing to have any link, however humble, and however remote, that connects you with a Secretary of State, or any member of the Administration. Political tergiversation is a great thing. Judicious ratting, at a critical period, will generally secure some one considerable reward. In a conservative institution to stand almost alone in professing very liberal opinions; or in a liberal institution to stand almost alone in professing conservative opinions : will probably cause you to Get On. The leaders of parties are likely to reward those who among the faithless are faithful to them ; and who hold by them under difficulties. Still, luck comes in here. While some will attain great rewards by professing opinions very inconsistent with their position, others by doing the same things merely bring themselves into universal ridicule and contempt. It is a powerful thing, to have abundant impudence: to be quite ready to ask for whatever you want. Worthier men wait till their merits are found out: you don't. You may possibly get what you ask: and then you may snap your fingers in the face of the worthier man. By a skilful dodge, A got something which ought to have come to B. Still, A can drive in dignity past B, covering him with mud from his chariot-wheels. There was a man in the last century who was made a bishop by George III., for having published a poem on the death of George II. That poem declared that George II. was removed by Providence to heaven, because he was too good for this world. You know what kind of man George II. was: you know whether even Bishop Porteus could possibly have thought he was speaking the truth in publishing that most despicable piece of toadyism. Yet Bishop Porteus was really a good man, and died in the odour of sanctity. He was merely a little yielding. Honesty would have stood in the way of his Getting On; and so honesty had to make way for the time. Many people know that a certain Bishop was to have been made Archbishop of Canterbury: but that he threw away his chance by an act of injudicious honesty. On one occasion, he opposed the court, under very strong conscientious convictions of duty. If he had just sat still, and refrained from bearing testimony to what he held for truth, he would have Got On much farther than he ever did. I am very sure the good man never regretted that he had acted honestly!

Judicious obscurity is often a reason for advancing a man. You know nothing to his prejudice. Eminent men have always some enemies: there are those who will secretly hate them just because they are eminent: and no one can say how or when the most insignificant enemy may have an opportunity to put a spoke in the wheel, and upset the coach in which an eminent man is advancing to what would have crowned his life. While nothing can be more certain than that if you know nothing at all about a man, you know no harm of him. There are many people who will oppose a man seeking for any end, just because they know him. They don't care about a total stranger gaining the thing desired: but they cannot bear that any one they know should reach it. They cannot make up their mind to *that*. You remember a curious fact brought out by Cardinal Wiseman in his *Lives of the Last Four Popes*. There are certain European kings who have the right to veto a Pope. Though the choice of the conclave fall on him, these kings can step in and say, No. They are called to give no reason. They merely say, Whoever is to be Pope, it shall not be that man. And the Cardinal shows us, that as surely as any man seems likely to be elected Pope who has ever been Papal Ambassador at the court of any of those kings;

so surely does the king at whose court he was veto him ! In short, the king is a man: and he cannot bear that any one he knows should be raised to the mystical dignity of the Papacy. But the monarch has no objection to the election of a man whom he knows nothing about. And as the more eminent cardinals are sure to have become known, more or less intimately, to all the kings who have the right to veto, the man elected Pope is generally a very obscure and insignificant Cardinal. Then there is a pleasant feeling of superiority and patronage in advancing a small man, a man smaller than yourself. You may have known men who were a good deal consulted as to the filling up of vacant offices in their own profession, who made it their rule strongly to recommend men whose talent was that of decent mediocrity, and never to mention men of really shining ability. And if you suggest to them the names of two or three persons of very high qualifications, as suitable to fill the vacant place, you will find the most vigorous methods instantly employed to make sure that whoever may be successful, it shall not be one of these. ' Oh, *he* would never do ! '

It is worth remembering, as further proof how little you can count on any means certainly conducing to the end of Getting On, that the most opposite courses of conduct have led men to great success. To be the toady of a great man is a familiar art of self-advancement: there once was a person who by doing extremely dirty work for a notorious peer, attained a considerable place in the government of this country. But it is a question of luck, after all. Sometimes it has been the making of a man, to insult a Duke, or to bully a Chief-Justice. It made him a popular favourite: it enlisted general sympathy on his side: it gained him credit for nerve and courage. But public feeling, and the feeling of the dispensers of patronage in all walks of life, oscillates so much, that at different times, the most contradictory qualities may commend a man for preferment. You may have known a man who was much favoured by those in power, though he was an extremely outspoken, injudicious, and almost reckless person. It is only at rare intervals that such a man finds favour: a grave, steady, and reliable man, who will never say or do anything outrageous, is for the most part preferred. And now and then you may find a highly cultivated congregation, wearied by having had for its minister for many years a remarkably correct and judicious though tiresome preacher, making choice for his successor of a brilliant and startling orator, very deficient in taste and sense. A man's luck, in all these cases, will appear, if it bring him into notice just at the time when his special characteristics are held in most estimation. If for some specific purpose, you desire to have a horse which has only three legs, it is plain that if two horses present themselves for your choice, one with three legs and the other with four, you will select and prefer the animal with three. It will be the best, so far as concerns you. And its good luck will appear in this: that it has come to your notice just when your liking happened to be a somewhat peculiar one. In like manner, you may find people say, In filling up this place at the present time, we don't want a clever man, or a well-informed man, or an accomplished and presentable man: we want a meek man, a humble man, a man who will take snubbing freely, a rough man, a man like ourselves. And I have known many cases, in which, of several competitors, one was selected just for the possession of qualities which testified his inferiority to the others. But then, in this case, that which was absolutely the worst, was the best for the particular case. The people *wanted* a horse with three legs: and when such an animal presented itself, they very naturally preferred him to the other horses which had four legs. The horses with four legs naturally complained of the choice; and thought themselves badly used when the screw was taken in preference. They were wrong. There are places for which a rough man is better than a smooth one: a dirty man than a clean one: in the judgment (that is) of the people who have the filling up of the place. I certainly think their judgment is wrong. But it *is* their judgment; and of course they act upon it.

As regards the attainment of very great and unusual wealth, by business or the like, it is very plain how much there is of luck. A certain degree of business talent is of course necessary, in the man who rises in a few years from nothing to enormous wealth : but it is Providence that says who shall draw the great prize : for other men with just as much ability and industry entirely fail. Talent and industry in business may make sure, unless in very extraordinary circumstances, of decent success: but Providence fixes who shall make four hundred thousand a year. The race is not to the swift, nor the battle to the strong, nor riches to men of understanding : that is, their riches are not necessarily in proportion to their understanding. Trickery and cheating, not crossed by ill luck, may gain great wealth. I shall not name several instances which will occur to every one. But I suppose, my friend, that you and I would cut off our right hand before we should Get On in worldly wealth by such means as these. You must make up your mind, however, that you will not be envious when you see the fine house, and the horses and carriages, of some successful trickster. All this indeed might have been had : but *you* would not have it at the price. That worldly success is a great deal too dear, which is to be gained only by sullying your integrity! And I gladly believe that I know many men, whom no material bribe would tempt to what is mean or dishonest.

There is something curious in the feeling which many people cherish towards an acquaintance who becomes a successful man. Getting On gives some people mortal offence. To them, success is an unpardonable crime. They absolutely hate the man that

Gets On. Timon, you remember, lost the affection of those who knew him when he was ruined: but depend upon it there are those who would have hated Timon much worse had he suddenly met some great piece of good fortune. I have already said that these envious and malicious people can better bear the success of a man whom they do not know. They cannot stand it, when an old school-companion shoots ahead. They cannot stand it, when a man in their own profession attains to eminence. They diligently thwart such an one's plans; and then chuckle over their failure; saying, with looks of deadly malice, 'Ah, this will do him a great deal of good!'

But now, my reader, I am about to stop. Let me briefly sum up my philosophy of Getting On. It is this: A wise man in this world will not set his heart on Getting On; and will not push very much to Get On. He will do his best: and humbly take, with thankfulness, what the Hand above sends him. It is not worth while to push. The whole machinery that tends to earthly success, is so capricious and uncertain in its action, that no man can count upon it, and no wise man will. A chance word, a look, the turning of a straw, may make your success or mar it. A man meets you on the street; and says, Who is the person for such a place, great or small: You suddenly think of somebody; and say, He is your man: and the thing is settled. A hundred poor fellows are disappointed. You did not know about them; or their names did not occur to you. You put your hand into a hat, and drew out a name. You stuck a hook into your memory, and this name came out. And *that* has made the man's fortune. And the upshot of the whole matter is, that such an infinitude of little fortuitous circumstances may either further or prevent our Getting On: the whole game is so complicated: that the right and happy course is humbly to do your duty and leave the issue with God. Let me say it again: 'Seekest thou great things for thyself? Seek them not!' It is not worth while. All your seeking will not make you sure of getting them: the only things you will make sure of will be fever and toil and suspense. We shall not push, or scheme, or dodge, for worldly success. We shall succeed exactly as well; and we shall save ourselves much that is wearisome and degrading. Let us trust in God, my friend; and do right: and we shall Get On as much as He thinks good for us. And it is not the greatest thing to Get On. I mean, to Get On in matters that begin and end upon this world. There is a progress in which we are sure of success, if we earnestly aim at it; which is the best Getting On of all. Let us 'grow in grace.' Let us try, by God's aid, to grow better, kinder, humbler, more patient, more earnest to do good to all. If the germ of the better life be implanted in us by the Blessed Spirit, and tended by Him day by day: if we trust our Saviour and love our God: then our whole existence, here and hereafter, will be a glorious progress from good to better. We shall always be Getting On!

CHAPTER X.

CONCERNING MAN AND HIS DWELLING-PLACE.*

WHEN my friend Smith's drag comes round to his door, as he and I are standing on the steps ready to go out for a drive, how cheerful and frisky the horses look! I think I see them, as I saw them yesterday, coming round from the stable-yard, with their glossy coats and the silver of their harness glancing in the May sunshine, the May sunshine mellowed somewhat by the green reflection of two great leafy trees. They were going out for a journey of twenty miles. They were, in fact, about to begin their day's work, and they knew they were; yet how buoyant and willing they looked! There was not the faintest appearance of any disposition to shrink from their task, as if it were a hard and painful one. No; they were eager to be at it: they were manifestly enjoying the anticipation of the brisk exertion in the midst of which they would be in five

---

* *Man and his Dwelling Place*; An Essay towards the Interpretation of Nature. London: 1859.

minutes longer. And by the time we have got into our places, and have wrapped those great fur robes comfortably about our limbs, the chafing animals have their heads given them; and instantly they fling themselves at their collars, and can hardly be restrained from breaking into a furious gallop. Happy creatures, you enjoy your work; you wish nothing better than to get at it!

And when I have occasionally beheld a ploughman, bricklayer, gardener, weaver, or blacksmith, begin his work in the morning, I have envied him the readiness and willingness with which he took to it. The ploughman, after he has got his horses harnessed to the plough, does not delay a minute: into the turf the shining share enters, and away go horses, plough, and man. It costs the ploughman no effort to make up his mind to begin. He does not stand irresolute, as you and I in childish days have often done when taken down to the sea for our morning dip, and when trying to get courage to take the first plunge under water. And the bricklayer lifts and places the first brick of his daily task just as easily as the last one. The weaver, too, sits down without mental struggle at his loom, and sets off at once. How different is the case with most men whose work is mental; more particularly how different is the case with most men whose work is to write—to spin out their thoughts into compositions for other people to read or to listen to! How such men, for the most part, shrink from their work—put it off as long as may be; and even when the paper is spread out and the pen all right, and the ink within easy reach, how they keep back from the final plunge! And after they have begun to write, how they dally with their subject; shrink back as long as possible from grappling with its difficulties; twist about and about, talking of many irrelevant matters, before they can summon up resolution to go at the real point they have got to write about! How much unwillingness there is fairly to put the neck to the collar!

Such are my natural reflections, suggested by my personal feelings at this present time. I know perfectly well what I have got to do. I have to write some account, and attempt some appreciation, of a most original, acute, well-expressed, and altogether remarkable book—the book, to wit, which bears the comprehensive title of *Man and his Dwelling Place*. It is a metaphysical book; it is a startling book; it is a very clever book; and though it is published anonymously, I have heard several acquaintances say, with looks expressive of unheard-of stores of recondite knowledge, that they have reason to believe that it is written by this and that author, whose name is already well known to fame. It may be so, but I did not credit it a bit the more because thus assured of it. In most cases the people who go about dropping hints of how much they know on such subjects, know nothing earthly about the matter; but still the premises (as lawyers would say) make it to be felt that the book is a serious one to meddle with. Not that in treating such a volume, plainly containing the careful and deliberate views and reflections of an able and well-informed man, I should venture to assume the dignified tone of superiority peculiar to some reviewers in dissecting works which they could not have written for their lives. There are not a score of men in Britain who would be justified in reviewing such a book as this *de haut en bas*. I intend the humbler task of giving my readers some description of the work; stating its great principle, and arguing certain points with its eminently clever author; and under the circumstances in which this article is written, it discards the dignified and undefined *We*, and adopts the easier and less authoritative first person singular. The work to be done, therefore, is quite apparent: there is no doubt about *that*. But the writer is most unwilling to begin it. Slowly was the pen taken up; oftentimes was the window looked out of. I am well aware that I shall not settle steadily to my task till I shall have had a preliminary canter, so to speak. Thus have I seen schoolboys, on a warm July day, about to jump from a sea-wall into the azure depths of ocean. But after their garments were laid aside, and all was ready for the plunge, long time sat they upon the tepid stones, and paddled with idle feet in the water.

How shall I better have that preliminary and moderate exercitation which serves to get up the steam, than by talking for a little about the scene around me? Through diamond-shaped panes the sunshine falls into this little chamber; and going to the window you look down upon the tops of tall trees. And it is pleasant to look down upon the tops of tall trees. The usual way of looking at trees, it may be remarked, is from below. But this chamber is high up in the tower of a parish church far in the country. Its furniture is simple as that of the chamber of a certain prophet, who lived long ago. There are some things here, indeed, which he had not; for yesterday's *Times* lies upon the floor drying in the morning sunbeams, and a certain Magazine, dear to the writer, is on a chair by the window. Why does that incomparable monthly act blisteringly upon the writer's mind? It never did so till now. Why does he put it for the time out of sight? Why, but because, for once, he has read in that Magazine an article—by a very eminent man, too—written in what he thinks a thoroughly mistaken spirit, and setting out views which he thinks to be utterly false and mischievous. Not such, the writer knows well, are the views of his dear friend the Editor; not such are the doctrines which the Magazine teaches to a grateful world. In the latter pages of his review of *Mill on Liberty*, Mr. Buckle spoke solely for himself; he did not express the opinions which that Magazine upholds, nor commit for one moment the staff of men who write in it; and, as one insignificant individual who has penned a good many pages of it, I beg to express my keen disapprobation of Mr. Buckle's views upon the subject of Christianity. They may be right, but I firmly believe they are wrong; they may be true, but I think them false. I repudiate any share in them: let their author bear their responsibility for himself. Alas, say I, that so able a man should sincerely think (I give him credit for entire sincerity) that man's best refuge and most precious hope is vain delusion! Very jarringly to my mind sound those eloquent periods, so inexpressibly sad and dreary, amid pages penned by some men at least, who for the truth of Christianity would, God helping them, lay down their lives. So, you May magazine, get meanwhile out of sight: I don't want to think of you. Rather let me stay this impatient throbbing of heart by looking down on the green tops of those great silent trees.

Thick ivy frames this mullioned window, with its three lance-shaped lights. Seventy feet below, the grassy graves of the churchyard swell like green waves. The white headstones gleam in the sun. Ancient oaks line the lichened wall of the churchyard: their leaves not yet so thick as they will be a month hereafter. Beyond the wall, I see a very verdant field, between two oaks; six or seven white lambs are lying there, or frisking about. The silver gleam of a river bounds the field; and beyond are thick hedges, white with hawthorn blossoms. In the distance there is a great rocky hill, which bounds the horizon. There is not a sound, save when a little flaw of air brushes a twig against the wall some feet below me. The smoke of two or three scattered cottages rises here and there. The sky is very bright blue, with many fleecy clouds. Quiet, quiet! And all this while the omnibuses, cabs, carriages, drays, horses, men, are hurrying, sweltering, and fretting along Cheapside!

Man and his Dwelling Place! Truly a comprehensive subject. For man's dwelling-place is the universe; and remembering this, it is plain that there is not much to be said which might not be said under that title. But, of course, there are sweeping views and opinions which include man and the universe, and which colour all beliefs as to details. And the author of this remarkable book has arrived at such a sweeping view. He holds, that whereas we fancy that we are living creatures, and that inanimate nature is inert, or without life, the truth is just the opposite of this fancy. He holds that man wants life, and that his dwelling-place possesses life. We are dead, and the world is living. No doubt it would be easy to laugh at all this; but I can promise the thoughtful reader that, though after reading the book he may still differ from its author, he will not laugh at him. Very moderately informed folk are quite aware of this—that the fact of any doctrine seeming startling at the first mention of it, is no argument whatever against its truth. Some centuries since you could hardly have startled men more than by saying that the earth moves, and the sun stands still. Nay, it is not yet forty years since practical engineers judged George Stephenson mad, for saying that a steam-engine could draw a train of carriages along a railway at the rate of fourteen miles an hour. It is certainly a startling thing to be told that I am dead, and that the distant hill out there is living. The burden of proof rests with the man who propounds the theory; the *primâ facie* case is against him. Trees do not read newspapers; hills do not write articles. We must try to fix the author's precise meaning when he speaks of *life*; perhaps he may intend by it something quite different from that which we understand. And then we must see what he has to say in support of a doctrine which at the first glance seems nothing short of monstrous and absurd.

No: I cannot get on. I cannot forget that May magazine that is lying in the corner. I must be thoroughly done with it before I can fix my thoughts upon the work which is to be considered. Mr. Buckle has done a service to my mind, entirely analogous to that which would be done to a locomotive engine by a man who should throw a handful of sand into its polished machinery. I am prepared, from personal experience, to meet with a flat contradiction his statement that a man does you no harm by trying to cast doubt and discredit upon the doctrines you hold most dear. Mr. Buckle, by his article, has done me an injury. It is an injury, irritating but not dangerous.

For the large assertions, which if they stated truths, would show that the religion of Christ is a miserable delusion, are unsupported by a tittle of proof: and the general tone in regard to Christianity, though sufficiently hostile, and very eloquently expressed, appears to me uncommonly weak in logic. I do not intend to argue against Mr. Buckle's opinions. This is not the time or place for such an undertaking. And Mr. Buckle, in his article, has not argued but dogmatically asserted, and then called hard names at those who may conscientiously differ from him. Let me suggest to Mr. Buckle that such names can very easily be retorted. Any man who *would* use them, very easily *could*. Mr. Buckle says that any man who would punish by legal means the publication of blasphemous sentiments, should be regarded as a *noxious animal*. It is quite easy for me to say that the man who advocates the free publication of blasphemous sentiments, is a noxious animal. So there we are placed on an equal footing; and what progress has been made in the argument of the question in debate? Then Mr. Buckle very strongly disapproves a certain judgment of one of the best judges who ever sat on the English Bench: I mean Mr. Justice Coleridge. That judge on one occasion sentenced to imprisonment a poor ignorant man, convicted of having written certain blasphemous words upon a gate. I am prepared to justify every step that was taken in the prosecution and punishment of that individual. That, however, is not the point at issue. Even supposing that the magistrates who committed, and the judge who sentenced, that miserable wretch, had acted wrongly and unjustly, could not Mr. Buckle suppose that they had acted conscientiously? What right had he to speak of Mr. Justice Coleridge as a 'stony-hearted man?' What right had he to say that the judge and the magistrates, in doing what they honestly believed to be right, were 'criminals,' who had 'committed a great crime?' What right had he to say that their motives were 'the pride of their power and the wickedness of their hearts?' What right had he to call one of the most admirable men in Britain 'this unjust and unrighteous judge?' And where did Mr. Buckle ever see anything to match the statement, that Mr. Justice Coleridge grasped at the opportunity of persecuting a poor blasphemer in a remote county, where his own wickedness was likely to be overlooked, while he durst not have done as much in the face of the London press? Who will believe that Mr. Justice Coleridge is distinguished for his 'cold heart and shallow understanding?' But I feel much more comfortable now, when I have written upon this page that I, as one humble contributor to the Magazine in question, utterly repudiate Mr. Buckle's sentiments with regard to Sir J. T. Coleridge, and heartily condemn the manner in which he has expressed them.

If there be any question which ought to be debated with scrupulous calmness and fairness, it is the question whether it is just that human laws should prevent and punish the publication of views commonly regarded as blasphemous. I deny Mr. Buckle's statement, that all belief is involuntary. I say that in a country like this, every man of education is responsible for his religious belief; but of course responsible only to his Maker. Thus, on totally different grounds from Mr. Buckle, I agree with him in thinking that no human law should interfere with a man's belief. I am not prepared without much longer thought than I have yet given to the subject, to agree with Mr. Buckle and Mr. Mill, that human law should never interfere with the publication of opinions, no matter how blasphemous they may be esteemed by the great majority of the nation to which they are published. I might probably say that I should not interfere with the publication of any book, however false and mischievous I might regard the religious doctrines it taught, provided the book were written in the interest of truth—provided its author manifestly desired to set out doctrines which he regarded as true and important. But if the book set out blasphemous doctrine in such a tone and temper as made it evident that the writer's main intention was to irritate and distress those who held the belief regarded as orthodox, I should probably suppress or punish the publication of such a book. Sincere infidelity is a sad thing, with little of the propagandist spirit. Even if it should think that those Christian doctrines which afford so much comfort and support to men are fond delusions, I think its humane feeling would be,—Well, I shall not seek to shatter hopes which I cannot replace. I know that such was the feeling of the most amiable of unbelievers—David Hume. I know how he regularly attended church, anxious that he might not by his example dash in humble minds the belief which tended to make them good and happy, though it was a belief which he could not share. My present notion is, that laws ought to punish coarse and abusive blasphemy. They may let thoughtful and philosophic scepticism alone. It will hardly reach, it will never distress, the masses. But if a blackguard goes up to a parsonage door, and bellows out blasphemous remarks about the Trinity; or if a man who is a blockhead as well as a malicious wretch writes blasphemous words upon a parsonage gate, I cannot for an instant recognise in these men the champions of freedom of religious thought and speech. Even Mr. Buckle cannot think that their purpose is to teach the clergyman important truth. They don't intend to proselytise. Their object is to insult and annoy and shock. And I think it is right to punish them. They are not punished for setting out their peculiar opinions. They are punished for designedly and maliciously injuring their neighbours. Mr. Justice Coleridge punished the blasphemer in Cornwall, not because he held wrong views, not because he expressed wrong views. He might have expressed them in a decent way as long as he liked, and no one would have interfered with him. He was punished because, with malicious and insulting intention, he wrote blasphemous words where he thought they would cause pain and horror. He was punished for *that*: and rightly. Mr. Buckle seeks to excite sympathy for the man, by mixing up with the question whether or no his crime deserved punishment, the wholly distinct question, whether or no the man was so far sane as to deserve punishment for any crime whatever. These two questions have no connexion; and it is unfair to mingle them. The question of the man's sanity or insanity was for the jury to decide. The jury decided that he was so sane as to be responsible. Mr. Buckle's real point is, that however sane the man might have been, it was wicked to punish him; and I do not hesitate to say, for myself, that looking to the entire circumstances of the case, the magistrates who committed that nuisance of his neighbourhood, and the judge who sent him to jail, did no more than their duty.

There are several statements made by Mr. Buckle which must not be regarded as setting forth the teaching of the Magazine in which they were made. Mr. Buckle says that no man can be sure that any doctrine is divinely revealed: that whoever says so must be 'absurdly and immodestly confident in his own powers.' I deny that. Mr. Buckle says that it is part of Christian doctrine that rich men cannot be saved. I deny that. Christ's statement as to the power of worldly possessions to concentrate the affections upon this world, went not an inch further than daily experience goes. What said Samuel Johnson when Garrick showed him his grand house? 'Ah, David, these are the things that make death terrible!' Mr. Buckle says that Christianity gained ground in early ages because its doctrines were combated. They were not combated. Its professors were persecuted, which is quite another thing. Mr. Buckle says that the doctrine of Immortality was known to the world before Christianity was heard of, or any other revealed religion. I deny that. Greek and Roman philosophers of the highest class regarded that doctrine as a delusion of the vulgar. Did Mr. Buckle ever read the letter of condolence which Sulpicius wrote to Cicero after the death of Cicero's daughter? A beautiful letter, beautifully expressed; stating many flimsy and wretched reasons for drying one's tears; but containing not a hint of any hope of meeting in another world. And the same may be said of Cicero's reply. As for Mr. Buckle's argument for Immortality, I think it extremely weak and inconclusive. It certainly goes to prove, if it proves anything, that my cousin Tom, who lately was called to the bar, is quite sure to be Lord Chancellor; and that Sam Lloyd, who went up from our village last week to a merchant's counting-house in Liverpool, is safe to rival his eminent namesake in wealth. Mr. Buckle's argument is just this: that if your heart is very much set upon a thing, you are perfectly sure to get it. Of course everybody has read the soliloquy in Addison's *Cato*, where Mr. Buckle's argument is set forth. I deem it not worth a rush. Does any man's experience of this life tend to assure him, that because some people (and not all people) would like to see their friends again after they die, therefore they shall? Do things usually turn out just as we particularly wish that they should turn out? Has not many a young girl felt, like Cato, a 'secret dread and inward horror' lest the pic-nic day should be rainy? Did *that* ensure its being fine? Was not I extremely anxious to catch the express train yesterday, and did not I miss it? Does not every child of ten years old know, that this is a world in which things have a wonderful knack of falling out just in the way least wished for? If I were an infidel, I should believe that some spiteful imp of the perverse had the guidance of the affairs of humanity. I know better than *that*: but for my knowledge I have to thank Revelation. But is it philosophical, is it common sense, in a man who rejects Revelation, and who must be guided in his opinions of a future life by the analogy of the present, to argue that because here the issue all but constantly defeats our wishes and hopes, therefore an end on which (as he says) human hearts are very much set shall certainly be attained hereafter? 'If the separation were final,' says Mr. Buckle, in a most eloquent and pathetic passage, 'how could we stand up and live?' Fine feeling, indeed, but impotent logic. When a man has worked hard and accumulated a little competence, and then in age loses it all in some swindling bank, and sees his daughters, tenderly reared, reduced to starvation, I doubt not he may think 'How can I live?' but will all this give him his fortune back again? Has not many a youthful heart, crushed down by bitter disappointment, taken up the fancy that surely life would now be impossible; but did the fancy, by the weight of a feather, affect the fact? I remember, indeed, seeing Mr. Buckle's question put with a wider reach of meaning. Poor Uncle Tom, torn from his family, is sailing down the Mississippi, and finding comfort as he reads his well-worn Bible. How could that poor negro weigh the arguments on either side, and be sure that the blessed Faith, which was then his only support, was true? With better logic than Mr. Buckle's, he drew his best evidence from his own consciousness. 'It fitted him so well: it was so exactly what he needed. It *must* be true, or how could he live?'

Having written all this, I feel that I can now think without distraction of *Man and his Dwelling Place*. I have mildly vented my indignation; and I now, in a moral sense, extend my hand to my eminent friend. Had he come up that corkscrew stair an hour or two ago, I am not entirely certain that I might not have taken him by the collar and shaken him. And had

I found him standing on a chair in the green behind my church, and indoctrinating my simple parishioners with his peculiar notions, I have an entire conviction that I should have forgotten my theoretical assent to the doctrine of religious toleration, and by a gentle hint to my sturdy friends, procured him an invigorating bath in that gleaming river. I have got rid of that feeling now. And although Mr. Buckle is the last man who would find fault with any honest opposition, I yet desire to express my regret if I have written any word that passes the limit of goodnatured though sturdy conflict. I respect Mr. Buckle's earnestness and moral courage: I heartily admire his eloquence: I give him credit for entire sincerity in the opinions he holds, though I think them sadly mistaken.

So now for *Man and his Dwelling Place.* Twice already has the writer put his mind at that book, but it has each time swerved, like a middling hunter from a very stiff fence, and taken a circle round the field. Now at last the thing must really be done.

If you, my reader, are desirous of discovering a book which shall entirely knock up your previous views upon all possible subjects, read this *Essay Towards the Interpretation of Nature.* It does, indeed, interpret Nature, and Man too, in a fashion which, to the best of my knowledge, is thoroughly original. And the book is distinguished not more by originality than by piety, earnestness, and eloquence. Its author is an enthusiastic Christian; and indeed his peculiar views in metaphysics and science are founded upon his interpretation of certain passages in the New Testament. It is from the sacred volume that he derives his theory that man is at present dead. The work appears likely to appeal to a limited circle of readers; it will be understood and appreciated by few. Though its style is clear, the abstruseness of the subjects discussed and the transcendental scope of its author, make the train of thought often difficult to follow. Possibly the fault is not in the book, but in the reader: possibly it may result from the book having been read rapidly and while pressed by many other concerns; but there seems to me a certain want of clearness and sharpness of presentment about it. The great principle maintained is indeed set forth with unmistakeable force; but, it is hard to say how, there appears in details a certain absence of method, and what in Scotland is called a *drumliness* of style. There is a good deal of repetition too; but for *that* one is rather thankful than otherwise; for the great idea of the deadness of man and the life and spirituality of nature grows much better defined, and is grasped more completely and intelligently, as we come upon it over and over again, put in many different ways and with great variety of illustration. It is a humiliating confession for a reviewer to make, but, to say the truth, I do not know what to make of this book. If its author should succeed in indoctrinating the race with his views, he will produce an intellectual revolution. Every man who thinks at all will be constrained for the remainder of his days (I must not say of his *life*) to think upon all subjects quite differently from what he has ever hitherto thought. As for readers for amusement, and for all readers who do not choose to read what cannot be read without some mental effort, they will certainly find the first half-dozen pages of this work quite sufficient for them. Without pretending to follow the author's views into the vast number of details into which they reach, I shall endeavour in a short compass to draw the great lines of them.

There is an interesting introduction, which gradually prepares us for the announcement of the startling fact that all men hitherto have been entirely mistaken in their belief both as to themselves and the universe which surrounds them. It is first impressed upon us that things may be in themselves very different indeed from that which they appear to us: that phenomenon may be something far apart from actual being. Yet though our conceptions, whether given by sense or intellect, do not correspond with the truth of things, still they are the elements from which truth is to be gathered. The following passage, which occurs near the beginning of the introduction, is the sharp end of the wedge:—

> All advance in knowledge is a deliverance of man from himself. Slowly and painfully we learn that he is not the measure of truth, that the fact may be very different from the appearance to him. The lesson is hard, but the reward is great. So he escapes from illusion and

error, from ignorance and failure. Directing his thoughts and energies no longer according to his own impressions, but according to the truth of things, he finds himself in possession of an unimaginable power alike of understanding and of acting. To a truly marvellous extent he is the lord of nature.

But the conditions of this lordship are inexorable. They are the surrender of prepossessions, the abandonment of assumption, the confession of ignorance: the open eye and the humble heart. Hence in all passing from error to truth we learn something respecting ourselves, as well as something respecting the object of our study. Simultaneously with our better knowledge we recognise the reason of our ignorance, and perceive what defect on our part has caused us to think wrongly.

Either the world is such as it appears to us, or it is not. If it be not, there must be some condition affecting ourselves which modifies the impression we receive from it. And this condition must be operative upon all mankind: it must relate to man as a whole rather than to individual men.

Thus does the author lay down the simple general principle from which he is speedily to draw conclusions so startling. Nothing can be more innocuous than all this. Every one must agree in it. Now come the further steps.

The study of nature leads to the conclusion that there is a defectiveness in man which modifies his perception of all external things; and that thus in so far as the actual fact of the universe differs from our impression of it, the actual fact is better, higher, more complete, than our impression of it. There are qualities, there is a glory about the universe, which our defective condition prevents our seeing or discerning. The universe, or nature, is not in itself such as it is to man's feeling; and man's feeling of it differs from the fact *by defect*. All that we discern in the universe is there: and a great deal besides.

Now, we think of nature as existing in a certain way which we call *physical*. We call the world the *physical world*. This mode of existence involves *inertness*. That which is physical does not act, except passively, as it is acted upon. Inertness is inaction. That which is inert, therefore, differs from that which is not inert by *defect*. The inert *wants something* of being active.

Next, we have a conception of another mode of being besides the inert. We conceive of being which possesses a spontaneous and primary activity. This kind of being is called *spiritual*. This kind of being has shaken off the reproach of inertness. It can act, and originate action. The physical thus differs from the spiritual (as regards inertness) by defect. The physical *wants something* of being spiritual.

So far, my reader, we do not of necessity start back from anything our author teaches us. Quite true, we think of matter, a kind of being which can *do nothing* of itself. Quite true, we think of spirit, a kind of being which can *do*. And no doubt that which is able to do is (*quoad hoc*) a higher and more noble kind of being than that which cannot do, but only be done to. But remember here, I do not admit that in this point lies the *differentia* between matter and spirit. I do not grant that by taking from matter the reproach of inertness, you would make it spirit. The essential difference seems to me not to lie there. We could conceive of matter as capable of originating action, and yet as material. This is by the bye—but now be on your guard. Here is our author's great discovery—

It is man's defectiveness which makes him feel the world as thus defective. Nature is really not inert, though it appears so to man. We have been wont to think that nature, the universe, is inert or physical; that man is not-inert, or spiritual. Now, there is no doubt at all that there is inertness somewhere. Here are the two things, Man and Nature; with which thing does the inertness lie? Our author maintains that it lies with man, not with nature. Science has proved to us that nature is not-inert. As there is inertness somewhere, and as it is not in nature, of course the conclusion is that it is in man. Inertness is in the phenomenon; that is, in nature as it appears to us. There cannot be any question that nature *seems to us* to be inert. But the author of this book declares that this inertness, though in the phenomenon, is not in the fact. Nature LOOKS inert; it IS not-inert. How does the notion of inertness come at all, then? Now comes the very essence of the new theory; I give it in its author's words:—

> The inertness is introduced by man. He perceives defect without him, only because there is defect within him.
>
> To be inert has the same meaning as to be dead. So we speak of nature, thinking it to be inert, as 'dead matter.' To say that man introduces inertness into nature, implies a deadness in him: it is to

say that he wants life. This is the proposition which is affirmed. This condition which we call our life, is not the true life of man.

The Book that has had greater influence upon the world than all others, differs from all others, in affirming that man wants life, and in making that statement the basis of all that it contains respecting the past and present and future of mankind.

Science thus pays homage to the Bible. What that book has declared as if with authority, so long ago, she has at last decyphered on the page of nature. This is not man's true life.

And who is there that can doubt, looking at man as he is now, and then thinking of what he is to be in another world, that there is about him, now, great defect? There is truly much wanting which it is hoped will one day be supplied. What shall we call this lacking thing—this one thing lacking whose absence is felt in every fibre of our being? Our author chooses to call it life; I am doubtful with how much felicity or naturalness of expression. Of course we all know that in the New Testament *life* does not mean merely existence continued; *eternal life* does not mean merely existence continued for ever: it means the highest and purest form of our being continued for ever;—happiness and holiness continued for ever. We know, too, that holy Scripture describes the step taken by any man in becoming an earnest believer in Christ, as 'passing from death to life;' we remember such a text as 'This is life eternal, that they may know Thee, the only true God, and Jesus Christ whom Thou hast sent.' We know that a general name for the Gospel, which grasps its grand characteristics, is ' The Word of Life ;' and that, in religious phrase, Christianity is concerned with the revealing, the implanting, the sustaining, the crowning, of a certain better life. Nor is it difficult to trace out such analogies between natural and spiritual death, between natural and spiritual life, as tend to prove that spiritual life and death are not spoken of in Scripture merely as the strongest words which could be employed, but that there is a further and deeper meaning in their constant use. But I do not see any gain in forcing figurative language into a literal use. Everybody knows what *life* and *death*, in ordinary language, imply. Life means sensibility, consciousness, capacity of acting, union with the living. Death means senselessness, helplessness, separation. No doubt we may trace analogies, very close and real, between the natural and the spiritual life and death. But still they are no more than analogies. You do not identify the physical with the spiritual. And it is felt by all that the use of the words in a spiritual sense is a figurative use. To the common understanding, a man is living, when he breathes and feels and moves. He is dead when he ceases to do all that. And it is a mere twisting of words from their understood sense to say that in reality, and without a figure, a breathing, feeling, moving man is *dead*, because he lacks some spiritual quality, however great its value may be. It may be a very valuable quality; it may be worth more than life; but it is not life, as men understand it; and as words have no meaning at all except that which men agree to give these arbitrary sounds, it matters not at all that this higher quality is what you may call true life, better life, real life. If you enlarge the meaning of the word *life* to include, in addition to what is generally understood by it, a higher power of spiritual action and discernment, why, all that can be said is, that you understand by *life* something quite different from men in general. If I choose to enlarge the meaning of the word *black* to include *white*, of course I might say with truth (relatively to myself) that white forms the usual clothing of clergymen. If I extend the meaning of the word *fast* to include *slow*, I might boldly declare that the Great Northern express is a slow train. And the entire result of such use of language would be, that no mortal would understand what I meant.

Thus it is that I demur to any author's right to tell me that such and such a thing is, or is not, 'the true life of man.' And when he says 'that man wants life, means that the true life of man is of another kind from this,' I reply to him, Tell me what is the blessing man needs; Tell me, above all, where and how he is to get it: but as to its name, I really do not care what you call it, so you call it by some name that people will understand. Call it so that people will know what you mean—Salvation, Glory, Happiness, Holiness, Redemption, or what else you please. Do not mystify us by saying we *want life*, and then, when we are startled by the perfectly intelligible assertion, edge off by explaining that by *life* you mean something quite different from what we do. There is no good in *that*. If I were to declare that this evening, before I sleep, I shall cross the Atlantic and go to America, my readers would think the statement a sufficiently extraordinary one; but if, after thus surprising them, I went on to explain that by the Atlantic I did not mean the ocean, nor by America the western continent, but that the Atlantic meant the village green, and America the squire's house on the other side of it, I should justly gain credit for a very silly mystification. As Nicholas Nickleby very justly remarked, If Dotheboys Hall is not a hall, why call it one? Mr. Squeers, in his reply, no doubt stated the law of the case: If a man chooses to call his house an island, what is to hinder him? If the author of *Man and his Dwelling Place* means to tell us only that we want some spiritual capacity, which it pleases him to call life, but which not one man in a million understands by that word, is he not amusing himself at our expense by telling us we *want life*? *We* know what we mean by being dead: our author means something quite different. Let him speak for himself:—

> That man wants life means that the true life of man is of another kind from this. It corresponds to that true, absolute Being which he as he now is cannot know.
> He cannot know it, because he is out of relation with it. THIS IS HIS DEADNESS. To know it is to have life.

Yes, reader—*this is his deadness*! Something, that is, which no plain mortal would ever understand by the word. When I told you, a long time ago, that this book taught that man is dead and nature living, was *this* what the words conveyed to you?

Still, though there may be something not natural in the word, the author's meaning is a broad and explicit one. For the want of *that* which he calls our true life (he maintains) utterly distorts and deforms this world to our view. Here is his statement as to the things which surrounds us:—

> There is not a physical world and a spiritual world besides; but the spiritual world which alone is is physical to man, *the physical being the mode in which man by his defectiveness perceives the spiritual.* We feel a physical world to be: that which is is the spiritual world.

The phenomenon, that is, is physical: the fact is spiritual. A tree looks to us material, because we want life: if we had life, we should see that it is spiritual. Really, there is no such thing as matter. Our own defectiveness make us fancy that to be material which in truth is spiritual. So I was misinterpreting the author, when I said that all that we see in nature is there, and a great deal more. The defect in us, it appears, not only subtracts from nature: it transforms it. Not merely do we fail to discern that which is in nature: we do actually discern that which is not in nature.

And to be delivered from all this deadness and delusion, what we have to do is to betake ourselves to the Saviour. Christianity is a system which starts from the fundamental principle that man is dead, and proposes to make him alive. Under its working man gains true life, otherwise called eternal life; and in gaining that life he finds himself *ipso facto* conveyed into a spiritual world. This world ceases to be physical to him, and becomes spiritual.

Such are the great lines of the new theory as to Man and his Dwelling Place. Thus does our author interpret Nature. I trust and believe that I have not in any way misrepresented or caricatured his opinions. His *Introduction* sets out in outline the purport of the entire book. The remainder of the volume is given to carrying out these opinions into detail, as they are suggested by or as they affect the entire system of things. It is divided into four *Books*. Book I. treats *Of Science*; Book II. *Of Philosophy*; Book III. *Of Religion*; Book IV. *Of Ethics*; and the volume is closed by four *Dialogues* between the *Writer* and *Reader*, in which, in a desultory manner, the principles already set forth are further explained and enforced.

Early in the first chapter of the Book *Of Science*, the author anticipates the obvious objection to his use of the terms *Life* and *Death*. I do not think he succeeds in justifying the fashion in which he employs them. But let him speak for himself:—

> It may seem unnatural to speak of a conscious existence as a state of death. But what is affirmed is, that a sensational existence such

as ours is not the life of MAN; that a consciousness of physical life does itself imply a deadness. The affirmations that we are living men, and that man has not true and absolute life, are not opposed. Life is a relative term. Our possession of a conscious life in relation to the things that we feel around us, is itself the evidence of man's defect of life in a higher and truer sense.

Let a similitude make the thought more clear. Are not we, as individuals, at rest, steadfast in space; evidently so to our own consciousness, demonstrably so in relation to the objects around us? But is man at rest in space? By no means. We are all partakers of a motion. Nay, if we were truly at rest, we could not have this relative steadfastness, we should not be at rest to the things around us: they would fleet and slip away. Our relative rest and consciousness of steadfastness, depend upon our being not at rest. There are moving things, to which he only can be steadfast who is moving too. Even such is the life of which we have consciousness. We have a life in relation to these physical things, because man wants life. True life in man would alter his relation to them. They could not be the realities any more: he could not have a life in them. As rest to moving things is not truly rest, but motion; so life to inert things is not truly life, but deadness.

Very ingeniously thought out: very skilfully put, with probably the only illustration which would go on all fours. But to me all this is extremely unsatisfactory: and unsatisfactory in a much farther sense than merely that it is using terms in a non-natural sense. I know, of course, that to look at Nature through blue spectacles will make Nature blue: but I cannot see that to look at Nature through dead eyes should make Nature dead. I see no proof that Nature, in fact, is living and active, though it admittedly looks inert and dead. And I can discover nothing more than a daring assertion, in the statement that we are dead, and that we project our own deadness upon living nature. I cannot see how to the purest and most elevated of beings, a tree should look less solid than it does to me. I cannot discover how greater purity of heart, and more entire faith in Christ, should turn this material world into a world of spirit. I doubt the doctrine that spirit in itself, as usually understood (apart from its power of originating action) is a higher and holier existence than matter. It seems to me that very much from a wrong idea that it is, come those vague, unreal, intangible notions as to the Christian Heaven, which do so much to make it a chilly, unattractive thing, to human wishes and hopes. It is hard enough for us to feel the reality of the things beyond the grave, without having the additional stumbling-block cast in our way, of being told that truly there is nothing real there for us to feel. As for the following eloquent passage, in which our author subsequently returns to the justification of his great doctrine, no more need be said than that it is rhetoric, not logic :—

> That man has not his true life, must have taken him long to learn. All our prepossessions, all our natural convictions, are opposed to that belief. If these activities, these powers, these capacities of enjoyment and suffering, this consciousness of free will, this command of the material world, be not life, what is life? What more do we want to make us truly man? This is the feeling that has held men captive, and biassed all their thoughts so that they could not perceive what they themselves were saying.
>
> Yet the sad undercurrent has belied the boast. From all ages and all lands the cry of anguish, the prayer for life, unconscious of itself, has gone up to heaven. In groans and curses, in despair and cruel rage, man pours out his secret to the universe ; writing it in blood,

and lust, and savage wrong, upon the fair bosom of the earth; he alone not knowing what he does. If this be the life of man, what is his death?

No doubt this would form a very eloquent and effective paragraph in a popular sermon. But in a philosophic treatise, where an author is tied to the severely precise use of terms, and where it will not do to call a thing death merely because it is very bad, nor to call a thing life merely because it is very good, the argument appears to have but little weight.

You must see, intelligent reader, that one thing which we are entitled to require our author to satisfactorily prove, is the fact that Nature is not inert, as it appears to man. If you can make it certain that Nature is living and active, then, no doubt, some explanation will be needful as to how it comes to look so different to us; though, even then, I do not see that it necessarily follows that the inertness is to be supposed to exist in ourselves. But unless the author can prove that Nature is not inert, he has no foundation to build on. He states three arguments, from which he derives the grand principle :—

1. Inertness necessarily belongs to all phenomena. That which is only *felt* to be, and does not truly or absolutely exist, must have the character of inaction. It must be felt as passive. A phenomenon must be inert *because it is a phenomenon*. We cannot argue from inertness in that which appears to us, to inertness in that which is. Of whatsoever kind the essence of nature may be, if it be unknown, the phenomenon must be equally inert. We have no ground, therefore, in the inertness which we feel, for affirming of nature that it *is* inert. We must feel it so, by virtue of our known relation to it, as not perceiving its essence.

2. The question, therefore, rests entirely upon its own evidence. Since we have no reason, from the inertness of the phenomenal, for inferring the inertness of the essential, can we know whether that essential be inert or not? We can know. Inertness, as being absolute inaction, cannot belong to that which truly is. Being and absolute inaction, are contraries. Inertness, therefore, must be a property by which the phenomenal differs from the essential or absolute.

3. Again, nature does act: it acts upon us, or we could not perceive it at all. The true being of nature is active therefore. That we feel it otherwise shows that we do not feel it as it is. We must look for the source of nature's apparent or felt inertness in man's condition. Never should man have thought to judge of nature without remembering his own defectiveness.

Such are the grounds upon which rests the belief, that nature is not inert. It appears to me that there is little force in them. To a great extent they are mere assumptions and assertions; and anything they contain in the nature of argument is easily answered.

First: Why must every phenomenon be felt as inert? Why must a 'phenomenon *be inert because it is a phenomenon*?' I cannot see why. We know nothing but phenomena; that is, things as they appear to us. Where did we get the ideas of life and activity, if not from phenomena? Many things *appear to us* to have life and activity. That is, there are phenomena which are not inert.

Secondly: Wherefore should we conclude that the phenomenon differs essentially from the fact? The phenomenon is the fact-as-discerned-by-us. And granting that our defectiveness forbids our having a full and complete discernment of the fact, why should we doubt that our discernment is right *so far as it goes?* It is incomparably more likely that things (not individual things, but the entire system, I mean) *are* what they *seem*, than that they *are not*. Why believe that we are gratuitously and needlessly deluded? God made the universe; He placed us in it; He gave us powers whereby to discern it. Is it reasonable to think that He did so in a fashion so blundering or so deceitful that we can only discern it wrong? And if nature *seems* inert, is not the rational conclusion that it *is* so?

Thirdly: Why cannot 'inertness, as being absolute inaction, belong to that which truly is?' Why cannot a thing *exist* without *doing* anything? Is not *that* just what millions of things actually do? Or if you intend to twist the meaning of the substantive verb, and to say that merely to *be* is to do something—that simply to exist is a certain form of exertion and action—I shall grant, of course, that nothing whatever that exists is in that sense inert; but I shall affirm that you use the word *inert* in quite a different sense from the usual one. And in that extreme and non-natural sense of the word, the phenomenon is no more inert than is the essence. Certainly things *seem to us to be*: and if just *to be* is to *be active*, then no phenomenon is inert: no single thing discerned by us appears to be inert.

Fourthly: I grant that ' nature does act upon us, or we could not perceive it at all.' But then I maintain that this kind of action is not action as men understand the word. This kind of action is quite consistent with the general notion of inertness. A thing may be inert, as mankind understand the word; and also active, as the author of this book understands the word. To discern this sort of activity and life in nature we have no need to 'pass from death to life' ourselves. We simply need to have the thing pointed out to us, and it is seen at once. It is playing with words to say that *nature acts upon us, or we could not perceive it*. No doubt, when you stand before a tree, and look at it, it does act in so far as that it depicts itself upon your retina; but that action is quite consistent with what we understand by inertness. It does not matter whether you say that your eye takes hold of the tree, or that the tree takes hold of your eye. When you hook a trout, you may say either that you catch the fish, or that the fish catches you. Is the alternative worth fighting about? Which is the natural way of speaking: to say that the man *sees the tree*, or that *the tree shows itself* to the man? All the activity which our author claims for nature goes no farther than that. Our reply is that *that* is not activity at all. If that is all he contends for, we grant it at once; and we say that it is not in the faintest degree inconsistent with the fact of nature's being inert, as that word is understood. You come and tell me that Mr. Smith has just passed your window *flying*. I say No; I saw him; he was not flying, but walking. Ah, you reply, I hold that walking is an inchoate flying; it is a rudimentary flying, the lowest form of flying; and therefore I maintain that he flew past the window. My friend, I answer, if it be any satisfaction to you to use words in that way, do so and rejoice; only do not expect any human being to understand what you mean; and beware of the lunatic asylum.

Why, I ask again, are we to cry down man for the sake of crying up nature? Why are we to depreciate the dweller that we may magnify the dwelling-place? Is not man (to say the least) *one* of the works of God? Did not God make both man and nature? And does not Revelation (which our author holds in so deep reverence) teach that man was the last and noblest of the handiworks of the Creator? And thus it is that I do not hesitate to answer such a question as that which follows, and to answer it contrariwise to what the author expects. It is from the human soul that glory and meaning are projected upon inanimate nature. To Newton, and to Newton's dog, the outward creation was physically the same; to the apprehension of Newton and of Newton's dog, how different! Hear the author:—

> To this clear issue the case is brought: Man does introduce into nature something from himself: either the inertness, the negative quality, the defect, or the beauty, the meaning, the glory. Either that whereby the world is noble comes from ourselves, or that whereby it is mean; that which it has, or that which it wants. Can it be doubtful which it is?

Not in the least! Give me the rational and immortal man, made in God's image, rather than the grandest oak which the June sunbeams will soon be warming—rather than the most majestic mountain which by and bye will be purple with the heather. Reason, immortality, love, and faith, are things liker God than ever so many cubic feet of granite, than ever so many loads of timber. 'Behold,' says Archer Butler, 'we stand alone in the universe! Earth, air, and ocean can show us nothing so awful as we!'

You fancy, says our author, that nature is inert, because it goes on in so constant and unvarying a course. You know, says he, what conscious exertion it cost you to produce physical changes; you can trace no such exertion in Nature. You would believe, says he, that Nature is active, but for the fact that her doings are all conformed to laws that you can trace. But invariableness, he maintains, is no proof of inaction. 'RIGHT ACTION is invariable; RIGHT ACTION is absolutely conformed to law. Why, therefore, should not the secret of nature's invariableness be, not passiveness, but rightness?' The unchanging uniformity of Nature's course proves her holiness—her willing, unvarying obedience to the Divine law. 'The invariableness of Nature bespeaks Holiness as its cause.'

May we not think upon all this (not dogmatically) in some such fashion as this?

Which is likelier

1. That Nature has it in her power to vary from the well-known laws of Nature; that she could disobey God if she pleased; but that she is so holy that she could not think of such a thing, and so through all ages has never swerved once. Or,

2. That Nature is bound by laws which she has not the power to disobey; that she is what she looks, an inanimate, passive, inert thing, actuated, as her soul and will, by the will of the Creator?

And to aid in considering which alternative is the likelier, let it be remembered that Revelation teaches that this is a fallen world: that experience proves that this world is not managed upon any system of optimism; that in this creation things are constantly going wrong; and especially, that all history gives no account of any mere creature whose will was free to do either good or ill; and yet who did not do ill frequently. Is it likely that to all this there is one entire exception; one thing, and that so large a thing as all inanimate nature, perfectly obedient, perfectly holy, perfectly right—and all by its own free will? I grant there is something touching in the author's eloquent words:—

> Because she is right, Nature is ours: more truly ours than we ourselves. We turn from the inward ruin to the outward glory, and marvel at the contrast. But we need not marvel: it is the difference of life and death: piercing the dimness even of man's darkened sense, jarring upon his fond illusion like waking realities upon a dream. Without is living holiness, within is deathly wrong.

Let the reader, ever remembering that in such cases

analogy is not argument but illustration—that it makes a doctrine clearer, but does not in any degree confirm it—read the chapter entitled 'Of the Illustration from Astronomy.' It will tend to make the great doctrine of *Man and his Dwelling Place* comprehensible; you will see exactly what it is, although you may not think it true. As astronomy has transferred the apparent movements of the planets from them to ourselves, so, says our author, has science transferred the seeming inertness of Nature from it to us. The phenomenon of Nature is physical and inert: the being is spiritual and active and holy. And if we now seem to have an insuperable conviction that Man is not inert and that Nature is inert, it is not stronger than our apparent consciousness that the earth is unmoving. Man lives under illusion as to himself and as to the universe. Reason, indeed, furnishes him with the means of correcting that illusion: but in that illusion is his want of life.

Strong in his conviction of the grand principle which he has established, as he conceives, in his first book, the author, in his second book, goes crashing through all systems of philosophy. His great doctrine makes havock of them all. All are wrong; though each may have some grain of truth in it. The Idealists are right in so far as that there is no such thing as Matter. Matter is the vain imagination of man through his wrong idea of Nature's inertness. But the Idealists are wrong if they fancy that because there is no Matter, there is nothing but Mind, and ideas in Mind. Nature, though spiritual, has a most real and separate existence. Then the Sceptics are right in so far as they doubt what our author thinks wrong; but they are wrong in so far as they doubt what our author thinks right. Positivism is right in so far as it teaches that we see all things relatively to ourselves, and so wrongly; but it is wrong in teaching that what things are in themselves is no concern of ours, and that we should live on as though things were what they seem.

If it were not that the reader of *Man and his Dwelling Place* is likely, after the shock of the first grand theory, that Man is dead and the Universe living, to receive with comparative coolness any further views set out in the book, however strange, I should say that probably the third Book, 'Of Religion,' would startle him more than anything else in the work. Although this Book stands third in the volume, it is first both in importance and in chronology. For the author tells us that his views *Of Religion* are not deduced from the theoretical conceptions already stated, but have been drawn immediately from the study of Scripture, and that from them the philosophical ideas are mainly derived. And indeed it is perfectly marvellous what doctrines men will find in Scripture, or deduce from Scripture. Is there not something curious in the capacity of the human mind, while glancing along the sacred volume, to find upon its pages both what suits its prevailing mood and its firm conviction at the time? You feel buoyant and cheerful: you open your Bible and read it; what a cheerful, hopeful book it is! You are depressed and anxious: you open your Bible; surely it was written for people in your present frame of mind! It is wonderful to what a degree the Psalms especially suit the mood and temper of all kinds of readers in every conceivable position. I can imagine the poor suicide, stealing towards the peaceful river, and musing on a verse of a psalm. I can imagine the joyful man, on the morning of a marriage day which no malignant relatives have embittered, finding a verse which will seem like the echo of his cheerful temper. And passing from feeling to understanding, it is remarkable how, when a man is possessed with any strong belief, he will find, as he reads the Bible, not only many things which appear to him expressly to confirm his view, but something in the entire tenor of what he reads that appears to harmonize with it. I doubt not the author of *Man and his Dwelling Place* can hardly open the Bible at random without chancing upon some passage which he regards as confirmatory of his opinions. I am quite sure that to ordinary men his opinions will appear flatly to conflict with the Bible's fundamental teaching. It has already been indicated in this essay in what sense the statements of the New Testament to the following effect are to be understood:—

The writers of the New Testament declare man to be dead. They speak of men as not having life, and tell of a life to be given them. If, therefore, our thoughts were truly conformed to the New Testament, how could it seem a strange thing to us that this state of man should be found a state of death; how should its very words, re-affirmed by science, excite our surprise? Would it not have appeared to us a natural result of the study of nature to prove man dead? Might we not, if we had truly accepted the words of Scripture, have anticipated that it should be so? For, if man be rightly called dead, should not that condition have affected his experience, and ought not a discovery of that fact to be the issue of his labours to ascertain his true relation to the universe? Why does it seem a thing incredible to us that man should be really, actually dead: dead in such a sense as truly to affect his being, and determine his whole state? Why have we been using words which affirm him dead in our religious speech, and feel startled at finding them proved true in another sphere of inquiry?

It is indeed true—it is a thing to be taken as a fundamental truth in reading the Bible—that in a certain sense man is dead, and is to be made alive; and the analogy which obtains between natural death and what in theological language is called spiritual death, is in several respects so close and accurate that we feel that it is something more than a strong figure when the New Testament says such things as 'You hath he quickened, who were *dead* in trespasses and sins.' But it tends only to confusion to seek to identify things so thoroughly different as natural and spiritual death. It is trifling with a man to say to him 'You are dead!' and having thus startled him, to go on to explain that you mean spiritually dead. 'Oh,' he will reply, 'I grant you that I may be dead in that sense, and possibly that is the more important sense; but it is not the sense in which words are commonly understood.' I can see, of course, various points of analogy between ordinary death and spiritual death. Does ordinary death render a man insensible to the presence of material things? Then spiritual death renders him heedless of spiritual realities, of the presence of God, of the value of salvation, of the closeness of eternity. Does natural death appear in utter helplessness and powerlessness? So does spiritual death render a man incapable of spiritual action and exertion. Has natural death its essence in the entire separation it makes between dead and living? So has spiritual death its essence in the separation of the soul from God. But, after all, these things do but show an analogy between natural death and spiritual: they do not show that the things are one; they do not show that in the strict unfigurative use of terms man's spiritual condition is one of death. They show that man's spiritual condition is *very like death*; that is all. It is so like as quite to justify the assertion in Scripture: it is not so identical as to justify the introduction of a new philosophical phrase. It is perfectly true that Christianity is described in Scripture as a means for bringing men *from death to life*; but it is also described, with equal meaning, as a means for bringing men *from darkness to light*. And it is easy to trace the analogy between man's spiritual condition and the condition of one in darkness—between man's redeemed condition and the condition of one in light; but surely it would be childish to announce, as a philosophical discovery, that all men are blind, because they cannot see their true interests and the things that most concern them. They are not blind in the ordinary sense, though they may be blind in a higher; neither are they dead in the ordinary sense, though they may be in a higher. And only confusion, and a sense of being misled and trifled with, can follow from the pushing figure into fact and trying to identify the two.

Stripping our author's views of the unusual phraseology in which they are disguised, they do, so far as regards the essential fact of man's loss and redemption, coincide exactly with the orthodox teaching of the Churches of England and of Scotland. Man is by nature and sinfulness in a spiritual sense dead; dead now, and doomed to a worse death hereafter. By believing in Christ he at once obtains some share of a better spiritual life, and the hope of a future life which shall be perfectly holy and happy. Surely this is no new discovery. It is the type of Christianity implied in our prayers, and weekly set out from our pulpits. The startling novelties of *Man and his Dwelling Place* are in matters of detail. It holds that fearful thing, *Damnation* which orthodox views push off into a future world, to be a present thing. It is now men are damned. It is now men are in hell. Wicked men are now in a state of damnation: they are now in hell. The common error arises from our thinking damnation a state of suffering. It is not. It is a state of something worse than suffering, viz., of sin :—

> We find it hard to believe that damnation can be a thing men like. But does not what every being likes depend on what it is? Is corruption less corruption, in man's view, because worms like it? Is damnation, less damnation in God's view, because men like it? And God's view is simply the truth. Surely one object of a revelation must be to show us things from God's view of them, that is, as they truly are. Sin truly is damnation, though to us it is pleasure. That sin is pleasure to us, surely is the evil part of our condition.

And indeed it is to be admitted that there is a great and much-forgotten truth implied here. It is a very poor, and low, and inadequate idea of Christianity, to think of it merely as something which saves from suffering—as something which saves us from hell, regarded merely as a place of misery. The Christian salvation is mainly a deliverance from sin. The deliverance is primarily from moral evil; and only secondarily from physical or moral pain. 'Thou shalt call His name Jesus, for He shall save His people *from their sins.*' No doubt this is very commonly forgotten. No doubt the vulgar idea of salvation and perdition founds on the vulgar belief that pain is the worst of all things, and happiness the best of all things. It is well that the coarse and selfish type of religion which founds on the mere desire to escape from burning and to lay hold of bliss, should be corrected by the diligent instilling of the belief, that sin is worse than sorrow. The Saviour's compassion, though ever ready to well out at the sight of suffering, went forth most warmly at the sight of sin.

Here I close the book, not because there is not much more in it that well deserves notice, but because I hope that what has here been said of it will induce the thoughtful reader to study it for himself, and because I have space to write no more. It is a May afternoon; *not* that on which the earliest pages of my essay were written, but a week after it. I have gone at the ox-fence at last, and got over it with several contusions. Pardon me, unknown author, much admired for your ingenuity, your earnestness, your originality, your eloquence, if I have written with some show of lightness concerning your grave book. Very far, if you could know it, was any reality of lightness from your reviewer's feeling. He is *non ignarus mali*: he has had his full allotment of anxiety and care; and he hails, with you, the prospect of a day when human nature shall cast off its load of death, and when sinful and sorrowful man shall be brought into a beautiful conformity to external nature. Would that *Man* were worthy of *his Dwelling-place* as it looks upon this summer-like day! Open, you latticed window: let the cool breeze come into this somewhat feverish room. Again, the tree tops; again the white stones and green graves; again the lambs, somewhat larger; again the distant hill. Again I think of Cheapside, far away. Yet there is trouble here. Not a yard of any of those hedges but has worried its owner in watching that it be kept tight, that sheep or cattle may not break through. Not a gate I see but screwed a few shillings out of the anxious farmer's pocket, and is always going wrong. Not a field but either the landlord squeezed the tenant in the matter of rent, or the tenant cheated the landlord. Not the smoke of a cottage but marks where pass lives weighted down with constant care, and with little end save the sore struggle to keep the wolf from the door. Not one of these graves, save perhaps the poor friendless tramp's in the corner, but was opened and closed to the saddening of certain hearts. Here are lives of error, sleepless nights, overdriven brains; wayward children, unnatural parents, though of these last, God be thanked, very few. No doubt we are dead: when shall we be quickened to a better life? Surely, as it is, the world is too good for man. And I agree, most cordially and entirely, with the author of this book, that there is but one Agency in the universe that can repress evil here, and extinguish it hereafter.

CHAPTER XI.

CONCERNING A GREAT SCOTCH PREACHER.*

MR. CAIRD'S name is already known to the English public as that of the author of a sermon on *Religion in Common Life*, which was published two or three years ago by her Majesty's command. Every Sunday during her autumn sojourn at Balmoral, the Queen and court worship at the little parish church of Crathie; and at various times several of the most popular preachers of the Church of Scotland have there preached in the presence of royalty. Mr. Norman McLeod of Glasgow, Dr. Cumming, Dr. Tulloch, and other eminent Scotch clergymen, have officiated at Crathie Church, and in more than one instance with so favourable an impression, that the manuscripts of the discourses have been

---

* *Sermons.* By the Rev. John Caird, M.A., Minister of the Park Church, Glasgow, Author of *Religion in Common Life*. Edinburgh and London: 1858. This Chapter was published in *Fraser's Magazine* for August 1858. Dr. Caird is now Professor of Divinity in the University of Glasgow.

required for the Queen's private perusal. But Mr. Caird was the first Scotch minister who received a royal command to give his sermon to the public; and indeed, with the exception of the Bishop of Oxford, the first preacher who had been so distinguished during her Majesty's reign. Many circumstances, apart from the merit of the discourse, contributed to secure for it a very large circulation in England as well as in Scotland; and we have been informed that no single sermon published in modern times has been so extensively read. Somewhere about a hundred thousand copies of it were exhausted in Britain: a still greater number were required for the United States, where the republicans were eager to know what sort of religious instruction was approved by a queen; and the sermon, being translated into the German tongue, was republished in Germany with a recommendatory preface by the Chevalier Bunsen. At that period it became known for the first time to the English public that there had arisen in Scotland a new luminary; a great pulpit orator who was held by many to be equal to any who had preceded him, Chalmers and Guthrie not being excepted. And the published sermon seemed almost to justify the enthusiasm of Mr. Caird's warmest admirers. We believe that among intelligent readers there was but one opinion of it, as an ingenious, eloquent, sensible, and interesting exposition of an important practical subject. Still, we have been told that some readers thought Mr. Caird's theology very defective; and it is not long since we read a letter in a newspaper which is the organ of a small religious sect, in which Mr. Caird was sadly torn to pieces as lacking all spiritual insight and knowledge of the gospel doctrines. And the ingenious writer of that letter stated that nothing could be more mistaken than the popular belief that the Queen, in commanding the publication of Mr. Caird's sermon, intended to express her approval of it. On the contrary, her Majesty's purpose was (so the writer of the letter assures us) to make an appeal to the sympathies of the religious public, and to say,—' Pity me, my subjects; here is a specimen of the kind of thing that I have to listen to in Scotland in autumn!'

Mr. Caird made his reputation as a preacher while minister of a church in Edinburgh; but about ten years since he retired from the bustle of a city clergyman's life to the country parish of Errol, in Perthshire. From his seclusion there he occasionally emerged to preach in the large towns of Scotland, and far from being forgotten or lost sight of in his country retirement, his popularity appeared ever on the increase. Whenever he preached in Edinburgh or Glasgow, the crowds that followed him had hardly been equalled since the great days of Dr. Chalmers; and the fame to which *Religion in Common Life* attained did not surpass the expectations of his Scotch admirers. A few months since Mr. Caird, now a clergyman of thirteen years' experience, was transferred from his country parish to the pretty church recently erected in the West-end Park at Glasgow, to which we are sorry to see its builders were too Protestant to give a saint's name. There, with undiminished fire and unslackening popularity, Mr. Caird preaches twice every Sunday. The stranger in Glasgow, if he wanders on Sunday afternoon in the direction of the Park, will see a well-dressed crowd hurrying towards the Park Church; and we understand that so overcrowded was the building at Mr. Caird's first coming, that it was found necessary to furnish the congregation with tickets, no one being admitted without producing one. Mr. Caird, we believe, is of opinion that in order to produce its full impression, a sermon ought not to be read, but to be delivered as if given *extempore*; but as the labour of committing a discourse to memory is great, he reads his forenoon discourse, and delivers without any manuscript that which he preaches in the afternoon. The afternoon appearance is thus the great one, and it is to that service that strangers who wish to hear the eminent preacher generally go. And although it is in the nature of things impossible that a great orator should be always at his best, we believe that hardly any one who goes to hear Mr. Caird of an afternoon, however high his expectations may have been, returns disappointed.

Let us suppose that by the kindness of some Glasgow acquaintance we have succeeded in procuring tickets of admission to the Park Church. In the midst of a throng which has converged from many points to the steep ascent which leads up to it, we approach the plain Gothic building, with its massive tower, which, standing on an elevated ridge of ground, looks on either hand over the distant din of thronging streets beneath to the quiet country hills far away. We find our way into the church; and we have time to look around us, for there is still half-an-hour before service begins. Is this really a Presbyterian church? What would John Knox say to it? For all the light within is the 'dim religious light' of the cathedral, mellowed in its passage through the windows of stained glass: there is the lofty vaulted roof of richly carved oak, and the double line of shafts parting the side aisles: far up, the amber-tinted clerestory windows throw shafts of sunset colour upon the oaken beams; and in the distance—for the church is a very long one—there is nothing less than a spacious chancel, parted from the church by a lofty pointed arch, partly filled up by a traceried screen of stone. And at the extremity of the chancel, but (something lacking still) at the *west* end of the church, there is an altar-window, whose fair proportions and rich tracery might have been designed by Pugin. No galleries cut these graceful shafts; and the seats are not pews, but open benches of oak. There is no organ, and no altar; but directly in front of the chancel a plain pulpit of oak.

It is just two o'clock. Every seat is crowded, and the passages have gradually filled with people who are content to stand. And as the last tones of the bell have died away, Mr. Caird ascends the pulpit, wearing, as Scotch ministers do, the black silk preaching gown and cassock. His appearance is natural and unaffected. Of the middle size, with dark complexion and long black hair, good but not remarkable forehead, a somewhat careworn and anxious expression, and looking like a retiring and hard-wrought student of eight-and-thirty—there we have Mr. Caird. He begins the service by reading the psalm which is to be sung; and we are struck at once by the solemnity and depth of his voice, and we feel already something of the charm there is about the whole man. The psalm is sung by a choir so efficient that the lack of the organ is hardly felt. Then the minister rises, and the congregation kneeling, offers a prayer. The Church of Scotland has no liturgy, and every clergyman has to prepare his own prayers. These are commonly understood to be given extemporaneously, and generally they are extemporaneous; but as we listen to those sentences, uttered with so much feeling, solemnity, quietude, and fluency, we soon know that the prayers, filled with happy turns of expression, containing many phrases and sentences borrowed from the Liturgy, and some (or we are much mistaken) translated from the Missal, and all conceived and expressed in the simple beautiful liturgical spirit, have been, if not written, at least most carefully thought over at home. At one time Mr. Caird's prayers were ambitious and oratorical; but now their perfect simplicity tells of more mature judgment and taste. We cannot say whether the congregation has so far mastered the essential difficulty of unliturgical common prayer as to be properly joining in those petitions: but the perfect stillness, the silence and stirlessness that prevail in church, testify that the congregation is at all events intently listening. The prayer is over—only a quarter of an hour. Then a lesson from each Testament is read, chosen at the discretion of the clergyman, a psalm being chanted between the two. Next a psalm is sung; and then, after a brief collect, comes the sermon. You cannot doubt, as you see the people arranging themselves for fixed attention, what portion of the worship of God is thought in Scotland the most important. The service in this country is essentially one of instruction rather than one of devotion. The text is read; it is generally such as we feel at once to be a suggestive one: it is sometimes striking, but never odd or strange. Then Mr. Caird begins his sermon. He has no manuscript before him, not a shred of what the humbler Scotch call *paper*, and abhor as they abhor a vestige of Rome; but who could for a moment be misled into imagining those felicitous sentences extemporaneous; or that masterly symmetrical discussion of the subject, so ingenious, so thoughtful, so rich in fine illustration, rising several times in the course of the sermon into a fervid rush of eloquence that you hold your breath to listen to—the excogitation of the moment? In hearing Mr. Caird you have nothing to *get over*. There is nothing that detracts from the general effect; none of those disagreeable peculiarities and awkwardnesses in utterance, in gesture, in appearance, in mode of thought, which grievously detract from the pleasure with which we listen to many distinguished speakers till we get accustomed to them, and learn to forget their defects in their merits and beauties. He begins quietly, but in a manner which is full of earnestness and feeling; every word is touched with just the right kind and degree of emphasis; many single words, and many little sentences which when you recal them do not seem very remarkable, are given in tones which make them absolutely thrill through you: you feel that the preacher has in him the elements of a tragic actor who would rival Kean. The attention of the congregation is riveted; the silence is breathless; and as the speaker goes on gathering warmth till he becomes impassioned and impetuous, the tension of the nerves of the hearer becomes almost painful. There is abundant ornament in style—if you were cooler you might probably think some of it carried to the verge of good taste; there is a great amount and variety of the most expressive, apt, and seemingly unstudied gesticulation; it is rather as though you were listening to the impulsive Italian speaking from head to foot, than to the cool and unexcitable Scot. After two or three such climaxes, with pauses between, the preacher gathers himself up for his peroration, which, with the tact of the orator, he has made more striking, more touching, more impressive, than by any preceding portion of his discourse. He is wound up often to an excitement which is painful to see. The full deep voice, so beautifully expressive, already taxed to its utmost extent, breaks into something which is almost a shriek; the gesticulation becomes wild; the preacher, who has hitherto held himself to some degree in check, seems to abandon himself to the full tide of his emotion: you feel that not even his eloquent lips can do justice to the rush of thought and feeling within. Two or three minutes in this impassioned strain and the sermon is done. A few moments of startling silence; you look round the church; every one is bending forward with eyes intent upon the pulpit; then there is a general breath and stir. You think the sermon has been a very short one: you consult your watch—it has lasted three quarters of an hour.

Then follow a brief collect, a hymn, and the benediction; and you come away, having heard the great Scotch preacher. We may very fitly call him so; for except Dr. Guthrie and Mr. McLeod, there is no one whom the popular judgment of Scotland in general places near Mr. Caird. And though every district of Scotland and every town has its popular preacher—and though many congregations have each their own favourite clergyman whom they prefer to all others—

still the very best that the warmest admirers of other Scotch ministers can find to say of them is, that they are better than Mr. Caird. He is the Scotch Themistocles. Even those who would place another preacher first, place Mr. Caird second.

It is rarely indeed that we find such a remarkable combination in one individual of the qualities which go to make an effective pulpit orator. Mr. Caird's mind has the knack of producing the precise kind of thought which shall be at once worthy of the attention of the best educated and most refined, and effective when addressed to a mixed congregation. And *that* is the practical talent for the preacher, after all. No depth, originality, or power of thought, will make up in a sermon for the absence of general interest. No thought or style is good in the pulpit, which is tiresome. There is an insufferable but lofty order of thought, which you listen to with an effort, feel to be extremely fine, and cease listening to as soon as possible. John Foster, who scattered congregations, was beyond doubt an abler preacher than Mr. Caird ; but he *did* scatter congregations, and therefore he was not a good preacher, finely as his published discourses read. There are other preachers who attract crowds by preaching sermons which revolt every one who possesses good sense or good taste ; but in distinction alike from the good unpopular preacher and the bad popular preacher, Mr. Caird has the talent to produce at will an order of thought elevated enough to please the most cultivated, and interesting enough to attract the masses. He has a good foundation of metaphysical acumen and power; strong practical sense; then great powers in the way of happy and striking illustration; indeed, he traces analogies between the material and the spiritual with a felicity which reminds us of Archbishop Whately. Mr. Caird has also that invaluable gift of the orator —a capacity of intense feeling; he can throw his whole soul into what he says, with an emotion which is contagious. Further, he has a remarkably telling and expressive voice, and a highly effective dramatic manner. Add to all these qualifications that, from natural bent, fostered and encouraged by unequalled success from his first entering the church, he has devoted himself steadfastly to the single end of becoming a great and distinguished preacher. That end he has completely attained. For at least ten years he has held in Scotland the position which he now holds; and the fortunate incident of his preaching at Crathie extended his reputation beyond the limits of Scotland. Mr. Caird is certainly the most generally popular preacher in the Scotch Church, and he deserves his popularity. We cannot, of course, go into the question of mute inglorious Miltons, and of flowers born to blush unseen. It is possible enough that among the Cumberland hills, or in curacies like Sydney Smith's on Salisbury Plain, or wandering sadly by the shore of Shetland fiords, there may be men who have in them the makings of better preachers than Bishop Wilberforce, Mr. Melvill, Mr. McLeod, or Mr. Caird. Of course there may be Folletts that never held a brief, Angelos that never built St. Peter's, and Vandycks who never got beyond their sixpence a day. There may be, of course, and there may not be; and what *is known* must for practical purposes be taken for what *is*.

It may readily be supposed that the announcement of a forthcoming volume of sermons by so distinguished a preacher did not fail to excite much interest in the district where he is best known. Little Tom Eaves, who at different times has given Mr. Thackeray so much valuable information, assured us, on his return from a recent visit to Edinburgh, that the eminent publishers who have sent forth this volume, were content to give for its copyright a sum which, for a volume of sermons, was quite extraordinary—as much, in fact, as Sir Walter Scott received for *Marmion*. Mr. Caird's book is sure to have many readers. Many educated people in England will feel curious to know what sort of preaching is at a premium in the Scotch Church. And we think we have been able to trace one or two indications in the volume, that Mr. Caird had an English audience in view. On at least two occasions we find the word *Sunday* ('a *Sunday* meditation,' '*Sunday*-school teachers') where we are mistaken if most Scotch preachers would not have employed the word *Sabbath*, which is in almost universal use north of the

Tweed. But in Scotland, no doubt, Mr. Caird will find the great majority of his readers. Numbers of people who have listened to the fiery orator will be anxious to find whether the discourses which struck them so much when aided by the accessories of a wonderfully telling manner, will stand the severer test of a quiet perusal at home. So here is Mr. Caird's volume.

Here, then, we have the spent thunderbolts, motionless and cold. Here we have the locomotive engine, which tore along at sixty miles an hour, with the fire raked out and the steam gone down. Here, in short, we have the sermons of the great Scotch pulpit orator, stripped of the fire, the energy, the eloquent voice, the abundant gesticulation, which did so much to give them their charm when delivered and heard. There is but one story told as to the share which *manner* has always had in producing the practical effect which has been felt in listening to all great orators from Demosthenes to Chalmers. Manner has always been the first, second, and third thing; and Mr. Caird could not publish his manner. We can examine his sermons calmly, and make up our mind about their merits deliberately now. To do so was quite impossible while we were hurried away by the rushing eloquence of the living voice.

No doubt, then, this volume will disappoint the less intelligent class of Mr. Caird's admirers, who expect to be as deeply impressed in reading these discourses as they were in hearing them. No words standing quietly on the printed page can possibly have the effect of the same words spoken by the human voice, with immense feeling, and with all the arts of oratory. To expect that they should have an equal effect is to expect that the sword laid upon the table should cut as deeply as it did when grasped in a strong and skilful swordsman's hand. Mr. Caird's manner we know is a remarkably effective one; and of course the better the speaker's manner, the more his speech loses by being dissociated from it.

Still, after making every deduction, they are noble sermons; and we are not sure but that, with the cultivated reader, they will gain rather than lose by being read, not heard. There is a thoughtfulness and depth about them which can hardly be appreciated, unless when they are studied at leisure; and there are many sentences so felicitously expressed that we should grudge being hurried away from them by a rapid speaker, without being allowed to enjoy them a second time. And Mr. Caird, we feel as we read his pages, has succeeded in attaining a great end: he has shown that it is possible to produce sermons which shall be immensely popular, and popular with all classes of people; while yet all shall be so chaste and correct that the most fastidious taste could hardly take exception to a single word or phrase. In Mr. Caird's sermons there is nothing extravagant or eccentric either in thought or style. There is nothing unworthy of the clergyman and the scholar. There are no claptrap expedients to excite attention; nothing merely designed to make an audience gape; nothing that could possibly produce a titter. The solemnity of the house of God is never forgotten. Mr. Caird has no peculiar views, no special system of theology: he preaches the moderate and chastened Calvinism of the Church of Scotland,—precisely the doctrine of the Thirty-Nine Articles. He does not tell his hearers that the world is coming to an end; he finds nothing about Louis Napoleon in the Book of Revelation; he does not select queer texts, or out-of-the-way topics for discussion. It is no small matter to have proved in this age of pulpit drowsiness on the one hand, and pulpit extravagance on the other, that sound and temperate doctrine, logical accuracy, and classical language are quite compatible with great popularity. It is pleasant to find that discourses which are thoroughly manly and free from sentimentalism or cant prove attractive to a class which is too ready to run after such preachers as Mr. Charles Honeyman; and that sensible and judicious views, set forth in a style which is always scholarly and correct, and enforced by a manner in which there is no acting, howling, ventriloquizing, or gymnastic posturing, can hold vast crowds in a rapt attention, which would please even that slashing critic of the pulpit, *Habitans in Sicco.* Wide as the poles apart is such popularity as that of Mr. Caird from such popularity as that of

Mr. Spurgeon and his class. It is very often with contempt and indignation that people of sense and taste listen to 'popular preachers.' No doubt such preachers may be well fitted to please and even to profit the great multitude who have little sense and no taste at all; but it is a fresh and agreeable sensation to the reviewer when he discovers a man whose eminence as a preacher is the sequel to a brilliant career at the University; whose sermons indicate a mind stored with the fruits of extensive reading and study; who shrinks instinctively from whatever is coarse or grotesque; who abhors all clap-trap; who is perfectly simple and sincere without a trace of self-consciousness; in whose composition there is nothing spasmodic, nothing aiming to be subtle and succeeding in being unintelligible; and who seems, so far as it is possible to judge, to be actuated by an earnest desire to impress religious truth upon the minds of his hearers. And, indeed, when we think what is the great end of the preacher's endeavours, we feel that all mere literary qualities and graces are of no account whatever when compared with the presence of that efficacious element in the sermon which makes it such as that it shall be the means of saving souls. For ourselves, we should prefer a thousand times the magic spell which Miss Marsh (all honour to the name) exercised at Sydenham over *English Hearts*, to the church-crowding eloquence of Chalmers. And in that solemn sense, perhaps the greatest of all living preachers is the homely, pithy, earnest Mr. Ryle.

We confess that we do not think sermons, generally speaking, by any means attractive reading; and we have not read a sufficient number of them to be able to institute a comparison between the printed sermons of Mr. Caird and those of other distinguished preachers. Still, we may say that we do not find in Mr. Caird the originality of Mr. Melvill, or the talent of that eminent divine for eliciting from his text a great amount of striking and unexpected instruction. There is nothing of the daring ingenuity and the novel interpretations of Archbishop Whately. Mr. Caird will never found a school of disciples, like Dr. Arnold; nor startle steady-going old clergymen, like Mr. Robertson of Brighton. He is so clear and comprehensible that he will not, like Mr. Maurice, make many readers feel or fancy the presence of something very fine, if they could only be sure what the preacher would be at. He hardly sets a scene before us in such life-like reality as does Dr. Guthrie. And although people may go to hear him for the intellectual treat, they will never go to be amused, as by Mr. Spurgeon. He will never point a sentence at the expense of due solemnity, like a great Scotch preacher who contrasted men's profession and their practice by saying, 'Profession says, "On this hang the law and the prophets;" Practice says, "Hang the law and the prophets!"' He will not, like Mr. Cecil, arrest attention by beginning his sermon, 'A man was hanged this morning at Tyburn;' nor like Rowland Hill, by exclaiming 'Matches! matches! matches!'—nor like somebody or other, by saying as he wiped his face, 'It's damned hot!'—nor like Whitefield, by vociferating 'Fire! fire—in hell!' He will not imitate Sterne, who read out as his text, 'It is better to go to the house of mourning than to go to the house of feasting;' and then exclaimed, as the first words of his discourse, 'That I deny!'— making it appear in a little while that such was not the preacher's own sentiment, but what might be supposed to be the reflection of an irreligious man. He will never introduce into his discourses long dialogues and arguments between God and Satan, in which the latter is made to exhibit a deficiency in logical power which is, to say the least, remarkable in one who is believed not to lack intellect. He will not appear in the pulpit with his shirt-sleeves turned back over his cassock, in ball-room fashion; and after giving out his text, astonish the congregation by bellowing, 'Now, you young men there, listen to my sermon, and don't stare at my wrists!' All such arts for attracting or compelling interest and attention Mr. Caird eschews.

And when we read his sermons, though we feel their interest, we find it hard to say in what it lies. They are admirable sermons: but we should scarcely, *à priori*, have ventured to predict their vast popular effect. The finely-linked thought, the completeness and symmetry of the discussion, the beautifully appropriate illustrations, none stuck in for ornament, but all *bonâ fide* illustrating the subject; the general sobriety and good sense:—these are literary characteristics which we should say would prove hardly discernible, and certainly not appreciable, save by people of considerable cultivation. Must we, then, fall back upon Manner, and suppose that the charm which gives these sermons their popular effect lies in a great measure in the touching and thrilling tones, the tears in the voice, the enchaining earnestness, with which they are poured forth by an orator who, like Whitefield, could almost melt an audience to tears by saying *Mesopotamia*? Or may we not rather ask whether Mr. Caird, in his elaborate and fastidious preparation of these discourses for the press, has not cut out, or smoothed down, much which was most striking when the sermons were preached, but which might have appeared of doubtful taste when they were carefully and critically read over? Perhaps these sermons, while gaining in *finish* and perfection of literary construction, have lost some of the salient points, the roughness and raciness, which added to their piquancy when delivered. We have heard Mr. Caird preach two of those now published : and we find he has drawn his pen through several of those phrases which had stuck longest and most vividly in our memory. We think he has erred here. He has been over-cautious, over-fastidious. It is on the very borderland of good taste that the deepest popular impression is made : and there was no fear of Mr. Caird's crossing the border. And we believe that upon ordinary Sundays, by discourses of much less elaborate preparation, he produces even a greater effect upon his congregation than could be produced by any sermon in this volume, were it preached exactly as it is printed.

The published discourses are certainly very ambitious in thought and style. There is a want of repose in them; and when two or three are read successively, the effect upon the mind is a little wearisome. But no doubt they were written to be preached; and when they are listened to one at a time, and at intervals of a week, this result will not follow. It is well to have the attention riveted and the nerves tightened for half-an-hour in the week: but the process becomes painful when it lasts too long. We remark a little mannerism here and there. An extraordinary number of paragraphs begin with the word *Now* : and the term *yearning* is, we think, of much too frequent occurrence. The result of the abundant use of this word, and of the occasional heaping up of adjectives unconnected by any copulative, and of nearly the same meaning, is to leave an occasional impression of an excess of the *gushing* element. There is the least shade here and there of the cant of the present day about ' the response of our deepest nature,'—its 'instinctive throb,' and its 'instinctive yearnings,'—phrases which to plain folk mean just nothing at all. We confess that we do not like the word *fair* several times applied to the Almighty—'the alone Infinitely True and Holy and Fair.' The word suggests ideas which are not in harmony with so solemn an application of it. And as we are fault-finding at any rate, we may here state that in all the volume there is but a single passage which appears to us to be in glaringly and painfully bad taste : so much and so disagreeably so that we wonder that Mr. Caird should have published it. It is that passage in which heaven is described as a place—

Where, *heart to heart with God*, happy souls *revel* unsated, undazzled, in the Essential Element of Love.

The description appears to us most irreverent, and its entire strain most unbecoming. Mr. Spurgeon could hardly have said anything worse. We have drawn the pen through it in our copy, that our pleasure in reading the volume may not be interrupted by its jarring and irritating effect; and we trust that in the future editions which are sure to be wanted, Mr. Caird will strike the entire passage out. It is most unworthy of him.

We do not know whether Mr. Caird was accustomed to preach such sermons as those now published to his country congregation. There are many phrases and sentences in them which to rustics would be quite unintelligible. What could a ploughman make of the following question :—

What elements must we eliminate from suffering caused by sin in forming our ideal of suffering purity? (p. 171.)

But as we know that Madame Rachel, by her wonderfully expressive gesticulation, succeeded, while in Russia, in making her meaning intelligible to people who did not understand the language which she spoke, so Mr. Caird may have been able to get country folk to understand the general drift of sentences containing many words whose sense they did not know. And indeed the late Hugh Miller maintains that sermons which are in a considerable degree *over the heads* of a rural congregation, are the most likely both to interest and improve them.

By this time, we doubt not, our readers are impatient of our remarks, and would like to hear Mr. Caird speak for himself. We proceed to give a more specific account of the contents of the volume.

It contains eleven sermons, the fourth being divided into two parts, intended, we presume, to be preached at different times; and a glance at the Table of Contents at once makes us suspect that the sermons have, with a view to publication, been materially changed from what they were when they were preached. Sermons in Scotland, as in England, have a sort of average length, from which they do not deviate materially except on extraordinary occasions. But while Mr. Caird's first sermon occupies forty pages, the second occupies only twenty-five, the fourth twenty, and the fifth thirteen. The first sermon is thus three times as long as the fifth, and twice as long as the fourth. So if the fifth sermon be of the standard Scotch length of three quarters of an hour, the first would occupy in the delivery two hours and a quarter. Or if the first sermon is to be taken as the standard, the fifth would crumple up into the ' just fifteen minutes.'

The subject of the first sermon is *The Self-evidencing Nature of Divine Truth*; its text is, ' By manifestation of the truth commending ourselves to every man's conscience in the sight of God.' (2 Cor. iv. 2.) It is a scholarly and masterly production; but the thought which forms its staple is more severe than is usual in Mr. Caird's discourses. It is, in short, a view, set out with consummate tact and ingenuity, of the internal evidence of the truth of the Christian religion. We should ask university men and clergymen to read this sermon the first. They will find in it a strict and unerring logic, great skill in simplifying and illustrating abstract ideas, and a style which could scarcely be improved. But when we pass to the discourse which stands next in order we find much clearer indications of the power of the popular orator.

It is on *Self-Ignorance*; the text, ' Who can understand his errors.' (Psalm xix. 12.) We almost wonder in reading the former sermon how Mr. Caird can be so popular; but when we read this, more especially if we have heard Mr. Caird preach, and can imagine the fashion in which he would deliver many passages, we have less difficulty in understanding the matter. Here is the introduction, which would arrest attention at once:—

Of all kinds of **ignorance**, that which **is** the most strange, **and, in so far as** it is **voluntary, the** most culpable, **is** our ignorance **of self.** For not only is **the subject in** this case **that which** might be expected to possess **for us the greatest** interest, but it is the **one concerning which we have amplest facilities and** opportunities **of information.** Who of us would not think it a strange and unaccountable story, could it be told of any man now present, **that for years he** had **harboured under his** roof a guest whose face **he had never** seen—a constant inmate **of his** home, who was yet to him altogether unknown? It is no supposition, however, but unquestionable fact, that to not a few of us, from the first moment of existence there has been present, not beneath the roof, but within the breast, a mysterious resident, an inseparable companion, nearer to us than friend or brother, **yet of** whom after all we know little or nothing. What man of intelligence **amongst** us would not be ashamed **to** have had in his possession for **years some** rare or universally admired **volume** with its leaves uncut? **or to be the** proprietor of a repository filled with the most exquisite productions of genius, and the rarest specimens in science and art, **which yet he** himself never thought of entering? Yet surely no **book so worthy of perusal,** no chamber containing objects of study **so curious, so replete with interest** for us, as that which seldom or never attracts our observation—the **book,** the chamber of our **own hearts.** We sometimes reproach with folly those persons who have travelled far and seen much of distant countries, and yet have been content to remain comparatively unacquainted with their own. But how venial such folly compared with **that of** ranging over all other departments of knowledge, going abroad **with** perpetual inquisitiveness over earth and sea and sky, whilst there is a little world within the breast which is still to us an unexplored region. Other scenes and objects we can study only at intervals: they are not always accessible, or can be reached only by long and laborious journeys; but the bridge of consciousness is soon crossed—we have but to close the eye and withdraw .**the** thoughts from **the world** without in order at any moment to **wander** through **the** scenes **and** explore the phenomena of **the still more** wondrous **world** within. To examine other objects delicate and elaborate instruments are often necessary: the researches of the astronomer, the botanist, the chemist, can be prosecuted only by means of rare and costly apparatus; but the power of reflection, that faculty more wondrous than any mechanism which art has ever fashioned, is an instrument possessed by all—the poorest and most illiterate alike with the most cultured and refined have at their command an apparatus by which to sweep the inner firmament of the soul, and bring into view its manifold phenomena of thought and feeling and motive. And yet with all the unequalled facilities for acquiring this sort of knowledge, can it be questioned that it is the one sort of knowledge that is most commonly neglected, and that, even amongst those who would disdain the imputation of ignorance in history or science or literature, there are multitudes who have never acquired the merest rudiments of the knowledge of self?

By no means a far-fetched or difficult idea, the reader must see; and turned in many lights and brought out by a throng of illustrations; but a good and natural introduction to a sermon on self-ignorance, and quite sure, if given with a sort of *extempore* air, as if each successive comparison struck the speaker just at the moment, to get the people to listen with great stillness.

Then, restricting his view to the matter of a man's moral defects, Mr. Caird goes on to point out several reasons why the sinful man does not 'understand his errors.' The first is, that sin can be truly measured only when it is resisted. This principle indeed holds good of all forces:—

The rapid stream flows smooth and silent when there are no obstacles to stay its progress; but hurl a rock into its bed, and the roar and surge of the arrested current will instantly reveal its force. You cannot estimate the wind's strength when it rushes over the open plain; but when it reaches and wrestles with the trees of the forest, or lashes the sea into fury, then, resisted, you perceive its power. Or if, amid the ice-bound regions of the north, an altogether unbroken continuous winter prevailed, comparatively unnoticed would be its stern dominion; but it is the coming round of a more genial season, when the counteracting agency of the sun begins to prevail, that reveals, by the rending of the solid masses of ice, and by the universal stir and crash, the intensity of the bygone winter's cold.

The second reason is, that sin often makes a man afraid to know himself. The third, that sinful habits steal on men slowly and gradually. The fourth, that as character gradually deteriorates, there is a parallel deterioration of the standard by which we judge it. Such are the 'heads' of the sermon, as they are called in Scotland. They are all very clearly brought out and abundantly illustrated, and the sermon ends with a stirring 'practical application:'

It is possible now to seek the peace of self-forgetfulness,—to refuse to be disturbed,—to sink for a little longer into our dream of self-satisfaction; but it is a peace as transient as it is unreal. Soon, at the latest, and all the more terrible for the delay, the awakening must come. There are sometimes sad awakenings from sleep in this world. It is very sad to dream by night of vanished joys,—to revisit old scenes, and dwell once more among the unforgotten forms of our loved and lost,— to see in the dreamland the old familiar look, and hear the well-remembered tones of a voice long hushed and still, and then to wake with the morning light to the aching sense of our loneliness again. It were very sad for the poor criminal to wake from sweet dreams of other and happier days—days of innocence and hope, and peace, when kind friends, and a happy home, and an honoured or unstained name were his—to wake in his cell on the morning of his execution to the horrible recollection that all this is gone for ever, and that to-day he must die a felon's death. But inconceivably more awful than any awakening which earthly day-break has ever brought, shall be the awakening of the self-deluded soul when it is roused in horror and surprise from the dream of life—to meet Almighty God in judgment!

Of course all this has been very often said before: but probably those who heard Mr. Caird declaim these sentences, thought that it had never before been said so forcibly.

The third sermon is upon *Spiritual Influence*. Its text is that passage in the Saviour's speech to Nicodemus, 'The wind bloweth where it listeth,' &c. (S. John iii. 7, 8.) Here the preacher argues in defence of the Christian doctrine of Regeneration, maintaining that whatever difficulties surround that doctrine have their parallel in Nature. The 'heads' here are three. The analogy between Nature and Revelation is traced in regard to *Supernaturalness*, *Sovereignty*, or *apparent Arbitrariness*, and *Secrecy*. The gist of the first head is given in a sentence towards its close:—

> If not the slightest movement of matter can take place without the immediate agency of God, shall we wonder that His agency is needed in the higher and more subtle processes of mind?

The burden of the second head is given thus:—

> Marvel not nor be disquieted at your inability to explain the laws that regulate the operations of an infinite agent; for in a province much more within the range of human observation there are familiar agents at work, the operations of which are equally inscrutable, arbitrary, incalculable. Think it not strange that the ways of the Spirit of God are unaccountable to a mind by which even the common phenomena of the wind are irreducible to law.

Then, under the third division of the discourse, Mr. Caird shows that the fact that the Holy Spirit works unseen is no reason for doubting that he does really act:—

As you have surveyed the face of nature in some tranquil season—the unbreathing summer noon or the hushed twilight hour—every feature of the landscape has seemed suffused with calmness, every tree hung its motionless head, every unrippled brook crept on with almost inaudible murmuring, every plant, and flower, and leaf seemed as if bathed in repose. But anon you perhaps perceived a change passing over the scene, as if at the bidding of some invisible power;—a rushing sound, as of music evoked by invisible fingers from the harp of nature, began to fill your ear; the leaves began to quiver and rustle; the trees to bend and shake, the stream to dash onward with ruffled breast and brawling sound, and from every wood, and glade, and glen there came forth the intimation that a new and most potent agent was abroad and working around you. And yet while you marked the change on the face of nature, did you perceive the agent that effected it? Did the wind of heaven take visible form and appear as a winged messenger of God's will, hurrying hither and thither from object to object? Do you know and can you describe the way in which he worked,—how his touch fell upon the floweret and bade it wave, or his grasp seized the sturdy oak and strove with it till it quivered and bent? No, you cannot. You have not penetrated so far into the secrets of nature. You have seen only the effects, but not the agent or the process of his working. You have seen the wind's influences, but not itself. But do you therefore marvel, or hesitate to believe, that it has indeed been abroad and working over the face of the earth? or do you ever doubt whether there be any such agent as the wind at all? No; you have heard the sound thereof, you have witnessed the stir and commotion of nature that told of its presence, and so you believe in its existence, though you ' cannot tell whence it cometh or whither it goeth.'

The three ' heads ' having been illustrated, the sermon is wound up by various practical inferences, given at considerable length.

The fourth sermon is from the text, ' No man hath seen God at any time; the only-begotten Son, which is in the bosom of the Father, He hath declared him.' (S. John i. 18.) It is divided into two parts, the subject of the former being, *The Invisible God*, and that of the latter *The Manifestation of the Invisible God*. The preacher, having dwelt upon the fact that God is invisible to human eyes, and shown that not without destroying the character of our present state of being as a state of trial and training could the case be otherwise; goes on to show that the Saviour, by his person, his life and character, his sufferings and death, is a visible manifestation of the invisible God.

We believe that this sermon, when preached, was a very effective one; and probably the view which it sets out struck many ordinary hearers as novel and original. It is not, however, necessary to tell the well-informed reader that Mr. Caird has here done nothing more than present, in a somewhat more popular and rhetorical form, the substance of a sermon upon the same text, by Archbishop Whately, which, being detached from its text, is now published in the first series of the Archbishop's Essays.* The reader will find it interesting to do what we have done since writing the last sentence,—to peruse the two sermons together, and compare them. The Archbishop's sermon was addressed to a learned audience: it was preached before the University of Oxford; and accordingly it is the more critical and

---

* *Essays on some of the Peculiarities of the Christian Religion.* Essay II. 'On the Declaration of God in His Son,' pp. 98-118. Edition of 1856.

philosophical. Mr. Caird intended his sermon to be preached to ordinary congregations; and accordingly he quotes no Greek, and lengthens out his remarks upon those parts of his subject which most admit of popular illustration. Some observations early in the discourse, on the Invisibility of the Almighty, appear to have been suggested by Letter VI. in Foster's Essay *On a Man's writing Memoirs of Himself*, in which that topic is discussed with a power unparalleled in theological literature. And whoever wishes to find *The Manifestation of the Invisible God* through the personal Redeemer set out in a very interesting fashion, may find it in the first two chapters of a book of so popular a character as Jacob Abbott's *Corner-Stone*. The view taken by Abbott is precisely that of Archbishop Whately, as may be inferred from the motto prefixed to the first chapter, which is, ' The glory of God in the face of Jesus Christ.' It does not appear, however, that Abbott was acquainted with the Archbishop's discourse.

Although we cannot give Mr. Caird the credit of having thought out the idea which is pressed in this sermon, still he is entitled to the praise of having grasped it with great force, and of having set it forth in a discourse which would produce a strong popular effect. It must be said, however, that the style of this sermon is ambitious to a somewhat extravagant degree; in taste and accuracy it is very inferior to several of the other sermons in the volume. We should judge it to have been a comparatively juvenile production, which its author has got so fond of that he cannot now try it by the same severe standard as his recent compositions. And we are not sure if the phrase, *a woe that Deity could feel*, contains very sound theology. Deity can feel nothing like woe.

The sermon which comes next is, we think, one of the most eloquent in the book : it contains, perhaps, finer passages than any other. And although it is highly wrought up in several parts, there is not a word in it to which the severest critic could take exception. It is on *The Solitariness of Christ's Sufferings*: the text, 'I have trodden the wine-press alone.' It sets out with the following beautiful and natural introduction :—

> There is always a certain degree of solitude about a great mind. Even a mere human being cannot rise pre-eminently above the level of his fellow-men without becoming conscious of a certain solitariness of spirit gathering round him. The loftiest intellectual elevation, indeed, is nowise inconsistent with a genial openness and simplicity of nature, nor is there anything impossible or unexampled in the combination of a grasp of intellect that could cope with the loftiest abstractions of philosophy, and a playfulness that could condescend to sport with a child. Yet whilst it is thus true that the possessor of a great mind may be capable of sympathising with, of entering kindly into the views and feelings, the joys and sorrows of inferior minds, it must at the same time be admitted that there is ever a range of thought and feeling into which they cannot enter with him. They may accompany him, so to speak, a certain height up the mountain, but there is a point at which their feebler powers become exhausted, and if he ascend beyond that, his path must be a solitary one.
>
> What is thus true of all great minds must have been, beyond all others, characteristic of the mind of Him who, with all his real and

very humanity, could 'think it no robbery to be equal with God.' Jesus was indeed a lonely being in the world. With all the exquisite tenderness of his human sympathies—touched with the feeling of our every sinless infirmity—with a heart that could feel for a peasant's sorrow, and an eye that could beam with tenderness on an infant's face—he was yet one who, wherever he went, and by whomsoever surrounded, was, in the secrecy of his inner being, profoundly *alone*. You who are parents have, I dare say, often felt struck by the reflection, what a world of thoughts, and cares, and anxieties are constantly present to *your* minds into which your children cannot enter. You may be continually amongst them, holding familiar intercourse with them, condescending to all their childish thoughts and feelings, entering into all their childish ways—yet every day there are a thousand things passing through your mind, with respect, for instance, to your business or profession, your schemes and projects, your troubles, fears, hopes and ambitions in life, your social connexions, the incidents and events that are going on in the world around you,—there are a thousand reflections and feelings on such matters passing daily through your mind, of which your children know nothing. You never dream of talking to them on such subjects, and they could not understand or sympathise with you if you did. There is a little world in which the play of their passions is strong and vivid, but beyond that their sympathies entirely fail. And perhaps there is no spectacle so exquisitely touching as that which one sometimes witnesses in a house of mourning—the elder members of the family bowed down to the dust by some heavy sorrow, whilst the little children sport around in unconscious playfulness.

The bearing of this illustration is obvious. What children are to the mature-minded man, the rest of mankind were to Jesus.

The preacher goes on to say that he intends to follow out the thought of Christ's solitariness, with particular reference to his *sorrows*. And he does so with eloquence so impressive that we regret we can find room for no further specimens of it.

We have not space to do more than mention the subjects of the remaining sermons which make up the volume. The sermon which follows that on *The Solitariness of Christ's Sufferings*, is a sort of companion piece, on the text 'Rejoice, inasmuch as ye are partakers of the sufferings of Christ.' (1 Peter iv. 13.) There is a discourse on *Spiritual Rest* which we think less happy; a very able one on the text 'I wish that thou mayest prosper and be in health even as thy soul prospereth' (3 John 2); another admirable sermon on 'All things are yours,' which Mr. Caird preached before the Queen last autumn. There is a temperate and judicious sermon on *The Simplicity of Christian Ritual*, in which the author cautions us against attaching too much consequence to such things as church architecture and stately church services. At the same time Mr. Caird describes these perilous delights with such manifest gusto, that it is quite obvious he would have no serious objections to the cathedral worship and to York Minster. It is indeed quite true that—

> There is a semi-sensuous delight in religious worship imposingly conducted which may be felt by the least conscientious even more than by the sincerely devout. The soul that is devoid of true reverence towards God may be rapt into a spurious elation while in rich and solemn tones the loud-voiced organ peals forth his praise. The heart that never felt one throb of love to Christ may thrill with an ecstacy of sentimental tenderness while soft voices, now blending, now dividing, in combined or responsive strains, celebrate the glories of redeeming love. And not seldom the most sensual and profligate of men have owned to that strange, undefined, yet delicious feeling of awe and elevation that steals over the spirit in some fair adorned temple on which all the resources of art have been lavished, where soft light floods the air and mystic shadows play over pillar and arch and vaulted

roof, and the hushed and solemn stillness is broken only by the voice of prayer or praise.

All quite true; but though no doubt such feeling as Mr. Caird describes is not religion, it may prepare the way for receiving impressions which are properly religious. Nor can we evade the grand principle, that we ought to consecrate to the Almighty our very best in architecture and in melody as in everything else, by the reflection that such things, like all others in this world, may be abused. And, by the way, Mr. Caird appears to have forgotten to tell his hearers that if worshippers in the south may mistake their æsthetic enjoyment of beautiful church-worship for true devotion, there is at least as much risk that worshippers farther north may confuse their enjoyment of the intellectual treat of listening to impassioned and brilliant pulpit-oratory with a real reception of the great truths which are in such oratory set forth. If Anglicans must smash their stained-glass, board over their vaulted roofs, and turn off their cathedral choristers, then ought Mr. Caird to cut out his imagery, to destroy the rhythm of the last sentences of his paragraphs, and to cultivate a chronic sore-throat. If it be right for a clergyman to labour day and night to make his sermon beautiful, why not his church as well? And if the church must be only moderately beautiful, then the preaching must not be obtrusively so. Does Mr. Caird mean to insinuate a covert assurance, that however pleasing and admirable his discourses may be, he could, were it not for fear of exciting æsthetic emotion, make them a great deal better?

The last sermon in the volume is on *The Comparative Influence of* **Character** *and Doctrine.* The text is 'Take heed unto thyself and unto the doctrine.' (1 Tim. iv. 16.) And Mr. Caird, not perhaps with very critical accuracy, maintains that St. Paul in writing that text, placed the two matters to be attended to in the order of their importance: thus signifying that the life was of more moment than the instruction; that it was the preacher's duty to take heed, first to himself, and secondly, to his doctrine. Whether the **general** principle be implied in the text or not, there is no doubt it is a **sound one** : and the sermon enforces the old story, that example is better than precept, with extraordinary ability and eloquence.

Thus have we endeavoured, as regards these discourses of Mr. Caird, to do what we used to do every Sunday evening when we were children **at** home : to wit, to 'give an account of the sermons.' It was rather wearisome work then, we remember; we **trust** our readers have not found it so now. Let us add, that **fine as** are these published sermons, we are not sure that they are **Mr.** Caird's **best.** Authors are proverbially bad judges of their own productions, and preachers are no exceptions to the rule. And we have heard **from some** of the author's warm admirers fond recollections of sermons on the texts, *Every man shall bear his own burden,* **Surely** *I come quickly,* **There** *shall be no more pain,* **All** *things are become new,* *They have Moses and the prophets, let them hear them,*—which are said to contain passages which for telling effect upon a congregation are not equalled by anything in the printed volume. Perhaps the great preacher thought it as well not to give his followers the opportunity of examining the red-hot shot after it had grown cold.

An amusing proof of Mr. Caird's great popularity is afforded by the number of young preachers in Scotland who try to imitate him. And indeed it cannot be denied that several have succeeded in brushing their hair very like him. Others can walk up the pulpit-stair very much as Mr. Caird does so. Several have a happy knack of wiping their face like him at the close of each ' head,' and more have successfully imitated some tones of his voice, and the manner in which he pronounces certain words which he pronounces ill. The general impression left on the mind by any imitator of Mr. Caird, is that of a very fat goose attempting to fly like an eagle. It may be supposed that only the weakest of the aspirants to the clerical office will join the class of direct imitators. But Mr. Caird's success has had a powerful influence upon young men of a higher stamp, in leading them to cultivate a highly animated and impassioned kind of pulpit oratory. The calm, unexciting elegance of a former age is at a discount in the North. Dr. Blair would preach to empty benches now. And it must be admitted that the standard of Scotch preaching is at this time a very high one. The sermon is so completely the great thing in the Scotch service, that extraordinary labour is often spent upon it. Poor as is the worldly remuneration of the Scotch clergy, it is wonderful how the most able and accomplished students in the Universities of Scotland are found to devote themselves to that ill-paid ministry. A, who was first all through the classes, goes into the church, fills several important charges with great ability, and dies at the age of fifty, worn down by labour and excitement, an Edinburgh minister with six hundred a year. B, whom he easily beat in every competition, goes to the Scotch bar, does pretty fairly, is made (by the Whigs) a judge, draws his three or four thousand *per annum*, and by judiciously husbanding his bodily and mental energies, is able to adorn that high station to the age of eighty-six. In six months after A dies, the crowds he thrilled by his eloquence have entirely forgotten him. Yet possibly the work he did is remembered somewhere : and crowds of clever young lads in the academic shades of Edinburgh and Glasgow aim rather to be A than B.

A great deal has of late been said and written about preaching. It seems to be agreed on all hands that it will no longer do to have sermons such that people cannot listen to them. Assuming sound instruction as present in all sermons, the highest of all remaining qualities of the sermon is *interest*. Whatever literary characteristics tend to make a sermon *interesting*, are good ; and the very highest, if they make it uninteresting, are bad. Yet how great a proportion of the sermons one hears—however deserving in other respects—are utterly devoid of the grand quality, interest. The sermons are able, well-thought, and well-written compositions, but they are very *dry*. Yet Sydney Smith's saying of literature in general holds especially good of pulpit literature ; that every style is good, *except the tiresome*. We believe that church is the only place where people do not listen to what is said to them. 'I like so much,' said the labouring man in Southey's *Doctor*, ' to go to church on Sunday : when the sermon begins I lean back in the corner, and lay up my legs, and *think of nothing*.' We sympathise with that poor man. It is the clergyman's business to make his sermon such that while it is going on no one shall be able to ' think of nothing.'

There are two things which from our earliest youth have in our mind stood out together as equally desirable, and in the nature of things equally impossible. The one is, to bring matters to such a point that it shall be possible to get out of our snug warm bed on a cold winter morning without a very great effort ; the other is, that the service of the Church should be made such that it shall not be tiresome to be present at it. We believe that in the case of men in general the most insufferably tedious and wearisome hours they have **ever** spent, have been many of those which they have spent at church.

As to the prayers of the Anglican ritual, no doubt they are very beautiful, though with a calm scholarly beauty which **makes no** impression upon children or uneducated people. There are likewise by far too many of them; and we are persuaded that if the truth were told, most of our readers have experienced **that** sense of relief we used to feel in our youth, **when our** worthy pastor and master of those days reached that prayer of St. Chrysostom which signified that the long service was nearly over. **We** are not going to say anything of the devotional part of the Church service; because we fear that no beauty and no brevity will ever **make that** portion of it interesting except to the sincerely devout; and there we must leave the matter. But there **is** another part of the usual public worship which we really think need not be so horribly tedious as it is in most cases—we mean the sermon. **When** Edward Irving published a volume of discourses, instead of designating them by the usual name of sermons, he preferred to describe them on his title-page as *Orations*; mentioning as his reason the well-ascertained fact, that there is something in the very name of *sermon* that makes people grow sleepy, and that suggests dulness, yawning, and tediousness to the last degree.

We quite believe that in the nature of things it is properly impossible to render serious instruction as interesting as light amusement. Disguise it as we can, work will never be made so attractive as play. Boys are instantly aware when it is intended to benefit them under the pretext of amusing them; and the revulsion is instant and complete. When Dr. Chalmers said that the thing which above all others has tended to make *Robinson Crusoe* such a favourite book with boys is, that no book combines to such a degree instruction with amusement, he made a statement just as absurd and false as if he had said that black was white. But while we admit all this, we believe that the pill may be gilded so far, and that sermons need not be nauseous as medicines are, and never to be listened to but by a conscious effort and as an irksome task.

He would be a benefactor of his race who should succeed in laying down a code of rules, by obeying which, men of ordinary ability might succeed in preparing and preaching sermons, which should be interesting to an ordinary congregation, and at the same time characterized by good sense and good taste. These two ends have hardly ever been attained together. There are numbers of sensible and correct preachers, whom no one can listen to for ten minutes without becoming aware of that peculiar pricking of the veins, and disposition to fidget uneasily, which are associated with the last degree of weariness. There is really such a thing as *acute* tediousness. And of the much smaller number of pulpit orators who succeed systematically in keeping the attention of their congregations thoroughly alive from the beginning to the end of their discourses, most, if not all, deal to a great degree in what may be termed clap-trap. Their sermons are often outrageously revolting to men of refined taste, or filled with views which are extravagant and absurd.

It is a great end to get an entire congregation to listen with interested attention from first to last of a sermon; but this end may be attained at too considerable an expense. One can easily think of various expedients that would for a time attract a crowd, and get it to gaze stupidly for an hour. A person from America preached some time since in some dissenting meeting-house in this country, arrayed in skins and feathers as an Indian chief. He was described as a war-chief, of the Somethingorotherawaws; and vast crowds, with visions of scalping-knives and wampum-belts, came to hear him, till it was understood that he was only a porter at a steamboat wharf on the Mississippi, and that his strange attire would have excited much more surprise in his native place than it did at Manchester. A small boy of nine or ten years old was advertised to preach in a large building in Glasgow; and to the disgrace of that town some three or four thousand people crowded to hear him on more occasions than one. An individual calling himself the Angel Gabriel, held large assemblages of the

Modern Athenians in breathless attention by preaching with a trumpet in his hand, which he sounded at the end of each paragraph of his sermon. The usual tedium of a church would be dissipated were the officiating clergyman to turn a somersault at intervals. Any wretched mountebank may keep attention alive by shrieks and yells, rushings about his platform, imitations of the Yankee snuffle or the gibberish of Cockayne—in short, by degrading the pulpit beneath the level of the stage of a minor theatre. But the question is, how may a man, without sinking the clergyman, the scholar, and the gentleman—without becoming a buffoon or a melodramatic actor—without eccentricity in the choice of texts and topics, in illustration or gesture—make a sermon as interesting and attractive as in the nature of things religious instruction can be made.

There is one obvious rule which is very generally violated: a preacher should take some pains to make his meaning intelligible. Many a clergyman who would not think of giving orders to his man-servant in terms which that person could not by possibility understand, is yet accustomed every Sunday to address a rustic congregation in discourses which would be just as intelligible *to it* if they were preached in Hebrew. Let a preacher be direct and straightforward: let him avoid roundabout sentences; they are much more puzzling to the dull brain of a country bumpkin than are mere big words: let him put his meaning sharply and clearly. We believe that this is a great secret of interest. We might suggest the abundant use of illustration *which really illustrates* the subject; but every preacher has not the faculty which enables him to use this arm. Comparisons drawn from daily life are a tower of force. And we strongly recommend to all young clergymen whose pulpit manner is not yet hopelessly formed, the reading of a good deal of light literature. They should read *that* to see what kind of matter interests the majority of minds. Most preachers have a thoroughly mistaken notion on that point. A man who has brought himself to feel a deep interest in dry tomes of old Theology, or even in the more flimsy popular theological literature of the day, forgets that the human race in general takes no interest in such things; and fancies that when producing thought which he knows or thinks would interest *himself*, he is all right. He is far mistaken! Who reads Theology by choice? Ask the publisher of ordinary sermons. Let the preacher, then, make himself familiar with the kind of thought and style which people read because attracted and interested by it. We do not say that he should take that for his model, or imitate it in any way. But let him see there what sort of *pabulum* suits the common appetite; and let him aim at making his sermons if possible as easy and pleasant to be listened to as *that* is to be read. We believe that the main cause why sermons are so dull is that their writers do not seriously set it as a worthy aim to make them interesting. Most preachers—if we except those whose end is simply to cover their paper with the least possible trouble—aim at completeness of treatment, at elegance of style, at scholarly tone and finish,—all ends quite apart from the great end of *interest*. If interest were systematically made the great object of endeavour; if clergymen remembered that unless they get their congregation to listen to them, they might as well not preach at all,—we are convinced, with average talent and average industry on the preacher's part, there would be fewer dry sermons and fewer sleepers in church.

CHAPTER XII.

AT THE LAND'S END.

JUST a quarter of an hour ago, an aged man, the most intelligent and pleasant of ostlers, zealous in Methodism, and skilled in the characteristics of horses, said to the present writer, 'Stand on that rock.' And as he said the words, he pointed to a little flat expanse of granite, three or four feet square. The present writer obeyed. And then the aged and intelligent man added, emphatically and solemnly, 'Now, sir, you are standing on THE LAND'S HEND.'

When I used continually to read the life of that great and good man, Dr. Arnold (to whom, and to whose biographer, many thousands of human beings owe some of the most healthful influence that ever went to ameliorate their heart and life), I remember thinking, a good many times, that one subject in a list of subjects for English verses to be prescribed to the boys of the sixth class, was a most suggestive one. It was, as the intelligent reader has anticipated, *The Land's End.*

One had a vague idea, that a great many fine things were to be said upon that subject. But if I ever thought what they were, I am sorry to say that they have quite vanished from remembrance now. At present, I can only look and feel, in a very confused fashion. For this is the Land's End. Here I am, on the extreme verge of England: this paper is laid on a rough granite rock, in a little recess which keeps off the wind. All this little headland is granite, shattered and splintered as if by lightning. The granite is in many places covered with lichens: and here and there a bright sprig of heather looks out from a little nook in which it has been able to root itself. The sea is roaring eighty feet below. Eighty feet make all the elevation: of course the mere height is very poor when compared with that of many bits of the Scotch coast. The descent to the sea is perpendicular: the sea below is not deep just at this point. Out, a mile and a half, from shore, you might see the Longships Rocks: detached islets rising in a line, very sharply out of the sea; and running up almost into spires. On one of them is a lighthouse. Three men live in it. A few years ago, a young man who had been absent from his family for twelve years, came back to visit his old home hard by. His father was one of the keepers of the lighthouse; and as it was his turn to take charge of the lights that month, he could not come ashore to see his son till a few days should pass. The morning after the son's arrival, it was too stormy to go out to the lighthouse to visit his father: and he came to this spot, to have as near a view as might be of the place where his father was. He fell over the rocks, and was killed. It is a touching story.

Off on the right, at three miles' distance, is a black-looking promontory, called Cape Cornwall. When you visit the place, my reader, the old man will tell you it is the only cape in England. There are heads: there are points: there is a ness: but there is no other cape. You would think that Cape Cornwall reaches into the sea farther than the Land's End itself: but your eye deceives you. It falls short of its more famous neighbour by several hundred yards. Looking down from this recess, you may see a number of rocks, greater and less, rising out of the sea: each with a ring of white foam at its base. Far out, you may just trace the outline of Scilly: for the day is not very clear.

When you come to this spot, my friend, you will have all the sights shown you by that most intelligent old man already mentioned: that is, of course, if he and you are spared to meet. You will see, very near the End, the deep marks of a horse's hoofs in the turf, within two feet of the verge. A very silly person (he will tell you) once made a bet that he would ride on horseback to the Land's End: meaning to the very extremity of the little rocky headland.

He forced his horse down the steep and rugged descent from the heathery plateau above, and upon the neck of turf-covered rock that joins the headland to the shore. But when the horse reached this slippery neck, he testified how much more sense he had than the man who rode him, by refusing to go any farther. The rider goaded him with whip and spur: and slipping upon the short turf, the poor creature fell; and clung by his forefeet in the marks you see before making the awful plunge below. The fall was not into water, but upon sharp rocks; and the poor horse miserably perished. I lamented the horse's fate: and I could not but conclude that had his master been smashed instead of himself, relative justice would have been done. It is fifty-five years since the horse's hoofs clung to that last hope: but the deep marks have been diligently kept clear, and they remain as when the horse was wickedly killed: serving as a monument of his sad fate, and a memorial of his owner's common sense, and regard for the life of his beast. After standing on the rocky table which is emphatically styled the HEND, you will clamber down a rough path; and lie down at all your length on a very overhanging crag. Here your head will project much over the sea; and the intelligent old man will keep a tight hold of your feet. And now, looking away to the right, you will discern the reason why you were brought to this precarious position. You will see that the rocky neck joining the End to the shore, is penetrated clear through by a lofty Gothic arch, through which the waves fret in foam. You will be told of another lesser arch, which you cannot see. These have been worn in the lapse of ages: and some day, if the world stands, the superincumbent rock will fall, and the Land's End will become a little rocky islet. You can see many traces in the rocks near, of the like having happened before. Doubtless the Cornwall coast once reached at least as far seaward as those Longships Rocks. And coming up from this spot, you will reach the neck once more: and here the old man (skilful ostler and zealous Methodist), if he thinks you a fit person so to distinguish; if he sees you are a man or a woman who can sympathize with him and understand him; will point with reverence to a square block of granite that looks through the turf: and tell you that a good man whose memory *he* holds very dear, and whose memory can be indifferent to no human being who reverences simple-hearted devotion to the best good of his fellow-creatures, has been before you here. 'John Wesley stood on that stone, and made verses of poetry,' said the old man to me: and I am glad to say that he then went on, with much simple solemnity, to repeat the verses from end to end. I doubt not you know them. They are the verses in which the good man tells us how, standing physically 'between two seas:' standing on this narrow neck with the Atlantic chafing on either hand beneath ; he remembered that he, and every human being with him, stands morally and spiritually between two oceans more solemn than that ; and prayed humbly that the pilgrimage might end well for all. The writer is a churchman : churchman both by head and by heart : but when he heard again the simple lines (which he confesses struck him as extremely poor when tried by merely æsthetic rules), he could not but stand reverentially on the stone where Wesley's feet had stood ; and think of the old man, with his white hair, his kindly face, his warm heart, and his beautifully starched bands; and heartily ask, in a fashion very familiar to us all, for more of Wesley's single-minded spirit.

And now I have sent the old man away, thanking him very much for the intelligent and interesting way in which he told his story : and I wait here by myself. I have written these lines which you have read, since he departed. At a spot like this, a party of visitors along with you is fatal to your feeling the genius of the place : and after the most intelligent guide has told you all he can tell, it is a relief to get rid of him. I want to feel that I am here. And first, I am aware that I am not disappointed. I went many miles round to-day to see the Logan Rock. The Logan Rock is an imposition. It is a delusion and a snare. You are told it is a mass of granite weighing eighty tons : and that it is so balanced by nature on a pivot of stone, that a touch from the hand can make it rock back and forward. To rock back and forward is apparently an idea conveyed in Cornish speech by the verb *to log*; and the Rock, though its name be spelled as above, is called the *Loggin Rock*, to describe its nature. You drive or walk ten miles from Penzance, by fearfully steep roads the last miles, till you come to a very dirty little village at the top of a hill. I have seldom seen more squalid cottages. I wish I knew the name of the proprietor of the estate on which they are built. A man, who has been lounging about on the road to the village, approaches as you stop at the door of the neat little inn; and the driver of the vehicle which has borne you from Penzance introduces him as your guide. You follow him along a well-defined path, through fields of ripening grain, for about half-a-mile. Then you come upon a rocky height, from which you discern the sea below you on two sides, within two hundred yards. You can indistinctly trace the outline of the walls of an ancient fortress upon that rocky height. Then you scramble down upon a little isthmus, as at the Land's End: the isthmus spreads into a little headland, made of huge blocks of granite. On either hand below you can see a beach of silvery white sand. As you are scrambling down the descent to the isthmus, you observe a man leisurely walking up the opposite ascent: and you become aware of the extent to which the division of labour is carried in that little Cornish village. One man is your guide to the Rock: his business is to conduct you along a path you could not possibly miss, even without a guide. A second man waits your arrival at the Rock: his business is to give it a push with his shoulder, and set it *loggin*. The Rock is a large mass, which may possibly weigh eighty tons : it certainly does not look as if it did. It lies on the landward slope of the headland which you reach by the isthmus. And when the man puts his shoulder to it, and gives it a push, you may, if you shut one eye, and look very sharply with the other, see the rock move a distance of perhaps one inch : possibly two. Let me strongly advise the reader to spare himself the trouble of going to see that sight.

But sitting on a rock at the Land's End, you will not feel disappointed. The interest here is not the factitious one of seeing a large stone moved an inch or two. It is the interest of looking at a wild piece of rocky coast, round whose name there clusters a crowd of associations. How familiar the name is : how often, when a child, you pointed this place out on the map : how many times you have wondered what it would be like ; and wondered if you would ever see it ! A quarter of a mile out to sea, just below, there is a black-looking rock : on that rock at this minute there are sitting twelve cormorants. Now and then one of them skims off over the sea. The day has become overcast : there is not a soul near. You cannot help having an eerie kind of feeling. You think it wonderful to find yourself here.

Sitting here, I think of a passage in the works of the most pleasing of English essayists, whom the writer is so happy as to call his friend. You will find the passage in *Friends in Council*. In it, mention is made of an old lady, who firmly believed that three pounds given by her were equal to about five pound ten given by anybody else. Her money had cost so much thought and so much rigid saving to get it together. Sixpence by sixpence had been got together through patient self-denial: each separate shilling had formed the matter of long consideration. And the old lady felt it hard that the result of all this should be hardly and unsympathetically expressed by such words as three pounds. Of course the philosophic reader knows that it was merely that the poor old lady felt an interest in what was her own, which she could not feel in what belonged to anybody else. Had she been a person of greater enlightenment, she would have read in all her own little anxieties and schemings, the reflection of what was passing in the minds of those around her: and she would have concluded not that three pounds of her own were equal to six pounds of a neighbour's; but rather that three pounds, no matter to whom belonging, made a serious and important thing. But the poor old lady's feeling was natural. I am not able, at the present moment, quite to repress a feeling entirely like it. It seems to me a far stranger thing that I should be here, than it would be that any one of a great many people I know should be here. They are venturesome folk. They go about a great deal. Nothing strikes them as very remarkable. When Mr. Smith said in my hearing, that something or other happened when he was going into Jerusalem, I could not but look at Mr. Smith with great respect. But Mr. Jones, who has been everywhere himself, was quite free from any such feeling. You would hear or read quite coolly, my friend, that A or B had been at the Land's End. It is no great matter. But come yourself to this very spot where I am sitting: look round on this scene on which I have cast my eyes since I wrote the last sentence: and if you be a homely person who have never been beyond the limits of Britain, and who lead a quiet life from day to day somewhere in a quiet rural parish in Scotland, you will feel it curious to find yourself here. And if you be a sensible person, you will not think it a fine thing to pretend that you do not feel it so.

You remember what Sydney Smith said of Scotland. He said, no doubt, many things on that subject: but the thing to which I refer is the statement that Scotland is 'the knuckle-end of England.' There is a certain degree of truth in the statement. After you have spent a little while in Surrey, or Sussex, or Wiltshire, in a very richly wooded part of either county: if you get into an express train on the North-Western Railway on the morning of a summer day, and travel on by daylight through Staffordshire and Lancashire, through Cumberland and Lanarkshire, till you arrive at Glasgow, you will be aware that Sydney Smith's metaphor corresponds with your own feeling. You will be aware that as you travel towards the **North,** the trees are gradually growing smaller, the fields less rich, the whole landscape barer and bleaker: you will remember that nightingales do not sing north of Leeds, and you will think of other little traces of something like a physical decadence. But the impression made upon you will vary according to the line of country you pass through. I could take you to tracts in Scotland where the trees and hedges and fields are as rich, and the air as soft and pleasant, as anywhere in Britain: and where you add to the charms of the sweet English landscape, the long summer twilights which England wants. The true knuckle-end of England is here. And you will feel *that*, if you come to this place through the rich plains traversed by the Great Western Railway; or (better still) by that railway which comes by Salisbury, Sherborne, and Honiton to Exeter, through a country where at every turn you feel you are looking on a landscape which is your very ideal of beautiful England: and where churches and churchyards abound, so incomparably lovely in architecture and situation, that on a pleasant summer day one could hardly wish for better than to sit down on an ancient tombstone, and look for an hour at the fair piece of gray Gothic, at the green ivy, and the great elms. And the churches come so frequently, that one cannot but think of the happy life of duty and leisure which may well be led by the unambitious country parson there. His population is probably so small that he is free from that constant sense of pressure under which the clergy in many places are now compelled to live. He may write his sermon without being worried by the thought of a dozen things waiting to be attended to : and he may sit down under a large tree in the churchyard and meditate, without knowing that meditation is a luxury in which he has not time to indulge. But come on towards the West, and you will find the gradual approach to the knuckle-end. The juiciness and richness of the leg of mutton, pass slowly into tendon, skin, and bone. In Devonshire, you have Scotch irregularity of outline in the landscape; but there is English luxuriance in the hedges and wild-flowers; and more than English softness in the air. You enter Cornwall, over Brunel's wonderful but remarkably ugly suspension bridge at Saltash ; and you very soon feel that you have reached a tract entirely different from the ideal English country. The land is remarkably diversified in surface: steep ups and downs everywhere: and now and then, as you fly along in the railway train, you pass over a deep narrow gorge, spanned by the flimsiest wooden bridge that ever formed part of a line of railway. Sometimes these gorges are of vast depth. They occur perpetually: and they are always crossed

At the Land's End. 383

by the like unsubstantial structures. For many miles after entering Cornwall, the country is very richly wooded. You may see all kinds of forest trees growing luxuriantly; and many orchards, thickly crowded with apple-trees. But after you have passed Truro, there is a total change. The engine pants and struggles, as it hardly draws the train up inclines of extraordinary steepness; and you begin to see all round you heather and granite: great bare stretches of country with tin mines here and there, and rare woods of stunted pine. The railway brings you to Penzance, a pretty little town ten miles from the Land's End, which has the advantage of a climate of wonderful mildness. Granite is the stone here: almost every building is formed of it. The town is situated on one side of a considerable bay. Across the bay, three miles off, is St. Michael's Mount, rising out of the sea. St. Michael's Mount, it will be remembered, was in former days the residence of the Giant Cormoran, whose destruction formed the first recorded exploit of Jack the Giant-Killer. You leave Penzance and journey westward: probably in a phaeton drawn by a black horse. There is a rich country for the first two or three miles: then you enter a district very bleak and desolate. The cottages are rude and squalid; the churches, all of granite, are rare and large; and look as if they were accustomed to be battered by heavy storms. You pass through the last village, which is about a mile from the sea: and then you go along a lane, through a great field whose surface is made of granite, heather, and yellow furze as short as heather. You see the sea before you stretching far away: but the ground over which you are going swells so much, that it hides the rocky shore. Passing through that final large field, you might expect to come upon a sandy beach at last. At length you stand before a little cottage, an inscription on which tells you that it claims to be THE LAND'S END HOTEL: and here you will find the intelligent ostler, who guides you down a rough slope, not very steep, of granite, furze, and heather, till, after two hundred yards, you come upon the blunt promontory, whose extremity is by preeminence the End. The End does not reach into the sea so much as a hundred yards beyond the regular coast line. And the End is not the boldest portion of that rocky coast. Its height, as has been said, is about eighty feet perpendicular; while the rocks on either hand must be in many places at least a hundred and fifty. And now, looking back on the way you have come, you feel how gradually the scene around you grew barer, as you came on. It was like a bad man growing old. Trees and hedges were left behind: corn-fields and cottages with little gardens: for the beautiful churches of Somersetshire, you have only that rude and stern erection which you passed a little since: and now you have come to this, that you have no more than granite, and furze, and desolate sea. It is a most interesting spot to come to visit for a little while: but it would be a terrible thing to be condemned to live here for the remainder of your life. I cannot but think here of the unloved and unhonoured later days of some hoary reprobate: who, in a moral sense, has had his Somersetshire, then his Cornwall, and last his Land's End. And even though a man be not a reprobate, I believe that all life, apart from the presence of religion, is a going down hill. It is leaving behind, from year to year, the trees and flowers: leaving the soft green fields and the rich hedgerows: till you come at length to wastes of furze and heather; and end at last in stern rocks and pathless sea.

It was of this that the writer thought longest, sitting at the lonely Land's End; and this was something, let me confess, that never once occurred to me when reading Arnold's life, and musing on his theme for English verses. Another thing which will probably occur to the reader, when he shall visit the same place, will be, what a solitary and small being he himself will be there. The writer's home, at this moment, is seven hundred and forty miles away. Probably it is a good deal less, if you could go in a direct line; but such is the tale of the miles which he has traversed to reach this spot. And you will know, my friend, how misty and how far away your daily life and your home will seem, when you sit down by yourself in any lonely place, with all your belongings hundreds of miles distant. Going away alone, you truly leave great part of yourself behind.

Your mere individuality is a very small thing in size. Great men, such as kings and nobles, have occasionally had this truth disagreeably impressed upon them. A man with a magnificent estate must feel as though those green glades and magnificent trees were a portion of himself, and as if you must see all these things, and add them to himself, before you can understand how big an object he really is. But small men feel that too. They feel as though, to reckon what they are, you must add to the little object that sense reveals to you, the path they have come through life; the labour they have come through: the griefs and joys they have felt: the atmosphere and the surroundings amid which they live at home. I thought of this, one afternoon last winter. The ground was covered with snow: it had grown almost dark: going down a steep street, in which were a good many passers-by, I beheld the dim form of a poor fellow who has but one arm. There he was, a little figure, walking along as fast as he could, going home. You would have said, a more thoroughly insignificant atom of humanity could hardly be. But I knew all about that man's humble home: and I knew how much depended on him there. Not many weeks before, his poor, careworn wife had died: and at that minute, he was going home to his children, four little things, the eldest but seven years old, to whom he now had to be all. Anything befalling that insignificant man, would be to those four children an infinitely more important event than the separation of the Northern and Southern States of America. If we knew more about our humblest fellow-creatures, my reader: if we knew what they have borne and done, and what they have yet to bear and do: if round the unnoted little personality there were even the dim suggestion of its cares and belongings: we should feel more sympathy for every man;—we should regard no mortal as insignificant. I sometimes find people who talk of the great majority of their fellow-creatures as CADS: people who, in another country, would doubtless stand up vigorously for slavery. Let me say, that when I call to mind what I have known of those whom some heartless fools would call so;—when I think of their sufferings, their cares, their patience, their resignation, their sacrifices for one another;—my feeling towards the fools to whom I have alluded, passes from contempt, and turns to indignation. Would that we had all some of the truly Christian spirit of the heathen poet, who told us how much of sympathy with everything human he felt as incumbent upon him, forasmuch as he himself was a man!

But now, my friend, I must go. I shall never see the Land's End any more. But I have had it all to myself for these two hours; and it has become a possession for ever. Yesterday, it was a vague name; now, it is a clear picture, and it will always be so. It is not in the least like what I had expected. No person nor place you ever saw, is the least like what you expected. But now, I seem to have known it for a long time. And it is like parting from a friend to bid it good-bye. But the black horse has rested, and has been fed : and I have far to go to-day.

Good-bye !

CONCLUSION.

I WAS sitting by my study fire this evening in a rocking-chair, in the restful interval between dinner and tea; and thinking how I should conclude this volume. In that meditative state, my attention was drawn to a little girl who was sitting on the floor a little way off, sewing, and at the same time talking to herself.

These were her words: they were spoken slowly, in a pensive tone, and with considerable pauses between the sentences.

'Once I thought a great deal of a shilling. Now, I think nothing of it. I am accustomed to shillings. I think nothing even of a pound. I have got one myself, and I think nothing of it.'

You see, the freshness and edge of enjoyment were gone, through habit. Shillings had become too many: and so they were not now the great things they used to be. And after all, it was no very great number of shillings which had sufficed to produce this result.

Listening to the little girl's meditation, I thought of my volume. It is still a curious feeling to see one's thoughts in print. The page that bears what you have yourself written, my friend, has always a peculiar expression : an expression that is familiar, and yet strange. And there is still more of the singular feeling it imparts, when you look at an entire volume of your own. But more than one or two have preceded this : and the writer begins to feel towards a volume, as the little girl said she felt towards a shilling. Yet not quite as the little girl said she felt. The freshness is somewhat gone : yet the publication of a new book is a little epoch in a quiet life. I suppose the Editor of a daily newspaper, seeing himself in print every day of his life, if he pleases ; and often finding it his duty to write upon subjects in which he feels no great personal interest: must cease, in a few years, to feel any special attraction to the columns that have come from his own pen. There is less likelihood of *that*, in the case of a writer whose productions see the light at much longer intervals. And you may remember how Southey, who wrote probably more in quantity than any English author of the present century, with but two or three exceptions, tells us that he retained, to the last, the keen interest of a quite fresh writer in his own articles. When a new *Quarterly* appeared, he was quite impatient if it were a day too late in reaching him. I have no doubt he cut all the leaves before reading any : for

Southey was a man of an orderly turn: but I am sure he read his own paper the first. And he says he always found it very fresh and interesting reading: and he conveys that he generally thought it very good. As indeed it was. The shillings did not lose their value, many as they might grow.

There have been cases in which the successive shillings grew always more precious. You will think of Sterne, who appreciated his own writings so highly: and who used to write to his friends, as he was drawing each succeeding volume of *Tristram Shandy* to a close, that this new volume was to be by far the best. The present writer can say sincerely that each succeeding volume of these Essays which you may have read has been the result of more care and thought. He does not write now in the vague hope that perhaps somebody may read what he writes: he has the certainty of finding very many kindly readers. And he is not able to write now in the unconstrained way in which he wrote the first of those chapters, in days when not one of his rustic parishioners ever saw a page which he put forth. He is conscious now of the check which comes of the pervading sense, that a great many of the Flock intrusted to his care, recognize in what he writes, a familiar hand: and can compare what is written on these pages with what it is his duty to teach them elsewhere. He ventures to believe that, in spirit, there is no inconsistency. And he knows that in the judgment of those whose judgment he values most, there is none.

There is but little time, in the life of a hard-working parish clergyman, for writing anything beyond that which it is imperative to write. And one may sometimes think, with a wearied sigh, even in the midst of duty which is very dear, of the learned quiet and leisure of canonries and deaneries, such as our poor Church has not: sadly despoiled of that which is by right her own. Yet the habit of the pen grows into a second nature: and reserved folk never talk out their heart so freely as when talking to all the world. And if we live, friendly reader, I think we shall meet again.

[APRIL 1871.]

GENERAL LIST OF WORKS

PUBLISHED BY

MESSRS. LONGMANS, GREEN, AND CO.

PATERNOSTER ROW, LONDON.

History, Politics, Historical Memoirs, &c.

The HISTORY of ENGLAND from the Fall of Wolsey to the Defeat of the Spanish Armada. By JAMES ANTHONY FROUDE, M.A. late Fellow of Exeter College, Oxford.
LIBRARY EDITION, 12 VOLS. 8vo. price £8 18s.
CABINET EDITION, in 12 vols. crown 8vo. price 72s. each.

The HISTORY of ENGLAND from the Accession of James II. By Lord MACAULAY.
LIBRARY EDITION, 5 vols. 8vo. £4.
CABINET EDITION, 8 vols. post 8vo. 48s.
PEOPLE'S EDITION, 4 vols. crown 8vo. 16s.

LORD MACAULAY'S WORKS. Complete and Uniform Library Edition. Edited by his Sister, Lady TREVELYAN. 8 vols. 8vo. with Portrait, price £5 5s. cloth, or £8 8s. bound in tree-calf by Rivière.

An ESSAY on the HISTORY of the ENGLISH GOVERNMENT and Constitution, from the Reign of Henry VII. to the Present Time. By JOHN EARL RUSSELL. Fourth Edition, revised. Crown 8vo. 6s.

SELECTIONS from SPEECHES of EARL RUSSELL, 1817 to 1841, and from Despatches, 1859 to 1865; with Introductions. 2 vols. 8vo. 28s.

VARIETIES of VICE-REGAL LIFE. By Sir WILLIAM DENISON, K.C.B. late Governor-General of the Australian Colonies, and Governor of Madras. With Two Maps. 2 vols. 8vo. 28s.

On PARLIAMENTARY GOVERNMENT in ENGLAND: Its Origin, Development, and Practical Operation. By ALPHEUS TODD, Librarian of the Legislative Assembly of Canada. 2 vols. 8vo. price £1 17s.

A HISTORICAL ACCOUNT of the NEUTRALITY of GREAT BRITAIN DURING the AMERICAN CIVIL WAR. By MOUNTAGUE BERNARD, M.A. Chichele Professor of International Law and Diplomacy in the University of Oxford. Royal 8vo. 16s.

The CONSTITUTIONAL HISTORY of ENGLAND, since the Accession of George III. 1760—1860. By Sir THOMAS ERSKINE MAY, C.B. Second Edition. 2 vols. 8vo. 33s.

A

The **HISTORY of ENGLAND**, from the Earliest Times to the Year 1866. By C. D. YONGE, Regius Professor of Modern History in the Queen's University, Belfast. New Edition. Crown 8vo. price 7s. 6d.

The **OXFORD REFORMERS of 1498**—John Colet, Erasmus, and Thomas More; being a History of their Fellow-work. By FREDERIC SEEBOHM. Second Edition, enlarged. 8vo. 14s.

A **HISTORY of WALES**, derived from Authentic Sources. By JANE WILLIAMS, Ysgafell. 8vo. 14s.

LECTURES on the HISTORY of ENGLAND, from the earliest Times to the Death of King Edward II. By WILLIAM LONGMAN. With Maps and Illustrations. 8vo. 15s.

The **HISTORY of the LIFE and TIMES of EDWARD the THIRD**. By WILLIAM LONGMAN. With 9 Maps, 8 Plates, and 16 Woodcuts. 2 vols. 8vo. 28s.

The **OVERTHROW of the GERMANIC CONFEDERATION** by PRUSSIA in 1866. By Sir ALEXANDER MALET, Bart. K.C.B. With 5 Maps. 8vo. 18s.

The **MILITARY RESOURCES of PRUSSIA and FRANCE**, and RECENT CHANGES in the ART of WAR. By Lieut.-Col. CHESNEY, R.E. and HENRY REEVE, D.C.L. Crown 8vo. price 7s. 6d.

WATERLOO LECTURES: a Study of the Campaign of 1815. By Colonel CHARLES C. CHESNEY, R.E. late Professor of Military Art and History in the Staff College. New Edition. 8vo. with Map, 10s. 6d.

STAFF COLLEGE ESSAYS. By Lieutenant EVELYN BARING, Royal Artillery. 8vo. with 2 Maps, 8s. 6d.

DEMOCRACY in AMERICA. By ALEXIS DE TOCQUEVILLE. Translated by HENRY REEVE. 2 vols. 8vo. 21s.

HISTORY of the REFORMATION in EUROPE in the Time of Calvin. By J. H. MERLE D'AUBIGNÉ, D.D. VOLS. I. and II. 8vo. 28s. VOL. III. 12s. VOL. IV. 16s. VOL. V. price 16s.

CHAPTERS from FRENCH HISTORY; St. Louis, Joan of Arc, Henri IV. with Sketches of the Intermediate Periods. By J. H. GURNEY, M.A. New Edition. Fcp. 8vo. 6s. 6d.

MEMOIR of POPE SIXTUS the FIFTH. By Baron HUBNER. Translated from the Original in French, with the Author's sanction, by HUBERT E. H. JERNINGHAM. 2 vols. 8vo. [*In preparation.*

IGNATIUS LOYOLA and the EARLY JESUITS. By STEWART ROSE. New Edition, nearly ready.

The **HISTORY of GREECE**. By C. THIRLWALL, D.D. Lord Bishop of St. David's. 8 vols. fcp. 8vo. price 28s.

GREEK HISTORY from Themistocles to Alexander, in a Series of Lives from Plutarch. Revised and arranged by A. H. CLOUGH. New Edition. Fcp. with 44 Woodcuts, 6s.

CRITICAL HISTORY of the LANGUAGE and LITERATURE of Ancient Greece. By WILLIAM MURE, of Caldwell. 5 vols. 8vo. £3 9s.

The **TALE of the GREAT PERSIAN WAR**, from the Histories of Herodotus. By GEORGE W. COX, M.A. New Edition. Fcp. 3s. 6d.

HISTORY of the LITERATURE of ANCIENT GREECE. By Professor K. O. MÜLLER. Translated by the Right Hon. Sir GEORGE CORNEWALL LEWIS, Bart. and by J. W. DONALDSON, D.D. 3 vols. 8vo. 21s.

HISTORY of the CITY of ROME from its Foundation to the Sixteenth Century of the Christian Era. By THOMAS H. DYER, LL.D. 8vo. with 2 Maps, 15s.

The HISTORY of ROME. By WILLIAM IHNE. English Edition translated and revised by the Author. VOLS. I. and II. 8vo. price 30s.

HISTORY of the ROMANS under the EMPIRE. By the Very Rev. C. MERIVALE, D.C.L. Dean of Ely. 8 vols. post 8vo. 48s.

The FALL of the ROMAN REPUBLIC; a Short History of the Last Century of the Commonwealth. By the same Author. 12mo. 7s. 6d.

A STUDENT'S MANUAL of the HISTORY of INDIA, from the Earliest Period to the Present. By Colonel MEADOWS TAYLOR, M.R.A.S M.R.I.A. Crown 8vo. with Maps, 7s. 6d.

The HISTORY of INDIA, from the Earliest Period to the close of Lord Dalhousie's Administration. By JOHN CLARK MARSHMAN. 3 vols. crown 8vo. 22s. 6d.

INDIAN POLITY: a View of the System of Administration in India By Lieutenant-Colonel GEORGE CHESNEY, Fellow of the University of Calcutta. New Edition, revised; with Map. 8vo. price 21s.

HOME POLITICS; being a consideration of the Causes of the Growth of Trade in relation to Labour, Pauperism, and Emigration. By DANIEL GRANT. 8vo. 7s.

REALITIES of IRISH LIFE. By W. STEUART TRENCH, Land Agent in Ireland to the Marquess of Lansdowne, the Marquess of Bath, and Lord Digby. Fifth Edition. Crown 8vo. price 6s.

The STUDENT'S MANUAL of the HISTORY of IRELAND. By MARY F. CUSACK, Author of the 'Illustrated History of Ireland, from the Earliest Period to the Year of Catholic Emancipation.' Crown 8vo. price 6s.

CRITICAL and HISTORICAL ESSAYS contributed to the *Edinburgh Review*. By the Right Hon. LORD MACAULAY.
CABINET EDITION, 4 vols. post 8vo. 24s. LIBRARY EDITION, 3 vols. 8vo. 36s.
PEOPLE'S EDITION, 2 vols. crown 8vo. 8s. STUDENT'S EDITION, 1 vol. cr. 8vo. 6s

HISTORY of EUROPEAN MORALS, from Augustus to Charlemagne. By W. E. H. LECKY, M.A. Second Edition. 2 vols. 8vo. price 28s.

HISTORY of the RISE and INFLUENCE of the SPIRIT of RATIONALISM in EUROPE. By W. E. H. LECKY, M.A. Cabinet Edition being the Fourth. 2 vols. crown 8vo. price 16s.

GOD in HISTORY; or, the Progress of Man's Faith in the Moral Order of the World. By Baron BUNSEN. Translated by SUSANNA WINKWORTH; with a Preface by Dean STANLEY. 3 vols. 8vo. price 42s.

The HISTORY of PHILOSOPHY, from Thales to Comte. By GEORGE HENRY LEWES. Third Edition. 2 vols. 8vo. 30s.

The MYTHOLOGY of the ARYAN NATIONS. By GEORGE W. COX, M.A. late Scholar of Trinity College, Oxford, Joint-Editor, with the late Professor Brande, of the Fourth Edition of 'The Dictionary of Science, Literature, and Art,' Author of 'Tales of Ancient Greece,' &c. 2 vols. 8vo. 28s.

HISTORY of CIVILISATION in England and France, Spain and Scotland. By HENRY THOMAS BUCKLE. New Edition of the entire Work, with a complete INDEX. 3 vols. crown 8vo. 24s.

HISTORY of the CHRISTIAN CHURCH, from the Ascension of Christ to the Conversion of Constantine. By E. BURTON, D.D. late Prof. of Divinity in the Univ. of Oxford. Eighth Edition. Fcp. 3s. 6d.

SKETCH of the HISTORY of the CHURCH of ENGLAND to the Revolution of 1688. By the Right Rev. T. V. SHORT, D.D. Lord Bishop of St. Asaph. Eighth Edition. Crown 8vo. 7s. 6d.

HISTORY of the EARLY CHURCH, from the First Preaching of the Gospel to the Council of Nicæa, A.D. 325. By ELIZABETH M. SEWELL, Author of 'Amy Herbert.' New Edition, with Questions. Fcp. 4s. 6d.

The ENGLISH REFORMATION. By F. C. MASSINGBERD, M.A. Chancellor of Lincoln and Rector of South Ormsby. Fourth Edition, revised. Fcp. 8vo. 7s. 6d.

MAUNDER'S HISTORICAL TREASURY; comprising a General Introductory Outline of Universal History, and a series of Separate Histories. Latest Edition, revised and brought down to the Present Time by the Rev. GEORGE WILLIAM COX, M.A. Fcp. 6s. cloth, or 9s. 6d. calf.

HISTORICAL and CHRONOLOGICAL ENCYCLOPÆDIA; comprising Chronological Notices of all the Great Events of Universal History: Treaties, Alliances, Wars, Battles, &c.; Incidents in the Lives of Eminent Men and their Works, Scientific and Geographical Discoveries, Mechanical Inventions, and Social, Domestic, and Economical Improvements. By B. B. WOODWARD, B.A. and W. L. R. CATES. 1 vol. 8vo. [*In the press.*

Biographical Works.

The LIFE of ISAMBARD KINGDOM BRUNEL, Civil Engineer. By ISAMBARD BRUNEL, B.C.L. of Lincoln's Inn; Chancellor of the Diocese of Ely. With Portrait, Plates, and Woodcuts. 8vo. 21s.

The LIFE and LETTERS of FARADAY. By Dr. BENCE JONES, Secretary of the Royal Institution. Second Edition, thoroughly revised. 2 vols. 8vo. with Portrait, and Eight Engravings on Wood, price 28s.

FARADAY as a DISCOVERER. By JOHN TYNDALL, LL.D. F.R.S. Professor of Natural Philosophy in the Royal Institution. New and Cheaper Edition, with Two Portraits. Fcp. 8vo. 3s. 6d.

The LIFE and LETTERS of the Rev. SYDNEY SMITH. Edited by his Daughter, Lady HOLLAND, and Mrs. AUSTIN. New Edition, complete in One Volume. Crown 8vo. price 6s.

SOME MEMORIALS of R. D. HAMPDEN, Bishop of Hereford. Edited by his Daughter, HENRIETTA HAMPDEN. With Portrait. 8vo. price 12s.

A MEMOIR of G. E. L. COTTON, D.D. late Lord Bishop of Calcutta; with Selections from his Journals and Letters. Edited by Mrs. COTTON. With Portrait. 8vo. price 18s.

The LIFE and TRAVELS of GEORGE WHITEFIELD, M.A. By JAMES PATERSON GLEDSTONE. 8vo. price 14s.

LIVES of the LORD CHANCELLORS and KEEPERS of the GREAT SEAL of IRELAND, from the Earliest Times to the Reign of Queen Victoria. By J. R. O'FLANAGAN, M.R.I.A. Barrister-at-Law. 2 vols. 8vo. 36s.

DICTIONARY of GENERAL BIOGRAPHY; containing Concise Memoirs and Notices of the most Eminent Persons of all Countries, from the Earliest Ages to the Present Time. Edited by W. L. R. CATES. 8vo. 21s.

LIVES of the TUDOR PRINCESSES, including Lady Jane Grey and her Sisters. By AGNES STRICKLAND, Author of 'Lives of the Queens of England.' Post 8vo. with Portrait, &c. 12s. 6d.

LIVES of the QUEENS of ENGLAND. By AGNES STRICKLAND. Library Edition, newly revised; with Portraits of every Queen, Autographs, and Vignettes. 8 vols. post 8vo. 7s. 6d. each.

MEMOIRS of BARON BUNSEN. Drawn chiefly from Family Papers by his Widow, FRANCES Baroness BUNSEN. Second Edition, abridged; with 2 Portraits and 4 Woodcuts. 2 vols. post 8vo. 21s.

The LETTERS of the Right Hon. Sir GEORGE CORNEWALL LEWIS, Bart. to various Friends. Edited by his Brother, the Rev. Canon Sir G. F. LEWIS, Bart. 8vo. with Portrait, price 14s.

LIFE of the DUKE of WELLINGTON. By the Rev. G. R. GLEIG, M.A. Popular Edition, carefully revised; with copious Additions. Crown 8vo. with Portrait, 5s.

HISTORY of MY RELIGIOUS OPINIONS. By J. H. NEWMAN, D.D. Being the Substance of Apologia pro Vitâ Suâ. Post 8vo. 6s.

The PONTIFICATE of PIUS the NINTH; being the Third Edition of 'Rome and its Ruler,' continued to the latest moment and greatly enlarged. By J. F. MAGUIRE, M.P. Post 8vo. with Portrait, 12s. 6d.

FATHER MATHEW: a Biography. By JOHN FRANCIS MAGUIRE, M.P. for Cork. Popular Edition, with Portrait. Crown 8vo. 3s. 6d.

FELIX MENDELSSOHN'S LETTERS from *Italy and Switzerland*, and *Letters from* 1833 *to* 1847, translated by Lady WALLACE. New Edition, with Portrait. 2 vols. crown 8vo. 5s. each.

MEMOIRS of SIR HENRY HAVELOCK, K.C.B. By JOHN CLARK MARSHMAN. Cabinet Edition, with Portrait. Crown 8vo. price 3s. 6d.

VICISSITUDES of FAMILIES. By Sir J. BERNARD BURKE, C.B. Ulster King of Arms. New Edition, remodelled and enlarged. 2 vols. crown 8vo. 21s.

THE EARLS of GRANARD: a Memoir of the Noble Family of Forbes. Written by Admiral the Hon. JOHN FORBES, and edited by GEORGE ARTHUR HASTINGS, present Earl of Granard, K.P. 8vo. 10s.

ESSAYS in ECCLESIASTICAL BIOGRAPHY. By the Right Hon. Sir J. STEPHEN, LL.D. Cabinet Edition, being the Fifth. Crown 8vo. 7s. 6d.

MAUNDER'S BIOGRAPHICAL TREASURY. Thirteenth Edition, reconstructed, thoroughly revised, and in great part rewritten; with about 1,000 additional Memoirs and Notices, by W. L. R. CATES. Fcp. 6s.

LETTERS and LIFE of FRANCIS BACON, including all his Occasional Works. Collected and edited, with a Commentary, by J. SPEDDING, Trin. Coll. Cantab. VOLS. I. and II. 8vo. 24s. VOLS. III. and IV. 24s. VOL. V. price 12s.

Criticism, Philosophy, Polity, &c.

The INSTITUTES of JUSTINIAN; with English Introduction, Translation, and Notes. By T. C. SANDARS, M.A. Barrister, late Fellow of Orie Coll. Oxon. New Edition. 8vo. 15s.

SOCRATES and the SOCRATIC SCHOOLS. Translated from the German of Dr. E. ZELLER, with the Author's approval, by the Rev. OSWALD J. REICHEL, B.C.L. and M.A. Crown 8vo. 8s. 6d.

The STOICS, EPICUREANS, and SCEPTICS. Translated from the German of Dr. E. ZELLER, with the Author's approval, by OSWALD J. REICHEL, B.C.L. and M.A. Crown 8vo. price 14s.

The ETHICS of ARISTOTLE, illustrated with Essays and Notes. By Sir A. GRANT, Bart. M.A. LL.D. Second Edition, revised and completed. 2 vols. 8vo. price 28s.

The NICOMACHEAN ETHICS of ARISTOTLE newly translated into English. By R. WILLIAMS, B.A. Fellow and late Lecturer of Merton College, and sometime Student of Christ Church, Oxford. 8vo. 12s.

ELEMENTS of LOGIC. By R. WHATELY, D.D. late Archbishop of Dublin. New Edition. 8vo. 10s. 6d. crown 8vo. 4s. 6d.

Elements of Rhetoric. By the same Author. New Edition. 8vo. 10s. 6d. crown 8vo. 4s. 6d.

English Synonymes. By E. JANE WHATELY. Edited by Archbishop WHATELY. 5th Edition. Fcp. 3s.

BACON'S ESSAYS with ANNOTATIONS. By R. WHATELY, D.D. late Archbishop of Dublin. Sixth Edition. 8vo. 10s. 6d.

LORD BACON'S WORKS, collected and edited by J. SPEDDING, M.A. R. L. ELLIS, M.A. and D. D. HEATH. New and Cheaper Edition. 7 vols. 8vo. price £3 13s. 6d.

The SUBJECTION of WOMEN. By JOHN STUART MILL. New Edition. Post 8vo. 5s.

On REPRESENTATIVE GOVERNMENT. By JOHN STUART MILL. Third Edition. 8vo. 9s. Crown 8vo. 2s.

On LIBERTY. By JOHN STUART MILL. Fourth Edition. Post 8vo. 7s. 6d. Crown 8vo. 1s. 4d.

Principles of Political Economy. By the same Author. Sixth Edition. 2 vols. 8vo. 30s. Or in 1 vol. crown 8vo. 5s.

A System of Logic, Ratiocinative and Inductive. By the same Author. Seventh Edition. Two vols. 8vo. 25s.

ANALYSIS of Mr. MILL'S SYSTEM of LOGIC. By W. STEBBING, M.A. Fellow of Worcester College, Oxford. New Edition. 12mo. 3s. 6d.

UTILITARIANISM. By JOHN STUART MILL. Third Edition. 8vo. 5s.

**DISSERTATIONS and DISCUSSIONS, POLITICAL, PHILOSOPHI-
CAL, and HISTORICAL.** By JOHN STUART MILL. Second Edition, revised.
3 vols. 8vo. 36s.

EXAMINATION of Sir W. HAMILTON'S PHILOSOPHY, and of the
Principal Philosophical Questions discussed in his Writings. By JOHN
STUART MILL. Third Edition. 8vo. 16s.

An OUTLINE of the NECESSARY LAWS of THOUGHT: a Treatise
on Pure and Applied Logic. By the Most Rev. WILLIAM, Lord Archbishop of York, D.D. F.R.S. Ninth Thousand. Crown 8vo. 5s. 6d.

The ELEMENTS of POLITICAL ECONOMY. By HENRY DUNNING
MACLEOD, M.A. Barrister-at-Law. 8vo. 16s.

A Dictionary of Political Economy; Biographical, Bibliographical,
Historical, and Practical. By the same Author. VOL. I. royal 8vo. 30s.

The ELECTION of REPRESENTATIVES, Parliamentary and Muni-
cipal; a Treatise. By THOMAS HARE, Barrister-at-Law. Third Edition,
with Additions. Crown 8vo. 6s.

SPEECHES of the RIGHT HON. LORD MACAULAY, corrected by
Himself. People's Edition, crown 8vo. 3s. 6d.

**Lord Macaulay's Speeches on Parliamentary Reform in 1831 and
1832.** 16mo. 1s.

INAUGURAL ADDRESS delivered to the University of St. Andrews.
By JOHN STUART MILL. 8vo. 5s. People's Edition, crown 8vo. 1s.

A DICTIONARY of the ENGLISH LANGUAGE. By R. G. LATHAM,
M.A. M.D. F.R.S. Founded on the Dictionary of Dr. SAMUEL JOHNSON, as
edited by the Rev. H. J. TODD, with numerous Emendations and Additions.
In Four Volumes, 4to. price £7.

THESAURUS of ENGLISH WORDS and PHRASES, classified and
arranged so as to facilitate the Expression of Ideas, and assist in Literary
Composition. By P. M. ROGET, M.D. New Edition. Crown 8vo. 10s. 6d.

LECTURES on the SCIENCE of LANGUAGE, delivered at the Royal
Institution. By MAX MÜLLER, M.A. &c. Foreign Member of the French
Institute. Sixth Edition. 2 vols. crown 8vo. price 16s.

CHAPTERS on LANGUAGE. By FREDERIC W. FARRAR, F.R.S.
Head Master of Marlborough College. Crown 8vo. 8s. 6d.

WORD-GOSSIP; a Series of Familiar Essays on Words and their
Peculiarities. By the Rev. W. L. BLACKLEY, M.A. Fcp. 8vo. 5s.

A BOOK ABOUT WORDS. By G. F. GRAHAM, Author of 'English,
or the Art of Composition,' &c. Fcp. 8vo. price 3s. 6d.

The DEBATER; a Series of Complete Debates, Outlines of Debates,
and Questions for Discussion. By F. ROWTON. Fcp. 6s.

MANUAL of ENGLISH LITERATURE, Historical and Critical. By
THOMAS ARNOLD, M.A. Second Edition. Crown 8vo. price 7s. 6d.

SOUTHEY'S DOCTOR, complete in One Volume. Edited by the Rev.
J. W. WARTER, B.D. Square crown 8vo. 12s. 6d.

**HISTORICAL and CRITICAL COMMENTARY on the OLD TESTA-
MENT;** with a New Translation. By M. M. KALISCH, Ph.D. VOL. I.
Genesis, 8vo. 18s. or adapted for the General Reader, 12s. VOL. II. *Exodus,*
15s. or adapted for the General Reader, 12s. VOL. III. *Leviticus,* PART I.
15s. or adapted for the General Reader, 8s.

A HEBREW GRAMMAR, with EXERCISES. By M. M. KALISCH, Ph.D. PART I. *Outlines with Exercises*, 8vo. 12s. 6d. KEY, 5s. PART II. *Exceptional Forms and Constructions*, 12s. 6d.

A LATIN-ENGLISH DICTIONARY. By J. T. WHITE, D.D. of Corpus Christi College, and J. E. RIDDLE, M.A. of St. Edmund Hall, Oxford. Third Edition, revised. 2 vols. 4to. pp. 2,128, price 42s. cloth.

White's College Latin-English Dictionary (Intermediate Size), abridged for the use of University Students from the Parent Work (as above). Medium 8vo. pp. 1,048, price 18s. cloth.

White's Junior Student's Complete Latin-English and English-Latin Dictionary. New Edition. Square 12mo. pp. 1,058, price 12s.

Separately { The ENGLISH-LATIN DICTIONARY, price 5s. 6d.
The LATIN-ENGLISH DICTIONARY, price 7s. 6d.

An ENGLISH-GREEK LEXICON, containing all the Greek Words used by Writers of good authority. By C. D. YONGE, B.A. New Edition. 4to. 21s.

Mr. YONGE'S NEW LEXICON, English and Greek, abridged from his larger work (as above). Revised Edition. Square 12mo. 8s. 6d.

A GREEK-ENGLISH LEXICON. Compiled by H. G. LIDDELL, D.D. Dean of Christ Church, and R. SCOTT, D.D. Dean of Rochester. Sixth Edition. Crown 4to. price 36s.

A Lexicon, Greek and English, abridged from LIDDELL and SCOTT's *Greek-English Lexicon*. Twelfth Edition. Square 12mo. 7s. 6d.

A SANSKRIT-ENGLISH DICTIONARY, the Sanskrit words printed both in the original Devanagari and in Roman Letters. Compiled by T. BENFEY, Prof. in the Univ. of Göttingen. 8vo. 52s. 6d.

WALKER'S PRONOUNCING DICTIONARY of the ENGLISH LANGUAGE. Thoroughly revised Editions, by B. H. SMART. 8vo. 12s. 16mo. 6s.

A PRACTICAL DICTIONARY of the FRENCH and ENGLISH LANGUAGES. By L. CONTANSEAU. Fourteenth Edition. Post 8vo. 10s. 6d.

Contanseau's Pocket Dictionary, French and English, abridged from the above by the Author. New Edition, revised. Square 18mo. 3s. 6d.

NEW PRACTICAL DICTIONARY of the GERMAN LANGUAGE; German-English and English-German. By the Rev. W. L. BLACKLEY, M.A. and Dr. CARL MARTIN FRIEDLÄNDER. Post 8vo. 7s. 6d.

The MASTERY of LANGUAGES; or, the Art of Speaking Foreign Tongues Idiomatically. By THOMAS PRENDERGAST, late of the Civil Service at Madras. Second Edition. 8vo. 6s.

Miscellaneous Works and *Popular Metaphysics.*

The ESSAYS and CONTRIBUTIONS of A. K. H. B., Author of 'The Recreations of a Country Parson.' Uniform Editions:—

Recreations of a Country Parson. By A. K. H. B. FIRST and SECOND SERIES, crown 8vo. 3s. 6d. each.

The **COMMON-PLACE PHILOSOPHER in TOWN and COUNTRY.** By A. K. H. B. Crown 8vo. price 3s. 6d.

Leisure Hours in Town; Essays Consolatory, Æsthetical, Moral, Social, and Domestic. By A. K. H. B. Crown 8vo. 3s. 6d.

The Autumn Holidays of a Country Parson; Essays contributed to *Fraser's Magazine* and to *Good Words*. By A. K. H. B. Crown 8vo. 3s. 6d.

The Graver Thoughts of a Country Parson. By A. K. H. B. FIRST and SECOND SERIES, crown 8vo. 3s. 6d. each.

Critical **Essays of a Country** Parson, selected from **Essays** contributed to *Fraser's Magazine.* By A. K. H. B. Crown 8vo. 3s. 6d.

Sunday Afternoons at the Parish Church of a Scottish University City. By A. K. H. B. Crown 8vo. 3s. 6d.

Lessons of Middle Age; with some Account of various Cities and **Men.** By A. K. H. B. Crown 8vo. 3s. 6d.

Counsel and Comfort spoken from a **City Pulpit.** By A. K. H. B. Crown 8vo. price 3s. 6d.

Changed **Aspects of Unchanged Truths;** Memorials of St. Andrews Sundays. By A. K. H.B. Crown 8vo. 3s. 6d.

Present-day **Thoughts;** Memorials of St. Andrews Sundays. By A. K. H. B. Crown 8vo. 3s. 6d.

SHORT STUDIES on GREAT SUBJECTS. By JAMES ANTHONY FROUDE, M.A. late Fellow of Exeter Coll. Oxford. Third Edition. 8vo. 12s. SECOND SERIES, nearly ready.

LORD MACAULAY'S MISCELLANEOUS WRITINGS:—
LIBRARY EDITION. 2 vols. 8vo. Portrait, 21s.
PEOPLE'S EDITION. 1 vol. crown 8vo. 4s. 6d.

The **REV. SYDNEY SMITH'S MISCELLANEOUS WORKS;** including his Contributions to the *Edinburgh Review.* Crown 8vo. 6s.

The Wit and Wisdom of the Rev. Sydney Smith: a Selection of the most memorable Passages in his Writings and Conversation. 16mo. 3s. 6d.

TRACES of HISTORY in the NAMES of PLACES; with a Vocabulary of the Roots out of which Names of Places in England and Wales are formed. By FLAVELL EDMUNDS. Crown 8vo. 7s. 6d.

The ECLIPSE of FAITH; or, a Visit to a Religious Sceptic. By HENRY ROGERS. Twelfth Edition. Fcp. 5s.

Defence of the Eclipse of Faith, by its Author; a rejoinder to Dr. Newman's *Reply.* Third Edition. Fcp. 3s. 6d.

Selections from the Correspondence of R. E. H. Greyson. By the same Author. Third Edition. Crown 8vo. 7s. 6d.

FAMILIES of SPEECH, Four Lectures delivered at the **Royal** Institution of Great Britain. By the Rev. F. W. FARRAR, M.A. F.R.S. Head Master of Marlborough College. Post 8vo. with Two Maps, 5s. 6d.

CHIPS from a GERMAN WORKSHOP; being Essays on the Science of Religion, and on Mythology, Traditions, and Customs. By MAX MÜLLER, M.A. &c. Foreign Member of the French Institute. 3 vols. 8vo. £2.

B

ANALYSIS of the PHENOMENA of the HUMAN MIND. By JAMES MILL. A New Edition, with Notes, Illustrative and Critical, by ALEXANDER BAIN, ANDREW FINDLATER, and GEORGE GROTE. Edited, with additional Notes, by JOHN STUART MILL. 2 vols. 8vo. price 28s.

An INTRODUCTION to MENTAL PHILOSOPHY, on the Inductive Method. By J. D. MORELL, M.A. LL.D. 8vo. 12s.

ELEMENTS of PSYCHOLOGY, containing the Analysis of the Intellectual Powers. By the same Author. Post 8vo. 7s. 6d.

The SECRET of HEGEL: being the Hegelian System in Origin, Principle, Form, and Matter. By J. H. STIRLING. 2 vols. 8vo. 28s.

Sir William Hamilton; being the Philosophy of Perception: an Analysis. By the same Author. 8vo. 5s.

The SENSES and the INTELLECT. By ALEXANDER BAIN, M.D. Professor of Logic in the University of Aberdeen. Third Edition. 8vo. 15s.

The EMOTIONS and the WILL. By the same Author. New Edition, preparing for publication.

On the STUDY of CHARACTER, including an Estimate of Phrenology. By the same Author. New Edition, preparing for publication.

MENTAL and MORAL SCIENCE: a Compendium of Psychology and Ethics. By the same Author. Second Edition. Crown 8vo. 10s. 6d.

LOGIC, DEDUCTIVE and INDUCTIVE. By the same Author. In TWO PARTS, crown 8vo. 10s. 6d. Each Part may be had separately:—
PART I. *Deduction,* 4s. PART II. *Induction,* 6s. 6d.

TIME and SPACE; a Metaphysical Essay. By SHADWORTH H. HODGSON. (This work covers the whole ground of Speculative Philosophy.) 8vo. price 16s.

The Theory of Practice; an Ethical Inquiry. By the same Author. (This work, in conjunction with the foregoing, completes a system of Philosophy.) 2 vols. 8vo. price 24s.

STRONG AND FREE; or, First Steps towards Social Science. By the Author of 'My Life, and What shall I do with it?' 8vo. price 10s. 6d.

The PHILOSOPHY of NECESSITY; or, Natural Law as applicable to Mental, Moral, and Social Science. By CHARLES BRAY. Second Edition 8vo. 9s.

The Education of the Feelings and Affections. By the same Author. Third Edition. 8vo. 3s. 6d.

On Force, its Mental and Moral Correlates. By the same Author. 8vo. 5s.

A TREATISE on HUMAN NATURE; being an Attempt to Introduce the Experimental Method of Reasoning into Moral Subjects. By DAVID HUME. Edited, with Notes, &c. by T. H. GREEN, Fellow, and T. H. GROSE, late Scholar, of Balliol College, Oxford. [*In the press.*

ESSAYS MORAL, POLITICAL, and LITERARY. By DAVID HUME. By the same Editors. [*In the press.*

Astronomy, Meteorology, Popular Geography, &c.

OUTLINES of ASTRONOMY. By Sir J. F. W. HERSCHEL, Bart. M.A. Tenth Edition, revised; with 9 Plates and many Woodcuts. 8vo. 18s.

The SUN; RULER, LIGHT, FIRE, and LIFE of the PLANETARY SYSTEM. By RICHARD A. PROCTOR, B.A. F.R.A.S. With 10 Plates (7 coloured) and 107 Figures on Wood. Crown 8vo. 14s.

OTHER WORLDS THAN OURS; the Plurality of Worlds Studied under the Light of Recent Scientific Researches. By the same Author. Second Edition, with 14 Illustrations. Crown 8vo. 10s. 6d.

SATURN and its SYSTEM. By the same Author. 8vo. with 14 Plates, 14s.

SCHALLEN'S SPECTRUM ANALYSIS, in its application to Terrestrial Substances and the Physical Constitution of the Heavenly Bodies. Translated by JANE and C. LASSELL; edited by W. HUGGINS, LL.D. F.R.S. Crown 8vo. with Illustrations. [*Nearly ready.*

CELESTIAL OBJECTS for COMMON TELESCOPES. By the Rev. T. W. WEBB, M.A. F.R.A.S. Second Edition, revised, with a large Map of the Moon, and several Woodcuts. 16mo. 7s. 6d.

NAVIGATION and NAUTICAL ASTRONOMY (Practical, Theoretical, Scientific) for the use of Students and Practical Men. By J. MERRIFIELD F.R.A.S and H. EVERS. 8vo. 14s.

DOVE'S LAW of STORMS, considered in connexion with the Ordinary Movements of the Atmosphere. Translated by R. H. SCOTT, M.A. T.C.D 8vo. 10s. 6d.

M'CULLOCH'S DICTIONARY, Geographical, Statistical, and Historical, of the various Countries, Places, and Principal Natural Objects in the World. New Edition, with the Statistical Information brought up to the latest returns by F. MARTIN. 4 vols. 8vo. with coloured Maps, £4 4s.

A GENERAL DICTIONARY of GEOGRAPHY, Descriptive, Physical, Statistical, and Historical: forming a complete Gazetteer of the World. By A. KEITH JOHNSTON, LL.D. F.R.G.S. Revised Edition. 8vo. 31s. 6d.

A MANUAL of GEOGRAPHY, Physical, Industrial, and Political. By W. HUGHES, F.R.G.S. With 6 Maps. Fcp. 7s. 6d.

The STATES of the RIVER PLATE: their Industries and Commerce. By WILFRID LATHAM, Buenos Ayres. Second Edition, revised. 8vo. 12s.

MAUNDER'S TREASURY of GEOGRAPHY, Physical, Historical, Descriptive, and Political. Edited by W. HUGHES, F.R.G.S. Revised Edition, with 7 Maps and 16 Plates. Fcp. 6s. cloth, or 9s. 6d. bound in calf

Natural History and Popular Science.

ELEMENTARY TREATISE on PHYSICS, Experimental and Applied. Translated and edited from GANOT's *Éléments de Physique* (with the Author's sanction) by E. ATKINSON, Ph.D. F.C.S. New Edition, revised and enlarged; with a Coloured Plate and 620 Woodcuts. Post 8vo. 15s.

The ELEMENTS of PHYSICS or NATURAL PHILOSOPHY. By NEIL ARNOTT, M.D. F.R.S. Physician Extraordinary to the Queen. Sixth Edition, rewritten and completed. Two Parts, 8vo. 21s.

SOUND: a Course of Eight Lectures delivered at the Royal Institution of Great Britain. By JOHN TYNDALL, LL.D. F.R.S. New Edition, crown 8vo. with **Portrait** of *M. Chladni* and 169 Woodcuts, price 9s.

HEAT a MODE of MOTION. By Professor JOHN TYNDALL, LL.D. F.R.S. Fourth Edition. Crown 8vo. with Woodcuts, 10s. 6d.

RESEARCHES on **DIAMAGNETISM** and **MAGNE-CRYSTALLIC** ACTION; including the Question of Diamagnetic Polarity. By the same Author. With 6 Plates and many Woodcuts. 8vo. price 14s.

PROFESSOR TYNDALL'S ESSAYS on the **USE** and **LIMIT** of the IMAGINATION in SCIENCE. Being the Second Edition, with Additions, of his Discourse on the Scientific Use of the Imagination. 8vo. 3s.

NOTES of a **COURSE** of SEVEN LECTURES on ELECTRICAL PHENOMENA and THEORIES, delivered at the Royal Institution, A.D. 1870. By Professor TYNDALL. Crown 8vo. 1s. sewed, or 1s. 6d. cloth.

NOTES of a **COURSE** of **NINE LECTURES** on **LIGHT** delivered at the Royal Institution, A.D. 1869. By the same Author. Crown 8vo. price 1s. sewed, or 1s. 6d. cloth.

LIGHT: Its Influence on Life and Health. By FORBES WINSLOW, M.D. D.C.L. Oxon. (Hon.). Fcp. 8vo. 6s.

A TREATISE on **ELECTRICITY**, in Theory and Practice. By A. DE LA RIVE, Prof. in the Academy of Geneva. Translated by C. V. WALKER, F.R.S. 3 vols. 8vo. with Woodcuts, £3 13s.

The BEGINNING: its When and its How. By MUNGO PONTON, F.R.S.E. Post 8vo. with very numerous Illustrations, price 18s.

The FORCES of the UNIVERSE. By GEORGE BERWICK, M.D. Post 8vo. 5s.

The CORRELATION of PHYSICAL FORCES. By W. R. GROVE, Q.C. V.P.R.S. Fifth Edition, revised, and followed by a Discourse on Continuity. 8vo. 10s. 6d. The *Discourse on Continuity*, separately, 2s. 6d.

MANUAL of GEOLOGY. By S. HAUGHTON, M.D. F.R.S. Revised Edition, with 66 Woodcuts. Fcp. 7s. 6d.

VAN DER HOEVEN'S HANDBOOK of ZOOLOGY. Translated from the Second Dutch Edition by the Rev. W. CLARK, M.D. F.R.S. 2 vols. 8vo. with 24 Plates of Figures, 60s.

Professor **OWEN'S LECTURES** on the **COMPARATIVE ANATOMY** and Physiology of the Invertebrate Animals. Second Edition, with 235 Woodcuts. 8vo. 21s.

The COMPARATIVE ANATOMY and PHYSIOLOGY of the VERTE- brate Animals. By RICHARD OWEN, F.R.S. D.C.L. With 1,472 Woodcuts. 3 vols. 8vo. £3 13s. 6d.

The ORIGIN of CIVILISATION and the **PRIMITIVE CONDITION** of MAN; Mental and Social Condition of Savages. By Sir JOHN LUBBOCK, Bart. M.P. F.R.S. Second Edition, with 25 Woodcuts. 8vo. price 16s.

The PRIMITIVE INHABITANTS of SCANDINAVIA: containing a Description of the Implements, Dwellings, Tombs, and Mode of Living of the Savages in the North of Europe during the Stone Age. By SVEN NILSSON. With 16 Plates of Figures and 3 Woodcuts. 8vo. 18s.

BIBLE ANIMALS; being a Description of every Living Creature mentioned in the Scriptures, from the Ape to the Coral. By the Rev. J. G. WOOD, M.A. F.L.S. With about 100 Vignettes on Wood, 8vo. 21s.

HOMES WITHOUT HANDS: a Description of the Habitations of Animals, classed according to their Principle of Construction. By Rev. J. G. WOOD, M.A. F.L.S. With about 140 Vignettes on Wood, 8vo. 21s.

A FAMILIAR HISTORY of BIRDS. By E. STANLEY, D.D. F.R.S. late Lord Bishop of Norwich. Seventh Edition, with Woodcuts. Fcp. 3s. 6d.

The **HARMONIES** of **NATURE** and **UNITY** of **CREATION**. By Dr. GEORGE HARTWIG. 8vo. with numerous Illustrations, 18s.

The **SEA** and its **LIVING WONDERS**. By the same Author. Third (English) Edition. 8vo. with many Illustrations, 21s.

The **TROPICAL WORLD**. By Dr. GEO. HARTWIG. With 8 Chromoxylographs and 172 Woodcuts. 8vo. 21s.

The **POLAR** WORLD; a Popular Description of Man and **Nature** in the Arctic and Antarctic Regions of the Globe. By Dr. GEORGE HARTWIG. With 8 Chromoxylographs, 3 Maps, and 85 Woodcuts. 8vo. 21s.

KIRBY and **SPENCE'S INTRODUCTION** to **ENTOMOLOGY**, or Elements of the Natural History of Insects. 7th Edition. Crown 8vo. 5s.

MAUNDER'S TREASURY of **NATURAL** HISTORY, or Popular Dictionary of Zoology. Revised and corrected by T. S. COBBOLD, M.D. Fcp. with 900 Woodcuts, 6s. cloth, or 9s. 6d. bound in calf.

The TREASURY of BOTANY, or Popular Dictionary of the Vegetable Kingdom; including a Glossary of Botanical Terms. Edited by J. LINDLEY, F.R.S. and T. MOORE, F.L.S. assisted by eminent Contributors. With 274 Woodcuts and 20 Steel Plates. Two Parts, fcp. 12s. cloth, or 19s. calf.

The ELEMENTS of BOTANY for FAMILIES and SCHOOLS. Tenth Edition, revised by THOMAS MOORE, F.L.S. Fcp. with 154 Woodcuts, 2s. 6d.

The **ROSE AMATEUR'S GUIDE**. By THOMAS RIVERS. Ninth Edition. Fcp. 4s.

The **BRITISH FLORA**; comprising the Phænogamous or Flowering Plants and the Ferns. By Sir W. J. HOOKER, K.H. and G. A. WALKER-ARNOTT, LL.D. 12mo. with 12 Plates, 14s.

LOUDON'S ENCYCLOPÆDIA of PLANTS; comprising the Specific Character, Description, Culture, History, &c. of all the Plants found in Great Britain. With upwards of 12,000 Woodcuts. 8vo. 42s.

MAUNDER'S SCIENTIFIC and LITERARY TREASURY. New Edition, thoroughly revised and in great part re-written, with above 1,000 new Articles, by J. Y. JOHNSON, Corr. M.Z.S. Fcp. 6s. cloth, or 9s. 6d. calf.

A DICTIONARY of SCIENCE, LITERATURE, and ART. Fourth Edition, re-edited by W. T. BRANDE (the original Author), and GEORGE W. COX, M.A. assisted by contributors of eminent Scientific and Literary Acquirements. 3 vols. medium 8vo. price 63s. cloth.

Chemistry, Medicine, Surgery, and the Allied Sciences.

A DICTIONARY of CHEMISTRY and the Allied Branches of other Sciences. By HENRY WATTS, F.R.S. assisted by eminent Contributors. Complete in 5 vols. medium 8vo. £7 3s.

ELEMENTS of CHEMISTRY, Theoretical and Practical. By W. ALLEN MILLER, M.D. late Prof. of Chemistry, King's Coll. London. Fourth Edition. 3 vols. 8vo. £3. PART I. CHEMICAL PHYSICS, 15s. PART II. INORGANIC CHEMISTRY, 21s. PART III. ORGANIC CHEMISTRY, 24s.

A MANUAL of CHEMISTRY, Descriptive and Theoretical. By WILLIAM ODLING, M.B. F.R.S. PART I. 8vo. 9s. PART II. *just ready.*

OUTLINES of CHEMISTRY; or, Brief Notes of Chemical Facts. By WILLIAM ODLING, M.B. F.R.S. Crown 8vo. 7s. 6d.

A Course of Practical Chemistry, for the use of Medical Students. By the same Author. New Edition, with 70 Woodcuts. Crown 8vo. 7s. 6d.

Lectures on Animal Chemistry, delivered at the Royal College of Physicians in 1865. By the same Author. Crown 8vo 4s. 6d.

Lectures on the Chemical Changes of Carbon. Delivered at the Royal Institution of Great Britain. By the same Author. Crown 8vo. price 4s. 6d.

A TREATISE on MEDICAL ELECTRICITY, THEORETICAL and PRACTICAL; and its Use in the Treatment of Paralysis, Neuralgia, and other Diseases. By JULIUS ALTHAUS. M.D. &c. Second Edition, revised and partly re-written. Post 8vo. with Plate and 2 Woodcuts, price 15s.

The DIAGNOSIS, PATHOLOGY, and TREATMENT of DISEASES of Women; including the Diagnosis of Pregnancy. By GRAILY HEWITT, M.D. Second Edition, enlarged; with 116 Woodcut Illustrations. 8vo. 24s.

LECTURES on the DISEASES of INFANCY and CHILDHOOD. By CHARLES WEST, M.D. &c. Fifth Edition, revised and enlarged. 8vo. 16s.

A SYSTEM of SURGERY, Theoretical and Practical. In Treatises by Various Authors. Edited by T. HOLMES, M.A. &c. Surgeon and Lecturer on Surgery at St. George's Hospital, and Surgeon-in-Chief to the Metropolitan Police. Second Edition, thoroughly revised, with numerous Illustrations. 5 vols. 8vo. £5 5s.

The SURGICAL TREATMENT of CHILDREN'S DISEASES. By T. HOLMES, M.A. &c. late Surgeon to the Hospital for Sick Children. Second Edition, with 9 Plates and 112 Woodcuts. 8vo. 21s.

LECTURES on the PRINCIPLES and PRACTICE of PHYSIC. By Sir THOMAS WATSON, Bart. M.D. New Edition in October.

LECTURES on SURGICAL PATHOLOGY. By JAMES PAGET, F.R.S. Third Edition, revised and re-edited by the Author and Professor W. TURNER, M.B. 8vo. with 131 Woodcuts, 21s.

COOPER'S DICTIONARY of PRACTICAL SURGERY and Encyclopædia of Surgical Science. New Edition, brought down to the present time. By S. A. LANE, Surgeon to St. Mary's Hospital, assisted by various Eminent Surgeons. VOL. II. 8vo. completing the work. [*In the press.*

On CHRONIC BRONCHITIS, especially as connected with GOUT, EMPHYSEMA, and DISEASES of the HEART. By E. HEADLAM GREENHOW, M.D. F.R.C.P. &c. 8vo. 7s. 6d.

The CLIMATE of the SOUTH of FRANCE as SUITED to INVALIDS; with Notices of Mediterranean and other Winter Stations. By C. T. WILLIAMS, M.A. M.D. Oxon. Assistant-Physician to the Hospital for Consumption at Brompton. Second Edition. Crown 8vo. 6s.

REPORTS on the PROGRESS of PRACTICAL and SCIENTIFIC MEDICINE in Different Parts of the World, from June 1868, to June 1869. Edited by HORACE DOBELL, M.D. assisted by numerous and distinguished Coadjutors. 8vo. 18s.

PULMONARY CONSUMPTION; its Nature, Treatment, and Duration exemplified by an Analysis of One Thousand Cases selected from upwards of Twenty Thousand. By C. J. B. WILLIAMS, M.D. F.R.S. and C. T. WILLIAMS, M.A. M.D. Oxon. [Nearly ready.

CLINICAL LECTURES on DISEASES of the LIVER, JAUNDICE, and ABDOMINAL DROPSY. By CHARLES MURCHISON, M.D. Post 8vo. with 25 Woodcuts, 10s. 6d.

ANATOMY, DESCRIPTIVE and SURGICAL. By HENRY GRAY, F.R.S. With about 400 Woodcuts from Dissections. Fifth Edition, by T. HOLMES, M.A. Cantab. with a new Introduction by the Editor. Royal 8vo. 28s.

CLINICAL NOTES on DISEASES of the LARYNX, investigated and treated with the assistance of the Laryngoscope. By W. MARCET, M.D. F.R.S. Crown 8vo. with 5 Lithographs, 6s.

OUTLINES of PHYSIOLOGY, Human and Comparative. By JOHN MARSHALL, F.R.C.S. Surgeon to the University College Hospital. 2 vols. crown 8vo. with 122 Woodcuts, 32s.

ESSAYS on PHYSIOLOGICAL SUBJECTS. By GILBERT W. CHILD, M.A. Second Edition, revised, with Woodcuts. Crown 8vo. 7s. 6d.

PHYSIOLOGICAL ANATOMY and PHYSIOLOGY of MAN. By the late R. B. TODD, M.D. F.R.S. and W. BOWMAN, F.R.S. of King's College. With numerous Illustrations. VOL. II. 8vo. 25s.
VOL. I. New Edition by Dr. LIONEL S. BEALE, F.R.S. in course of publication; PART I. with 8 Plates, 7s. 6d.

COPLAND'S DICTIONARY of PRACTICAL MEDICINE, abridged from the larger work and throughout brought down to the present State of Medical Science. 8vo. 36s.

REIMANN'S HANDBOOK of ANILINE and its DERIVATIVES; a Treatise on the Manufacture of Aniline and Aniline Colours. Edited by WILLIAM CROOKES, F.R.S. With 5 Woodcuts. 8vo. 10s. 6d.

On the MANUFACTURE of BEET-ROOT SUGAR in ENGLAND and IRELAND. By WILLIAM CROOKES, F.R.S. Crown 8vo. with 11 Woodcuts, 8s. 6d.

A MANUAL of MATERIA MEDICA and THERAPEUTICS, abridged from Dr. PEREIRA's Elements by F. J. FARRE, M.D. assisted by R. BENTLEY. M.R.C.S. and by R. WARINGTON, F.R.S. 8vo. with 90 Woodcuts, 21s.

THOMSON'S CONSPECTUS of the BRITISH PHARMACOPŒIA. 25th Edition, corrected by E. LLOYD BIRKETT, M.D. 18mo. price 6s.

The Fine Arts, and Illustrated Editions.

IN FAIRYLAND; Pictures from the Elf-World. By RICHARD DOYLE. With a Poem by W. ALLINGHAM. With Sixteen Plates, containing Thirty-six Designs printed in Colours. Folio, 31s. 6d.

LIFE of JOHN GIBSON, R.A. SCULPTOR. Edited by Lady EASTLAKE. 8vo. 10s. 6d.

The LORD'S PRAYER ILLUSTRATED by F. R. PICKERSGILL, R.A. and HENRY ALFORD, D.D. Dean of Canterbury. Imp. 4to. price 21s. cloth.

MATERIALS for a HISTORY of OIL PAINTING. By Sir CHARLES LOCKE EASTLAKE, sometime President of the Royal Academy. 2 vols. 8vo. price 30s.

HALF-HOUR LECTURES on the HISTORY and PRACTICE of the Fine and Ornamental Arts. By WILLIAM B. SCOTT. New Edition, revised by the Author; with 50 Woodcuts. Crown 8vo. 8s. 6d.

ALBERT DURER, HIS LIFE and WORKS; including Autobiographical Papers and Complete Catalogues. By WILLIAM B. SCOTT. With Six Etchings by the Author, and other Illustrations. 8vo. 16s.

SIX LECTURES on HARMONY, delivered at the Royal Institution of Great Britain in the Year 1867. By G. A. MACFARREN. With numerous engraved Musical Examples and Specimens. 8vo. 10s. 6d.

The CHORALE BOOK for ENGLAND: the Hymns translated by Miss C. WINKWORTH; the tunes arranged by Prof. W. S. BENNETT and OTTO GOLDSCHMIDT. Fcp. 4to. 12s. 6d.

The NEW TESTAMENT, illustrated with Wood Engravings after the Early Masters, chiefly of the Italian School. Crown 4to. 63s. cloth, gilt top; or £5 5s. elegantly bound in morocco.

LYRA GERMANICA; the Christian Year. Translated by CATHERINE WINKWORTH; with 125 Illustrations on Wood drawn by J. LEIGHTON, F.S.A. 4to. 21s.

LYRA GERMANICA; the Christian Life. Translated by CATHERINE WINKWORTH; with about 200 Woodcut Illustrations by J. LEIGHTON, F.S.A. and other Artists. 4to. 21s.

The LIFE of MAN SYMBOLISED by the MONTHS of the YEAR. Text selected by R. PIGOT; Illustrations on Wood from Original Designs by J. LEIGHTON, F.S.A. 4to. 42s.

CATS' and FARLIE'S MORAL EMBLEMS; with Aphorisms, Adages, and Proverbs of all Nations. 121 Illustrations on Wood by J. LEIGHTON, F.S.A. Text selected by R. PIGOT. Imperial 8vo. 31s. 6d.

SHAKSPEARE'S MIDSUMMER-NIGHT'S DREAM, illustrated with 24 Silhouettes or Shadow-Pictures by P. KONEWKA, engraved on Wood by A. VOGEL. Folio, 31s. 6d.

SACRED and LEGENDARY ART. By Mrs. JAMESON.

Legends of the Saints and Martyrs. Fifth Edition, with 19 Etchings and 187 Woodcuts. 2 vols. square crown 8vo. 31s. 6d.

Legends of the Monastic Orders. Third Edition, with 11 Etchings and 88 Woodcuts. 1 vol. square crown 8vo. 21s.

Legends of the Madonna. Third Edition, with 27 Etchings and 165 Woodcuts. 1 vol. square crown 8vo. 21s.

The History of Our Lord, with that of his Types and Precursors. Completed by Lady EASTLAKE. Revised Edition, with 31 Etchings and 281 Woodcuts. 2 vols. square crown 8vo. 42s.

The Useful Arts, Manufactures, &c.

HISTORY of the GOTHIC REVIVAL; an Attempt to shew how far the taste for Mediæval Architecture was retained in England during the last two centuries, and has been re-developed in the present. By CHARLES L. EASTLAKE, Architect. With many Illustrations. [*Nearly ready.*

GWILT'S ENCYCLOPÆDIA of ARCHITECTURE, with above 1,600 Engravings on Wood. Fifth Edition, revised and enlarged by WYATT PAPWORTH. 8vo. 52s. 6d.

A MANUAL of ARCHITECTURE: being a Concise History and Explanation of the principal Styles of European Architecture, Ancient, Mediæval, and Renaissance; with their chief variations, and a Glossary of Technical Terms. By THOMAS MITCHELL. Crown 8vo. with 150 Woodcuts, 10s. 6d.

ITALIAN SCULPTORS; being a History of Sculpture in Northern, Southern, and Eastern Italy. By C. C. PERKINS. With 30 Etchings and 13 Wood Engravings. Imperial 8vo. 42s.

TUSCAN SCULPTORS, their Lives, Works, and Times. With 45 Etchings and 28 Woodcuts from Original Drawings and Photographs. By the same Author. 2 vols. imperial 8vo. 63s.

HINTS on HOUSEHOLD TASTE in FURNITURE, UPHOLSTERY, and other Details. By CHARLES L. EASTLAKE, Architect. Second Edition, with about 90 Illustrations. Square crown 8vo. 18s.

The ENGINEER'S HANDBOOK; explaining the Principles which should guide the Young Engineer in the Construction of Machinery. By C. S. LOWNDES. Post 8vo. 5s.

PRINCIPLES of MECHANISM, designed for the Use of Students in the Universities, and for Engineering Students generally. By R. WILLIS, M.A. F.R.S. &c. Jacksonian Professor in the University of Cambridge. Second Edition, enlarged; with 374 Woodcuts. 8vo. 18s.

LATHES and TURNING, Simple, Mechanical, and ORNAMENTAL. By W. HENRY NORTHCOTT. With about 240 Illustrations on Steel and Wood. 8vo. 18s.

URE'S DICTIONARY of ARTS, MANUFACTURES, and MINES. Sixth Edition, chiefly rewritten and greatly enlarged by ROBERT HUNT, F.R.S. assisted by numerous Contributors eminent in Science and the Arts, and familiar with Manufactures. With above 2,000 Woodcuts. 3 vols. medium 8vo. price £4 14s. 6d.

HANDBOOK of PRACTICAL TELEGRAPHY, published with the sanction of the Chairman and Directors of the Electric and International Telegraph Company, and adopted by the Department of Telegraphs for India. By R. S. CULLEY. Fourth Edition, nearly ready.

ENCYCLOPÆDIA of CIVIL ENGINEERING, Historical, Theoretical, and Practical. By E. CRESY, C.E. With above 3,000 Woodcuts. 8vo. 42s.

TREATISE on MILLS and MILLWORK. By Sir W. FAIRBAIRN, F.R.S. New Edition, with 18 Plates and 322 Woodcuts. 2 vols. 8vo. 32s.

USEFUL INFORMATION for ENGINEERS. By the same Author. FIRST, SECOND, and THIRD SERIES, with many Plates and Woodcuts. 3 vols. crown 8vo. 10s. 6d. each.

The **APPLICATION** of **CAST** and **WROUGHT IRON** to Building Purposes. By Sir W. FAIRBAIRN, F.R.S. Fourth Edition, enlarged; with 6 Plates and 118 Woodcuts. 8vo. price 16s.

IRON SHIP BUILDING, its History and Progress, as comprised in a Series of Experimental Researches. By the same Author. With 4 Plates and 130 Woodcuts. 8vo. 18s.

A **TREATISE** on the **STEAM ENGINE**, in its various Applications to Mines, Mills, Steam Navigation, Railways and Agriculture. By J. BOURNE, C.E. Eighth Edition; with Portrait, 37 Plates, and 546 Woodcuts. 4to. 42s.

CATECHISM of the STEAM ENGINE, in its various Applications to Mines, Mills, Steam Navigation, Railways, and Agriculture. By the same Author. With 89 Woodcuts. Fcp. 6s.

HANDBOOK of the **STEAM ENGINE**. By the same Author, forming a KEY to the Catechism of the Steam Engine, with 67 Woodcuts. Fcp. 9s.

BOURNE'S RECENT IMPROVEMENTS in the **STEAM ENGINE** in its various applications to Mines, Mills, Steam Navigation, Railways, and Agriculture. Being a Supplement to the Author's 'Catechism of the Steam Engine.' By JOHN BOURNE, C.E. New Edition, including many New Examples; with 124 Woodcuts. Fcp. 8vo. 6s.

A **TREATISE** on the **SCREW PROPELLER, SCREW VESSELS,** and Screw Engines, as adapted for purposes of Peace and War; with Notices of other Methods of Propulsion, Tables of the Dimensions and Performance of Screw Steamers, and detailed Specifications of Ships and Engines. By J. BOURNE, C.E. New Edition, with 54 Plates and 287 Woodcuts. 4to. 63s.

EXAMPLES of MODERN STEAM, AIR, and **GAS ENGINES** of the most Approved Types, as employed for Pumping, for Driving Machinery, for Locomotion, and for Agriculture, minutely and practically described. By JOHN BOURNE, C.E. In course of publication in 24 Parts, price 2s. 6d. each, forming One volume 4to. with about 50 Plates and 400 Woodcuts.

A **HISTORY** of the **MACHINE-WROUGHT HOSIERY** and **LACE** Manufactures. By WILLIAM FELKIN, F.L.S. F.S.S. Royal 8vo. 21s.

PRACTICAL TREATISE on **METALLURGY**, adapted from the last German Edition of Professor KERL'S *Metallurgy* by W. CROOKES, F.R.S. &c. and E. RÖHRIG, Ph.D. M.E. With 625 Woodcuts. 3 vols. 8vo. price £4 19s.

MITCHELL'S MANUAL of PRACTICAL ASSAYING. Third Edition, for the most part re-written, with all the recent Discoveries incorporated, by W. CROOKES, F.R.S. With 188 Woodcuts. 8vo. 28s.

The **ART of PERFUMERY**; the History and Theory of Odours, and the Methods of Extracting the Aromas of Plants. By Dr. PIESSE, F.C.S. Third Edition, with 53 Woodcuts. Crown 8vo. 10s. 6d.

Chemical, Natural, and Physical Magic, for Juveniles during the Holidays. By the same Author. Third Edition, with 38 Woodcuts. Fcp. 6s.

LOUDON'S ENCYCLOPÆDIA of AGRICULTURE: comprising the Laying-out, Improvement, and Management of Landed Property, and the Cultivation and Economy of the Productions of Agriculture. With 1,100 Woodcuts. 8vo. 21s.

Loudon's Encyclopædia of Gardening: comprising the Theory and Practice of Horticulture, Floriculture, Arboriculture, and Landscape Gardening. With 1,000 Woodcuts. 8vo. 21s.

BAYLDON'S ART of VALUING RENTS and TILLAGES, and Claims of Tenants upon Quitting Farms, both at Michaelmas and Lady-Day. Eighth Edition, revised by J. C. MORTON. 8vo. 10s. 6d.

Religious and Moral Works.

CONSIDERATIONS on the REVISION of the ENGLISH NEW TESTAMENT. By C. J. Ellicott, D.D. Lord Bishop of Gloucester and Bristol. Post 8vo. price 5s. 6d.

An EXPOSITION of the 39 ARTICLES, Historical and Doctrinal. By E. Harold Browne, D.D. Lord Bishop of Ely. Seventh Edit. 8vo. 16s.

The LIFE and EPISTLES of ST. PAUL. By the Rev. W. J. Conybeare, M.A., and the Very Rev. J. S. Howson, D.D. Dean of Chester:—
  Library Edition, with all the Original Illustrations, Maps, Landscapes on Steel, Woodcuts, &c. 2 vols. 4to. 48s.
  Intermediate Edition, with a Selection of Maps, Plates, and Woodcuts. 2 vols. square crown 8vo. 31s. 6d.
  Student's Edition, revised and condensed, with 46 Illustrations and Maps. 1 vol. crown 8vo. price 9s.

The VOYAGE and SHIPWRECK of ST. PAUL; with Dissertations on the Life and Writings of St. Luke and the Ships and Navigation of the Ancients. By James Smith, F.R.S. Third Edition. Crown 8vo. 10s. 6d.

A CRITICAL and GRAMMATICAL COMMENTARY on ST. PAUL'S Epistles. By C. J. Ellicott, D.D. Lord Bishop of Gloucester & Bristol. 8vo.

Galatians, Fourth Edition, 8s. 6d.

Ephesians, Fourth Edition, 8s. 6d.

Pastoral Epistles, Fourth Edition, 10s. 6d.

Philippians, Colossians, and Philemon, Third Edition, 10s. 6d.

Thessalonians, Third Edition, 7s. 6d.

HISTORICAL LECTURES on the LIFE of OUR LORD JESUS CHRIST; being the Hulsean Lectures for 1859. By C. J. Ellicott, D.D. Lord Bishop of Gloucester and Bristol. Fifth Edition. 8vo. price 12s.

EVIDENCE of the TRUTH of the CHRISTIAN RELIGION derived from the Literal Fulfilment of Prophecy. By Alexander Keith, D.D 37th Edition, with numerous Plates, in square 8vo. 12s. 6d.; also the 39th Edition, in post 8vo. with 5 Plates, 6s.

History and Destiny of the World and Church, according to Scripture. By the same Author. Square 8vo. with 40 Illustrations, 10s.

An INTRODUCTION to the STUDY of the NEW TESTAMENT, Critical, Exegetical, and Theological. By the Rev. S. Davidson, D.D. LL.D. 2 vols. 8vo. 30s.

HARTWELL HORNE'S INTRODUCTION to the CRITICAL STUDY and Knowledge of the Holy Scriptures, as last revised; with 4 Maps and 22 Woodcuts and Facsimiles. 4 vols. 8vo. 42s.

Horne's Compendious Introduction to the Study of the Bible. Re-edited by the Rev. John Ayre, M.A. With Maps, &c. Post 8vo. 6s.

HISTORY of the KARAITE JEWS. By William Harris Rule, D.D. Post 8vo. price 7s. 6d.

EWALD'S HISTORY of ISRAEL to the DEATH of MOSES. Translated from the German. Edited, with a Preface and an Appendix, by RUSSELL MARTINEAU, M.A. Second Edition. 2 vols. 8vo. 24s.

The HISTORY and LITERATURE of the ISRAELITES, according to the Old Testament and the Apocrypha. By C. DE ROTHSCHILD and A. DE ROTHSCHILD. Second Edition, revised. 2 vols. post 8vo. with Two Maps, price 12s. 6d.

The SEE of ROME in the MIDDLE AGES. By the Rev. OSWALD J. REICHEL, B.C.L. and M.A. 8vo. price 18s.

The EVIDENCE for the PAPACY, as derived from the Holy Scriptures and from Primitive Antiquity. By the Hon. COLIN LINDSAY. 8vo. price 12s. 6d.

The TREASURY of BIBLE KNOWLEDGE; being a Dictionary of the Books, Persons, Places, Events, and other matters of which mention is made in Holy Scripture. By Rev. J. AYRE, M.A. With Maps. 16 Plates, and numerous Woodcuts. Fcp. 8vo. price 6s. cloth, or 9s. 6d. neatly bound in calf.

The GREEK TESTAMENT; with Notes, Grammatical and Exegetical. By the Rev. W. WEBSTER, M.A. and the Rev. W. F. WILKINSON, M.A. 2 vols. 8vo. £2 4s.

EVERY DAY SCRIPTURE DIFFICULTIES explained and illustrated. By J. E. PRESCOTT, M.A. VOL. I. *Matthew* and *Mark*; VOL. II. *Luke* and *John*. 2 vols. 8vo. 9s. each.

The PENTATEUCH and BOOK of JOSHUA CRITICALLY EXAMINED. By the Right Rev. J. W. COLENSO, D.D. Lord Bishop of Natal. People's Edition, in 1 vol. crown 8vo. 6s. or in 5 Parts, 1s. each.

SIX SERMONS on the FOUR CARDINAL VIRTUES (Fortitude, Justice, Prudence, Temperance) in relation to the Public and Private Life of Catholics; with Preface and Appendices. By the Rev. ORBY SHIPLEY, M.A. Crown 8vo. with Frontispiece, price 7s. 6d.

The FORMATION of CHRISTENDOM. By T. W. ALLIES. PARTS I. and II. 8vo. price 12s. each Part.

ENGLAND and CHRISTENDOM. By ARCHBISHOP MANNING, D.D. Post 8vo. price 10s. 6d.

CHRISTENDOM'S DIVISIONS, PART I., a Philosophical Sketch of the Divisions of the Christian Family in East and West. By EDMUND S. FFOULKES. Post 8vo. price 7s. 6d.

Christendom's Divisions, PART II. Greeks and Latins, being a History of their Dissensions and Overtures for Peace down to the Reformation. By the same Author. Post 8vo. 15s.

The HIDDEN WISDOM of CHRIST and the KEY of KNOWLEDGE; or, History of the Apocrypha. By ERNEST DE BUNSEN. 2 vols. 8vo. 28s.

The KEYS of ST. PETER; or, the House of Rechab, connected with the History of Symbolism and Idolatry. By the same Author. 8vo. 14s.

The TYPES of GENESIS, briefly considered as Revealing the Development of Human Nature. By ANDREW JUKES. Second Edition. Crown 8vo. 7s. 6d.

The Second Death and the Restitution of All Things, with some Preliminary Remarks on the Nature and Inspiration of Holy Scripture. By the same Author. Second Edition. Crown 8vo. 3s. 6d.

A VIEW of the SCRIPTURE REVELATIONS CONCERNING a FUTURE STATE. By RICHARD WHATELY, D.D. late Archbishop of Dublin. Ninth Edition. Fcp. 8vo. 5s.

The POWER of the SOUL over the BODY. By GEORGE MOORE M.D. M.R.C.P.L. &c. Sixth Edition. Crown 8vo. 8s. 6d.

THOUGHTS for the AGE. By ELIZABETH M. SEWELL, Author of 'Amy Herbert' &c. Second Edition, revised. Fcp. 8vo. price 5s.

Passing Thoughts on Religion. By the same Author. Fcp. 8vo. 5s.

Self-Examination before Confirmation. By the same Author. 32mo. price 1s. 6d.

Readings for a Month Preparatory to Confirmation, from Writers of the Early and English Church. By the same Author. Fcp. 4s.

Readings for Every Day in Lent, compiled from the Writings of Bishop JEREMY TAYLOR. By the same Author. Fcp. 5s.

Preparation for the Holy Communion; the Devotions chiefly from the works of JEREMY TAYLOR. By the same Author. 32mo. 3s.

THOUGHTS for the HOLY WEEK for Young Persons. By the Author of 'Amy Herbert.' New Edition. Fcp. 8vo. 2s.

PRINCIPLES of EDUCATION Drawn from Nature and Revelation, and applied to Female Education in the Upper Classes. By the Author of 'Amy Herbert.' 2 vols. fcp. 12s. 6d.

The WIFE'S MANUAL; or, Prayers, Thoughts, and Songs on Several Occasions of a Matron's Life. By the Rev. W. CALVERT, M.A. Crown 8vo. price 10s. 6d.

SINGERS and SONGS of the CHURCH: being Biographical Sketches of the Hymn-Writers in all the principal Collections; with Notes on their Psalms and Hymns. By JOSIAH MILLER, M.A. Second Edition, enlarged. Post 8vo. price 10s. 6d.

LYRA GERMANICA, translated from the German by Miss C. WINKWORTH. FIRST SERIES, Hymns for the Sundays and Chief Festivals. SECOND SERIES, the Christian Life. Fcp. 3s. 6d. each SERIES.

'SPIRITUAL SONGS' for the SUNDAYS and HOLIDAYS throughout the Year. By J. S. B. MONSELL, LL.D. Vicar of Egham and Rural Dean. Fourth Edition, Sixth Thousand. Fcp. 4s. 6d.

The BEATITUDES: Abasement before God; Sorrow for Sin; Meekness of Spirit; Desire for Holiness; Gentleness; Purity of Heart; the Peacemakers; Sufferings for Christ. By the same. Third Edition. Fcp. 3s. 6d.

His PRESENCE—not his MEMORY, 1855. By the same Author, in Memory of his SON. Sixth Edition. 16mo. 1s.

LYRA EUCHARISTICA; Hymns and Verses on the Holy Communion, Ancient and Modern: with other Poems. Edited by the Rev. ORBY SHIPLEY, M.A. Second Edition. Fcp. 5s.

Lyra Messianica; Hymns and Verses on the Life of Christ, Ancient and Modern; with other Poems. By the same Editor. Second Edition, altered and enlarged. Fcp. 5s.

Lyra Mystica; Hymns and Verses on Sacred Subjects, Ancient and Modern. By the same Editor. Fcp. 5s.

The LIFE of MARGARET MARY HALLAHAN, better known in the religious world by the name of Mother Margaret. By her RELIGIOUS CHILDREN. Second Edition. 8vo. with Portrait, 10s.

ENDEAVOURS after the CHRISTIAN LIFE: Discourses. By JAMES MARTINEAU. Fourth Edition, carefully revised. Post 8vo. 7s. 6d.

INVOCATION of SAINTS and ANGELS, for the use of Members of the English Church. Edited by the Rev. ORBY SHIPLEY. 24mo. 3s. 6d.

WHATELY'S INTRODUCTORY LESSONS on the CHRISTIAN Evidences. 18mo. 6d.

FOUR DISCOURSES of CHRYSOSTOM, chiefly on the Parable of the Rich Man and Lazarus. Translated by F. ALLEN, B.A. Crown 8vo. 3s. 6d.

BISHOP JEREMY TAYLOR'S ENTIRE WORKS. With Life by BISHOP HEBER. Revised and corrected by the Rev. C. P. EDEN, 10 vols. price £5 5s.

Travels, Voyages, &c.

The PLAYGROUND of EUROPE. By LESLIE STEPHEN, late President of the Alpine Club. With 4 Illustrations engraved on Wood by E. Whymper. Crown 8vo. price 10s. 6d.

CADORE; or, TITIAN'S COUNTRY. By JOSIAH GILBERT, one of the Authors of 'The Dolomite Mountains.' With Map, Facsimile, and 40 Illustrations. Imperial 8vo. 31s. 6d.

NARRATIVE of the EUPHRATES EXPEDITION carried on by Order of the British Government during the years 1835-1837. By General F. R. CHESNEY, F.R.S. With Maps, Plates, and Woodcuts. 8vo. 24s.

TRAVELS in the CENTRAL CAUCASUS and BASHAN. Including Visits to Ararat and Tabreez and Ascents of Kazbek and Elbruz. By D. W. FRESHFIELD. Square crown 8vo. with Maps, &c. 18s.

PICTURES in TYROL and Elsewhere. From a Family Sketch-Book. By the Authoress of 'A Voyage en Zigzag,' &c. Second Edition. Small 4to. with numerous Illustrations, 21s.

HOW WE SPENT the SUMMER; or, a Voyage en Zigzag in Switzerland and Tyrol with some Members of the ALPINE CLUB. From the Sketch-Book of one of the Party. In oblong 4to. with 300 Illustrations, 15s.

BEATEN TRACKS; or, Pen and Pencil Sketches in Italy. By the Authoress of 'A Voyage en Zigzag.' With 42 Plates, containing about 200 Sketches from Drawings made on the Spot. 8vo. 16s.

MAP of the CHAIN of MONT BLANC, from an actual Survey in 1863-1864. By A. ADAMS-REILLY, F.R.G.S. M.A.C. Published under the Authority of the Alpine Club. In Chromolithography on extra stout drawing-paper 28in. × 17in. price 10s. or mounted on canvas in a folding case, 12s. 6d.

WESTWARD by RAIL; the New Route to the East. By W. F. RAE. With Map shewing the Lines of Rail between the Atlantic and the Pacific, and Sections of the Railway. Post 8vo. price 10s. 6d.

HISTORY of DISCOVERY in our AUSTRALASIAN COLONIES, Australia, Tasmania, and New Zealand, from the Earliest Date to the Present Day. By WILLIAM HOWITT. 2 vols. 8vo. with 3 Maps, 20s.

The CAPITAL of the TYCOON; a Narrative of a Three Years' Residence in Japan. By Sir RUTHERFORD ALCOCK, K.C.B. 2 vols. 8vo. with numerous Illustrations 42s.

ZIGZAGGING AMONGST **DOLOMITES**. By the Author of 'How we Spent the Summer, or a Voyage en Zigzag in Switzerland and Tyrol.' With upwards of 300 Illustrations by the Author. Oblong 4to. price 15s.

The DOLOMITE MOUNTAINS; Excursions through Tyrol, Carinthia, Carniola, and Friuli, 1861-1863. By J. GILBERT and G. C. CHURCHILL, F.R.G.S. With numerous Illustrations. Square crown 8vo. 21s.

GUIDE to the PYRENEES, for the use of Mountaineers. By CHARLES PACKE. 2nd Edition, with Map and Illustrations. Cr. 8vo. 7s. 6d.

The ALPINE GUIDE. By JOHN BALL, M.R.I.A. late President of the Alpine Club. Thoroughly Revised Editions, in Three Volumes, post 8vo. with Maps and other Illustrations:—

GUIDE to the WESTERN ALPS, including Mont Blanc, Monte Rosa, Zermatt, &c. Price 6s. 6d.

GUIDE to the CENTRAL ALPS, including all the Oberland District. Price 7s. 6d.

GUIDE to the EASTERN ALPS, price 10s. 6d.

Introduction on Alpine Travelling in General, and on the Geology of the Alps, price 1s. Each of the Three Volumes or Parts of the *Alpine Guide* may be had with this INTRODUCTION prefixed, price 1s. extra.

The HIGH ALPS WITHOUT GUIDES. By the Rev. A. G. GIRDLESTONE, M.A. late Demy in Natural Science, Magdalen College, Oxford. With Frontispiece and 2 Maps. Square crown 8vo. price 7s. 6d.

NARRATIVE of a SPRING TOUR in PORTUGAL. By A. C. SMITH, M.A. Ch. Ch. Oxon. Rector of Yatesbury. Post 8vo. price 6s. 6d.

ENGLAND to DELHI; a Narrative of Indian Travel. By JOHN MATHESON, Glasgow. With Map and 82 Woodcut Illustrations. 4to. 31s. 6d.

MEMORIALS of LONDON and LONDON LIFE in the 13th, 14th, and 15th Centuries; being a Series of Extracts, Local, Social, and Political, from the Archives of the City of London, A.D. 1276-1419. Selected, translated, and edited by H. T. RILEY, M.A. Royal 8vo. 21s.

COMMENTARIES on the HISTORY, CONSTITUTION, and CHARTERED FRANCHISES of the CITY of LONDON. By GEORGE NORTON, formerly one of the Common Pleaders of the City of London. Third Edition. 8vo. 14s.

The NORTHERN HEIGHTS of LONDON; or, Historical Associations of Hampstead, Highgate, Muswell Hill, Hornsey, and Islington. By WILLIAM HOWITT. With about 40 Woodcuts. Square crown 8vo. 21s.

VISITS to REMARKABLE PLACES: Old Halls, Battle-Fields, and Stones Illustrative of Striking Passages in English History and Poetry. By WILLIAM HOWITT. 2 vols. square crown 8vo. with Woodcuts, 25s.

The RURAL LIFE of ENGLAND. By the same Author. With Woodcuts by Bewick and Williams. Medium 8vo. 12s. 6d.

ROMA SOTTERRANEA; or, an Account of the Roman Catacombs, especially of the Cemetery of San Callisto. Compiled from the Works of Commendatore G. B. DE ROSSI by the Rev. J. S. NORTHCOTE, D.D. and the Rev. W. B. BROWNLOW. With numerous Illustrations. 8vo. 31s. 6d.

PILGRIMAGES in the PYRENEES and LANDES. By DENYS SHYNE LAWLOR. Crown 8vo. with Frontispiece and Vignette, price 15s.

Works of Fiction.

LOTHAIR. By the Right Hon. B. DISRAELI, M.P. Cabinet Edition (the Eighth), complete in One Volume, with a Portrait of the Author, and a New General Preface. Crown 8vo. price 6s.—By the Same Author, Cabinet Editions, revised, uniform with the above:—
- CONINGSBY, 6s.
- SYBIL, 6s.
- TANCRED, 6s.
- VENETIA, 6s.
- HENRIETTA TEMPLE, 6s.
- CONTARINI FLEMING AND RISE OF ISKANDER, 6s.
- ALROY; IXION; THE INFERNAL MARRIAGE; AND POPANILLA Price 6s.
- YOUNG DUKE AND COUNT ALARCOS, 6s.
- VIVIAN GREY, 6s.

The MODERN NOVELIST'S LIBRARY. Each Work, in crown 8vo. complete in a Single Volume:—
- MELVILLE'S GLADIATORS, 2s. boards; 2s. 6d. cloth.
- ———— GOOD FOR NOTHING, 2s. boards; 2s. 6d. cloth.
- ———— HOLMBY HOUSE, 2s. boards; 2s. 6d. cloth.
- ———— INTERPRETER, 2s. boards; 2s. 6d. cloth.
- ———— QUEEN'S MARIES, 2s. boards; 2s. 6d. cloth.
- TROLLOPE'S WARDEN, 1s. 6d. boards; 2s. cloth.
- ———— BARCHESTER TOWERS, 2s. boards; 2s. 6d. cloth.
- BRAMLEY-MOORE'S SIX SISTERS *of the* VALLEYS, 2s. boards; 2s. 6d. cloth.

IERNE; a Tale. By W. STEUART TRENCH, Author of 'Realities of Irish Life.' Second Edition. 2 vols. post 8vo. price 21s.

THREE WEDDINGS. By the Author of 'Dorothy,' 'De Cressy,' &c. Fcp. 8vo. price 5s.

STORIES and TALES by ELIZABETH M. SEWELL, Author of 'Amy Herbert,' Cabinet Edition, each work complete in a single Volume:—
- AMY HERBERT, 2s. 6d.
- GERTRUDE, 2s. 6d.
- EARL'S DAUGHTER, 2s. 6d.
- EXPERIENCE *of* LIFE, 2s. 6d.
- CLEVE HALL, 3s. 6d.
- IVORS, 3s. 6d.
- KATHARINE ASHTON, 3s. 6d.
- MARGARET PERCIVAL, 5s.
- LANETON PARSONAGE, 4s. 6d.
- URSULA, 4s. 6d.

STORIES and TALES. By E. M. SEWELL. Comprising:—Amy Herbert; Gertrude; The Earl's Daughter; The Experience of Life; Cleve Hall; Ivors; Katharine Ashton; Margaret Percival; Laneton Parsonage; *and* Ursula. The Ten Works, complete in Eight Volumes, crown 8vo. bound in leather, and contained in a Box, price 42s.

A Glimpse of the World. By the Author of 'Amy Herbert.' Fcp. 7s. 6d.

The Journal of a Home Life. By the same Author. Post 8vo. 9s. 6d.

After Life; a Sequel to 'The Journal of a Home Life.' Price 10s. 6d.

UNCLE PETER'S FAIRY TALE for the NINETEENTH CENTURY. Edited by E. M. SEWELL, Author of 'Amy Herbert,' &c. Fcp. 8vo. 7s. 6d.

THE GIANT; A Witch's Story for English Boys. By the same Author and Editor. Fcp. 8vo. price 5s.

WONDERFUL STORIES from NORWAY, SWEDEN, and ICELAND. Adapted and arranged by JULIA GODDARD. With an Introductory Essay by the Rev. G. W. COX, M.A. and Six Woodcut Illustrations from Designs by W. J. Weigand. Square post 8vo. 6s.

A VISIT to MY DISCONTENTED COUSIN. Reprinted, with some Additions, from *Fraser's Magazine*. Crown 8vo. price 7s. 6d.

BECKER'S GALLUS; or, Roman Scenes of the Time of Augustus: with Notes and Excursuses. New Edition. Post 8vo. 7s. 6d.

BECKER'S CHARICLES; a Tale illustrative of Private Life among the Ancient Greeks: with Notes and Excursuses. **New Edition.** Post 8vo. 7s. 6d.

NOVELS and TALES by G. J. WHYTE MELVILLE :—
   The GLADIATORS, 5s.   HOLMBY HOUSE, 5s.
   DIGBY GRAND, 5s.   GOOD *for* NOTHING, 6s.
   KATE COVENTRY, 5s.   The QUEEN'S MARIES, 6s.
   GENERAL BOUNCE, 5s.   The INTERPRETER, 5s.

TALES of ANCIENT GREECE. By GEORGE W. COX, M.A. late Scholar of Trin. Coll. Oxon. Being a Collective Edition of the Author's Classical Stories and Tales, complete in One Volume. Crown 8vo. 6s. 6d.

A MANUAL of MYTHOLOGY, in the form of Question and Answer. By the same Author. Fcp. 3s.

OUR CHILDREN'S STORY, by one of their Gossips. By the Author of 'Voyage en Zigzag,' 'Pictures in Tyrol,' &c. Small 4to. with Sixty Illustrations by the Author, price 10s. 6d.

Poetry and *The Drama.*

THOMAS MOORE'S POETICAL WORKS, the only Editions containing the Author's last Copyright Additions :—
   CABINET EDITION, 10 vols. fcp. 8vo. price 35s.
   SHAMROCK EDITION, crown 8vo. price 3s. 6d.
   RUBY EDITION, crown 8vo. with Portrait, price 6s.
   LIBRARY EDITION, medium 8vo. Portrait and Vignette, 14s.
   PEOPLE'S EDITION, square crown 8vo. with Portrait, &c. 10s. 6d.

MOORE'S IRISH MELODIES, Maclise's Edition, with 161 Steel Plates from Original Drawings. Super-royal 8vo. 31s. 6d.

Miniature Edition of Moore's Irish Melodies with Maclise's Designs (as above) reduced in Lithography. Imp. 16mo. 10s. 6d.

MOORE'S LALLA ROOKH. Tenniel's Edition, with 68 Wood Engravings from original Drawings and other Illustrations. Fcp. 4to. 21s.

SOUTHEY'S POETICAL WORKS, with the Author's last Corrections and copyright Additions. **Library Edition, in 1 vol. medium 8vo.** with Portrait and Vignette, 14s.

LAYS of ANCIENT ROME; with *Ivry* and the *Armada*. By the Right Hon. LORD MACAULAY. 16mo. 4s. 6d.

Lord Macaulay's Lays of Ancient Rome. With 90 Illustrations on Wood, from the Antique, from Drawings by G. SCHARF. Fcp. 4to. 21s.

Miniature Edition of Lord Macaulay's Lays of Ancient Rome, with the Illustrations (as above) reduced in Lithography. Imp. 16mo. 10s. 6d.

GOLDSMITH'S POETICAL WORKS, with Wood Engravings from Designs by Members of the ETCHING CLUB. Imperial 16mo. 7s. 6d.

POEMS OF BYGONE YEARS. Edited by the Author of 'Amy Herbert,' &c. Fcp. 8vo. price 5s.

POEMS. By JEAN INGELOW. Fifteenth Edition. Fcp. 8vo. 5s.

POEMS by Jean Ingelow. With nearly 100 Illustrations by Eminent Artists, engraved on Wood by the Brothers DALZIEL. Fcp. 4to. 21s.

D

MOPSA the FAIRY. By JEAN INGELOW. Pp. 256, with Eight Illustrations engraved on Wood. Fcp. 8vo. 6s.

A STORY of DOOM, and other Poems. By JEAN INGELOW. Third Edition. Fcp. 5s.

The STORY of SIR RICHARD WHITTINGTON, Thrice Lord Mayor of London, A.D. 1397, 1406-7, and 1419. Written in Verse and Illustrated by E. CARR. With Ornamental Borders &c. on Wood, and 11 Copper-Plates Royal 4to. 21s.

WORKS by EDWARD YARDLEY:—
FANTASTIC STORIES. Fcp. 3s. 6d.
MELUSINE AND OTHER POEMS. Fcp. 5s.
HORACE'S ODES, translated into English Verse. Crown 8vo. 6s.
SUPPLEMENTARY STORIES AND POEMS. Fcp. 3s. 6d.

GLAPHYRA, and OTHER POEMS By FRANCIS REYNOLDS, Author of 'Alice Rushton, and other Poems.' 16mo. price 5s.

BOWDLER'S FAMILY SHAKSPEARE, cheaper Genuine Editions: Medium 8vo. large type, with 36 Woodcuts, price 14s. Cabinet Edition, with the same ILLUSTRATIONS, 6 vols. fcp. 3s. 6d. each.

HORATII OPERA, Pocket Edition, with carefully corrected Text, Marginal References, and Introduction. Edited by the Rev. J. E. YONGE, M.A. Square 18mo. 4s. 6d.

HORATII OPERA. Library Edition, with Marginal References and English Notes. Edited by the Rev. J. E. YONGE. 8vo. 21s.

The ÆNEID of VIRGIL Translated into English Verse. By JOHN CONINGTON, M.A. New Edition. Crown 8vo. 9s.

ARUNDINES CAMI, sive Musarum Cantabrigiensium Lusus canori. Collegit atque edidit H. DRURY, M.A. Editio Sexta, curavit H. J. HODGSON, M.A. Crown 8vo. 7s. 6d.

HUNTING SONGS and MISCELLANEOUS VERSES. By R. E. EGERTON WARBURTON. Second Edition. Fcp. 8vo. 5s.

The SILVER STORE collected from Mediæval Christian and Jewish Mines. By the Rev. SABINE BARING-GOULD, M.A. Crown 8vo. 3s. 6d.

Rural Sports, &c.

ENCYCLOPÆDIA of RURAL SPORTS; a complete Account, Historical, Practical, and Descriptive, of Hunting, Shooting, Fishing, Racing, and all other Rural and Athletic Sports and Pastimes. By D. P. BLAINE. With above 600 Woodcuts (20 from Designs by JOHN LEECH). 8vo. 21s.

The DEAD SHOT, or Sportsman's Complete Guide; a Treatise on the Use of the Gun, Dog-breaking, Pigeon-shooting, &c. By MARKSMAN. Revised Edition. Fcp. 8vo. with Plates, 5s.

The FLY-FISHER'S ENTOMOLOGY. By ALFRED RONALDS. With coloured Representations of the Natural and Artificial Insect. Sixth Edition; with 20 coloured Plates. 8vo. 14s.

A BOOK on ANGLING; a complete Treatise on the Art of Angling in every branch. By FRANCIS FRANCIS. Second Edition, with Portrait and 15 other Plates, plain and coloured. Post 8vo. 15s.

The **BOOK of the ROACH.** By GREVILLE FENNELL, of 'The Field.'
Fcp. 8vo. price 2s. 6d.

WILCOCKS'S SEA-FISHERMAN; comprising the Chief Methods of Hook and Line Fishing in the British and other Seas, a Glance at Nets, and Remarks on Boats and Boating. Second Edition, enlarged; with 80 Woodcuts. Post 8vo. 12s. 6d.

HORSES and STABLES. By Colonel F. FITZWYGRAM, XV. the King's Hussars. With Twenty-four Plates of Illustrations, containing very numerous Figures engraved on Wood. 8vo. 15s.

The **HORSE'S FOOT, and HOW to KEEP IT SOUND.** By W. MILES, Esq. Ninth Edition, with Illustrations. Imperial 8vo. 12s. 6d.

A PLAIN TREATISE on HORSE-SHOEING. By the same Author. Sixth Edition. Post 8vo. with Illustrations, 2s. 6d.

STABLES and STABLE-FITTINGS. By the same. Imp. 8vo. with 13 Plates, 15s.

REMARKS on HORSES' TEETH, addressed to Purchasers. By the same. Post 8vo. 1s. 6d.

ROBBINS'S CAVALRY CATECHISM, or Instructions on Cavalry Exercise and Field Movements, Brigade Movements, Out-post Duty, Cavalry supporting Artillery, Artillery attached to Cavalry. 12mo. 5s.

BLAINE'S VETERINARY ART; a Treatise on the Anatomy, Physiology, and Curative Treatment of the Horse, Neat Cattle and Sheep. Seventh Edition, revised and enlarged by C. STEEL, M.R.C.V.S.L. 8vo. with Plates and Woodcuts, 18s.

The **HORSE**: with a Treatise on Draught. By WILLIAM YOUATT. New Edition, revised and enlarged. 8vo. with numerous Woodcuts, 12s. 6d.

The **Dog.** By the same Author. 8vo. with numerous Woodcuts, 6s.

The **DOG in HEALTH and DISEASE.** By STONEHENGE. With 70 Wood Engravings. Square crown 8vo. 10s. 6d.

The **GREYHOUND.** By STONEHENGE. Revised Edition, with 24 Portraits of Greyhounds. Square crown 8vo. 10s. 6d.

The **OX**; his Diseases and their Treatment: with an Essay on Parturition in the Cow. By J. R. DOBSON. Crown 8vo. with Illustrations, 7s. 6d.

Commerce, Navigation, and *Mercantile Affairs.*

The **ELEMENTS of BANKING.** By HENRY DUNNING MACLEOD, M.A. Barrister-at-Law. Post 8vo. [*Nearly ready.*

The **THEORY and PRACTICE of BANKING.** By the same Author Second Edition, entirely remodelled. 2 vols. 8vo. 30s.

A DICTIONARY, Practical, Theoretical, and Historical, of Commerce and Commercial Navigation. By J. R. M'CULLOCH, Esq. New and thoroughly revised Edition. 8vo. price 63s. cloth, or 70s. half-bd. in russia.

The **LAW of NATIONS** Considered as Independent Political Communities. By Sir TRAVERS TWISS, D.C.L. 2 vols. 8vo. 30s., or separately, PART I. *Peace,* 12s. PART II. *War,* 18s.

Works of *Utility* and *General Information*.

The CABINET LAWYER; a Popular Digest of the **Laws of England**, Civil, Criminal, and Constitutional: intended for Practical Use and General Information. Twenty-third Edition, corrected and brought up to the Present Date. Fcp. 8vo. price 7s. 6d.

PEWTNER'S COMPREHENSIVE SPECIFIER; A Guide to the Practical Specification of every kind of Building-Artificers' Work; with Forms of Building Conditions and Agreements, an Appendix, Foot-Notes, and a copious Index. Edited by W. YOUNG, Architect. Crown 8vo. price 6s.

The LAW RELATING to BENEFIT BUILDING SOCIETIES; with Practical Observations on the Act and all the Cases decided thereon; also a Form of Rules and Forms of Mortgages. By W. TIDD PRATT, Barrister. Second Edition. Fcp. 3s. 6d.

COLLIERIES and COLLIERS: a Handbook of the Law and **Leading** Cases relating thereto. By J. C. FOWLER, of the Inner Temple, Barrister, Stipendiary Magistrate for the District of Merthyr Tydfil and **Aberdare**. Second Edition. Fcp. 8vo. 7s. 6d.

The MATERNAL MANAGEMENT of CHILDREN in HEALTH and Disease. By THOMAS BULL, M.D. Fcp. 5s.

HINTS to MOTHERS on the MANAGEMENT of their HEALTH during the Period of Pregnancy and in the Lying-in Room. By the late THOMAS BULL, M.D. Fcp. 5s.

NOTES on HOSPITALS. By FLORENCE NIGHTINGALE. Third Edition, enlarged; with 13 Plans. Post 4to. 18s.

CHESS OPENINGS. By F. W. LONGMAN, Balliol College, Oxford. Fcp. 8vo. 2s. 6d.

A PRACTICAL TREATISE on BREWING; with Formulæ for Public Brewers, and Instructions for Private Families. By W. BLACK. 8vo. 10s. 6d.

MODERN COOKERY for PRIVATE FAMILIES, reduced to a System of Easy Practice in a Series of carefully-tested Receipts. By ELIZA ACTON. Newly revised and enlarged Edition; with 8 Plates of Figures and 150 Woodcuts. Fcp. 6s.

WILLICH'S POPULAR TABLES, for ascertaining, according to the Carlisle Table of Mortality, the value of Lifehold, Leasehold, and Church Property, Renewal Fines, Reversions, &c. Also Interest, Legacy, Succession Duty, and various other useful Tables. Seventh Edition, edited by MONTAGUE MARRIOTT, Barrister-at-Law. Post 8vo. price 10s.

COULTHART'S DECIMAL INTEREST TABLES at 24 Different Rates not exceeding 5 per Cent. Calculated for the use of Bankers. To which are added Commission Tables at One-Eighth and One-Fourth per Cent. 8vo. price 15s.

MAUNDER'S TREASURY of KNOWLEDGE and LIBRARY of Reference: comprising an English Dictionary and Grammar, Universal Gazetteer, Classical Dictionary, Chronology, Law Dictionary, a Synopsis of the Peerage, useful Tables, &c. Revised Edition. Fcp. 8vo. price 6s.

INDEX

ACTON'S Modern Cookery	28
ALCOCK'S Residence in Japan	22
ALLEN'S Four Discourses of Chrysostom	27
ALLIES on Formation of Christendom	20
Alpine Guide (The)	23
ALTHAUS on Medical Electricity	14
ARNOLD'S Manual of English Literature	7
ARNOTT'S Elements of Physics	11
Arundines Cami	26
Autumn Holidays of a Country Parson	9
AYRE'S Treasury of Bible Knowledge	20
BACON'S Essays, by WHATELY	6
——— Life and Letters, by SPEDDING	5
——— Works, edited by SPEDDING	6
BAIN'S Logic, Deductive and Inductive	10
——— Mental and Moral Science	10
——— on the Emotions and Will	10
——— on the Senses and Intellect	10
——— on the Study of Character	10
BALL'S Alpine Guide	23
BARING'S Staff College Essays	2
BAYLDON'S Rents and Tillages	18
Beaten Tracks	22
BECKER'S Charicles and Gallus	25
BENFEY'S Sanskrit Dictionary	8
BERNARD on British Neutrality	1
BERWICK'S Forces of the Universe	12
BLACK'S Treatise on Brewing	28
BLACKLEY'S Word-Gossip	7
——————— German-English Dictionary	8
BLAINE'S Rural Sports	26
——— Veterinary Art	27
BOURNE on Screw Propeller	18
BOURNE'S Catechism of the Steam Engine	18
——— Handbook of Steam Engine	18
——— Improvements in the Steam Engine	18
——— Treatise on the Steam Engine	18
——— Examples of Modern Engines	26
BOWDLER'S Family SHAKSPEARE	
BRAMLEY-MOORE'S Six Sisters of the Valleys	24
BRANDE'S Dictionary of Science, Literature, and Art	13
BRAY'S (C.) Education of the Feelings	10
——— Philosophy of Necessity	10
——— on Force	10
BROWNE'S Exposition of the 39 Articles	19
BRUNEL'S Life of BRUNEL	4
BUCKLE'S History of Civilization	4
BULL'S Hints to Mothers	28
——— Maternal Management of Children	28
BUNSEN'S (Baron) Ancient Egypt	4
——————— God in History	3
——————— Memoirs	5
BUNSEN (E. DE) on Apocrypha	20
——————— 's Keys of St. Peter	20

BURKE'S Vicissitudes of Families	5
BURTON'S Christian Church	4
Cabinet Lawyer	28
CALVERT'S Wife's Manual	28
CARR'S Sir R. WHITTINGTON	21
CATES'S Biographical Dictionary	5
CATS' and FARLIE'S Moral Emblems	16
Changed Aspects of Unchanged Truths	9
CHESNEY'S Euphrates Expedition	22
——— Indian Polity	3
——— Waterloo Campaign	2
——— and REEVE'S Military Resources of Prussia and France, &c.	2
CHILD'S Physiological Essays	15
Chorale Book for England	16
CLOUGH'S Lives from Plutarch	2
COLENSO (Bishop) on Pentateuch	20
Commonplace Philosopher	9
CONINGTON'S Translation of the Æneid	26
CONTANSEAU'S French-English Dictionaries	8
CONYBEARE and HOWSON'S St. Paul	19
COTTON'S (Bishop) Life	
COOPER'S Surgical Dictionary	14
COPLAND'S Dictionary of Practical Medicine	15
COULTHART'S Decimal Interest Tables	28
Counsel and Comfort from a City Pulpit	9
Cox's Aryan Mythology	3
——— Manual of Mythology	25
——— Tale of the Great Persian War	2
——— Tales of Ancient Greece	25
CRESY'S Encyclopædia of Civil Engineering	17
Critical Essays of a Country Parson	9
CROOKES on Beet-Root Sugar	15
CULLEY'S Handbook of Telegraphy	17
CUSACK'S History of Ireland	3
D'AUBIGNE'S History of the Reformation in the time of CALVIN	2
DAVIDSON'S Introduction to New Testament	19
Dead Shot (The), by MARKSMAN	26
DE LA RIVE'S Treatise on Electricity	12
DENISON'S Vice-Regal Life	1
DE TOCQUEVILLE'S Democracy in America	2
DISRAELI'S Lothair	24
——— Novels and Tales	24
DOBELL'S Medical Reports	15
DOBSON on the Ox	27
DOVE on Storms	1
DOYLE'S Fairyland	16
DYER'S City of Rome	3
EASTLAKE'S Hints on Household Taste	17

EASTLAKE'S History of Oil Painting 16
——————— Gothic Revival 17
——————— Life of Gibson 18
EDMUNDS'S Names of Places 9
Elements of Botany 13
ELLICOTT on the Revision of the English New Testament............. 19
——————'s Commentary on Ephesians 19
——————— Commentary on Galatians 19
——————————————— Pastoral Epist. 19
——————————————— Philippians,&c. 19
——————————————— Thessalonians 19
——————— Lectures on the Life of Christ.. 19
Essays and Contributions of A. K. H. B..... 8
EWALD'S History of Israel................. 20

FAIRBAIRN on Iron Shipbuilding 18
——————'s Applications of Iron 18
——————— Information for Engineers .. 17
——————— Mills and Millwork 17
FARADAY'S Life and Letters................ 4
FARRAR'S Families of Speech 9
——————— Chapters on Language 7
FELKIN on Hosiery and Lace Manufactures 18
FENNELL'S Book of the Roach............. 27
FFOULKES'S Christendom's Divisions 20
FITZWYGRAM on Horses and Stables 27
FORBES'S Earls of Granard 5
FOWLER'S Collieries and Colliers 28
FRANCIS'S Fishing Book................... 26
FRESHFIELD'S Travels in the Caucasus..... 22
FROUDE'S History of England............. 1
——————— Short Studies on Great Subjects 9

GANOT'S Elementary Physics 11
GILBERT'S Cadore, or Titian's Country 22
GILBERT and CHURCHILL'S Dolomites 23
GIRDLESTONE'S High Alps without Guides 24
GLEDSTONE'S Life of WHITEFIELD 4
GODDARD'S Wonderful Stories 24
GOLDSMITH'S Poems, Illustrated 25
GOULD'S Silver Store 26
GRAHAM'S Book about Words 7
GRANT'S Home Politics 3
——————— Ethics of Aristotle 6
Graver Thoughts of a Country Parson...... 9
GRAY'S Anatomy 15
GREENHOW on Bronchitis 15
GROVE on Correlation of Physical Forces .. 12
GURNEY'S Chapters of French History 2
GWILT'S Encyclopædia of Architecture 17

HAMPDEN'S (Bishop) Memorials 4
HARE on Election of Representatives 7
HARTWIG'S Harmonies of Nature 13
——————— Polar World................... 13
——————— Sea and its Living Wonders .. 13
——————— Tropical World 13
HAUGHTON'S Manual of Geology 12
HERSCHEL'S Outlines of Astronomy........ 11
HEWITT on Diseases of Women 14
HODGSON'S Theory of Practice 10
——————— Time and Space 10
HOLMES'S System of Surgery 14
——————— Surgical Diseases of Infancy 14
HOOKER'S British Flora.................. 13
HORNE'S Introduction to the Scriptures.... 19
——————— Compendium of ditto 19
How we Spent the Summer 22
HOWITT'S Australian Discovery............ 22
——————— Northern Heights of London.... 23
——————— Rural Life of England.......... 23

HOWITT'S Visits to Remarkable Places.... 23
HÜBNER'S Memoir of Sixtus V............. 2
HUGHES'S (W.) Manual of Geography 11
HUME'S Essays 10
——————— Treatise on Human Nature 10

IHNE'S Roman History 3
INGELOW'S Poems 25
——————— Story of Doom 26
——————— Mopsa 26

JAMESON'S Saints and Martyrs 16
——————— Legends of the Madonna........ 16
——————— Monastic Orders................ 16
JAMESON and EASTLAKE'S Saviour 16
JOHNSTON'S Geographical Dictionary..... 11
JUKES on Second Death 20
——————— on Types of Genesis 21

KALISCH'S Commentary on the Bible 7
——————— Hebrew Grammar 8
KEITH on Fulfilment of Prophecy.......... 19
——————— Destiny of the World 19
KERL'S Metallurgy 18
——————— ROHRIG 18
KIRBY and SPENCE'S Entomology.......... 13

LATHAM'S English Dictionary............. 7
——————— River Plate 11
LAWLOR'S Pilgrimages in the Pyrenees 23
LECKY'S History of European Morals 3
——————— Rationalism 3
Leisure Hours in Town 9
Lessons of Middle Age 9
LEWES' History of Philosophy 3
LEWIS'S Letters 5
LIDDELL and SCOTT'S Two Lexicons 8
Life of Man Symbolised 16
Life of Margaret M. Hallahan............. 21
LINDLEY and MOORE'S Treasury of Botany 13
LINDSAY'S Evidence for the Papacy....... 20
LONGMAN'S Edward the Third 2
——————— Lectures on the History of England 2
——————— Chess Openings 28
Lord's Prayer Illustrated 16
LOUDON'S Agriculture 18
——————— Gardening 18
——————— Plants 13
LOWNDES'S Engineer's Handbook 13
LUBBOCK on Origin of Civilisation........ 12
Lyra Eucharistica 21
——————— Germanica 16, 21
——————— Messianica 21
——————— Mystica 21

MACAULAY'S (Lord) Essays ....
——————— History of England .. 1
——————— Lays of Ancient Rome 25
——————— Miscellaneous Writings 9
——————— Speeches 7
——————— Complete Works...... 1
MACFARREN'S Lectures on Harmony 16
MACLEOD'S Elements of Political Economy 7
——————— Dictionary of Political Economy 7
——————— Elements of Banking.......... 27
——————— Theory and Practice of Banking 27

NEW WORKS PUBLISHED BY LONGMANS AND CO.   31

McCULLOCH's Dictionary of Commerce.... 27
———————— Geographical Dictionary .. 11
MAGUIRE's Life of Father Mathew......... 5
——————— Pope Pius IX................ 5
MALET's Overthrow of the Germanic Confederation by Prussia................. 2
MANNING's England and Christendom 20
MARCET on the Larynx 15
MARSHALL's Physiology.................... 15
MARSHMAN's Life of Havelock 5
——————— History of India 3
MARTINEAU's Christian Life 22
MASSINGBERD's History of the Reformation
MATHESON's England to Delhi 23
MAUNDER's Biographical Treasury........ 5
——————— Geographical Treasury 11
——————— Historical Treasury 4
——————— Scientific and Literary Treasury.............................. 13
——————— Treasury of Knowledge...... 28
——————— Treasury of Natural History 13
MAY's Constitutional History of England.. 1
MELVILLE's Novels and Tales .... 24 & 25
Memoir of Bishop COTTON.................. 4
MENDELSSOHN's Letters 5
MERIVALE's Fall of the Roman Republic.. 3
——————— Romans under the Empire 3
MERRIFIELD and EVER's Navigation 11
MILES on Horse's Foot and Horseshoeing.. 27
——— Horses' Teeth and Stables 27
MILL (J.) on the Mind 10
MILL (J. S.) on Liberty 6
——— on Representative **Government** 6
——— on Utilitarianism................ 6
MILL's (J. S.) Dissertations and Discussions 7
——————— Political Economy 6
——————— System of Logic........... 6
——————— Hamilton's Philosophy..... 7
——————— Inaugural Address 7
——————— Subjection of Women....... 6
MILLER's Elements of Chemistry 14
——————— Hymn-Writers................ 21
MITCHELL's Manual of Architecture 17
——————— Manual of Assaying 18
MONSELL's Beatitudes..................... 21
——————— His Presence not his Memory 21
——————— 'Spiritual Songs'............ 21
MOORE's Irish Melodies 25
——————— Lalla Rookh 25
——————— Poetical Works................ 25
——————— Power of the Soul over the **Body** 21
MORELL's Elements of Psychology 10
——————— Mental Philosophy 10
MULLER's (MAX) Chips from a **German** Workshop 19
——————— Lectures on the Science of Language............ 7
——————— (K. O.) Literature of **Ancient** Greece 8
MURCHISON on Liver Complaints......... 15
MURE's Language and Literature of Greece 2

New Testament, Illustrated Edition........ 16
NEWMAN's History of his Religious Opinions 5
NIGHTINGALE's Notes on Hospitals 28
NILSSON's Scandinavia 12
NORTHCOTE's Sanctuaries of the Madonna 23
NORTHCOTT's Lathes and Turning 17
NORTON's City of London 23

ODLING's Animal Chemistry 14
——————— Course of Practical Chemistry.. 14
——————— Manual of Chemistry 14
——————— Lectures on Carbon 14
——————— Outlines of Chemistry........ 14

O'FLANAGAN's Irish Chancellors 5
Our Children's Story...................... 25
OWEN's Lectures on the Invertebrate Animals 12
——————— Comparative Anatomy and Physiology of Vertebrate Animals 12

PACKE's Guide to the Pyrenees 23
PAGET's Lectures on Surgical Pathology .. 14
PEREIRA's Manual of Materia Medica 15
PERKIN's Italian and Tuscan Sculptors.... 17
PEWTNER's Comprehensive Specifier 28
Pictures in Tyrol......................... 22
PIESSE's Art of Perfumery 18
——————— Natural Magic................ 18
PONTON's Beginning...................... 12
PRATT's Law of Building Societies 28
PRENDERGAST's Mastery of Languages.... 8
PRESCOTT's Scripture Difficulties 20
Present-Day Thoughts..................... 9
PROCTOR on Plurality of Worlds 11
——————— Saturn and its System...... 11
——————— The Sun 11

RAE's Westward by Rail................... 22
Recreations of a Country Parson........... 8
REICHEL's See of Rome.................... 20
REILY's Map of Mont Blanc............... 22
REIMANN on Aniline Dyes................. 15
REYNOLDS' Glaphyra, and other Poems ... 25
RILEY's Memorials of London.............. 23
RIVERS' Rose Amateur's Guide 13
ROBBIN's Cavalry Catechism 27
ROGER's Correspondence of Greyson 9
——————— Eclipse of Faith............ 9
——————— Defence of ditto............ 9
ROGET's English Words and **Phrases**...... 7
Roma Sotterranea........................ 24
RONALD's Fly-Fisher's Entomology 26
ROSE's Ignatius Loyola.................... 2
ROTHSCHILD's Israelites.................. 20
ROWTON's Debater 7
RULE's Karaite Jews 19
RUSSELL's (Earl) Speeches and Despatches 1
——————— on Government and Constitution 1

SANDAR's Justinian's Institutes 61
SCHALLEN's Spectrum Analysis............ 11
SCOTT's Lectures on the Fine Arts 6
——————— Albert Durer 16
SEEBOHM's Oxford Reformers of 1498 2
SEWELL's After Life...................... 24
——————— Amy Herbert 24
——————— Cleve Hall.................... 24
——————— Earl's Daughter.............. 24
——————— Examination for Confirmation .. 21
——————— Experience of Life 24
——————— Gertrude.................... 24
——————— Giant....................... 24
——————— Glimpse of the World........ 24
——————— History of the Early Church.. 24
——————— Ivors........................ 24
——————— Journal of a Home Life 24
——————— Katharine Ashton........... 24
——————— Laneton Parsonage........... 24
——————— Margaret Percival........... 24
——————— Passing Thoughts on **Religion**.. 21
——————— Poems of Bygone Years...... 25
——————— Preparations for Communion.... 21
——————— Principles of Education........ 21
——————— Readings for Confirmation.... 21
——————— Readings for Lent............. 21
——————— Tales and Stories 24
——————— Thoughts for the Age......... 21
——————— Ursula...................... 34
——————— Thoughts for the Holy **Week**.... 21

SHAKESPEARE'S Midsummer Night's Dream
   illustrated with Silhouettes 16
SHIPLEY'S Four Cardinal Virtues.......... 20
——————— Invocation of Saints 22
SHORT'S Church History.................... 4
SMART'S WALKER'S Dictionary 8
SMITH'S (A. C.) Tour in Portugal.......... 23
——— (J.) Paul's Voyage and Shipwreck 19
——— (SYDNEY) Miscellaneous Works.. 9
——————————— Wit and Wisdom 9
——————————— Life and Letters........ 4
SOUTHEY'S Doctor 7
——————— Poetical Works 25
STANLEY'S History of British Birds 13
STEBBING'S Analysis of MILL'S Logic 6
STEPHEN'S Ecclesiastical Biography 5
——————— Playground of Europe.......... 22
STIRLING'S Secret of Hegel 10
——————— Sir WILLIAM HAMILTON 10
STONEHENGE on the Dog 27
——————— on the Greyhound............. 27
STRICKLAND'S Tudor Princesses............ 5
——————— Queens of England 5
Strong and Free 10
Sunday Afternoons at the Parish Church of
  a Scottish University City (St. Andrews).. 9

TAYLOR'S History of India 3
——— (Jeremy) Works, edited by EDEN 22
THIRLWALL'S History of Greece............ 2
THOMPSON'S (Archbishop) Laws of Thought 7
——————— (A. T.) Conspectus 15
Three Weddings............................. 24
TODD (A.) on Parliamentary Government 1
TODD and BOWMAN'S Anatomy and Physiology of Man.............................. 15
TRENCH'S Ierne, a Tale 24
——————— Realities of Irish Life 3
TROLLOPE'S Barchester Towers 24
——————— Warden 24
TWISS'S Law of Nations..................... 27
TYNDALL on Diamagnetism................. 12
——————— Electricity..................... 12
——————— Heat........................... 12
——————— Imagination in Science 12
——————— Sound 12

TYNDALL'S Faraday as a Discoverer 4
——————— Lectures on Light............. 12

UNCLE PETER'S Fairy Tale 24
URE'S Arts, Manufactures, and Mines...... 17

VAN DER HOEVEN'S Handbook of Zoology 12
Visit to my Discontented Cousin 24

WARBURTON'S Hunting Songs 26
WATSON'S Principles and Practice of Physic 14
WATTS'S Dictionary of Chemistry 14
WEBB'S Objects for Common Telescopes .. 11
WEBSTER and WILKINSON'S Greek Testament 20
WELLINGTON'S Life, by GLEIG 5
WEST on Children's Diseases............... 14
WHATELY'S English Synonymes 6
——————— Logic 6
——————— Rhetoric 6
WHATELY on a Future State 21
——————— Truth of Christianity 22
WHITE'S Latin-English Dictionaries...... 8
WILCOCK'S Sea Fisherman.................. 27
WILLIAMS'S Aristotle's Ethics 6
——————— History of Wales 2
WILLIAMS on Climate of South of France 15
——————— Consumption 15
WILLICH'S Popular Tables 28
WILLIS'S Principles of Mechanism 17
WINSLOW on Light 13
WOOD'S Bible Animals 13
——————— Homes without Hands 12
WOODWARD and CATES'S Encyclopædia.. 4

YARDLEY'S Poetical Works................. 26
YONGE'S English-Greek Lexicons.......... 8
——————— Editions of Horace............. 26
——————— History of England 2
YOUATT on the Dog 27
——————— on the Horse 27

ZELLER'S Socrates 6
——————— Stoics, Epicureans, and Sceptics.. 6
Zigzagging amongst Dolomites 23

LONDON: PRINTED BY
SPOTTISWOODE AND CO., NEW-STREET SQUARE
AND PARLIAMENT STREET

www.ingramcontent.com/pod-product-compliance
Lightning Source LLC
Chambersburg PA
CBHW020543300426
44111CB00008B/781